Administering SAP™ R/3: SD-Sales and Distribution Module

Administering SAP™ R/3: SD-Sales and Distribution Module

ASAP World Consultancy
Jonathan Blain
and Bernard Dodd

Contributions by
Maggie Fitzgibbon

Administering SAP R/3: SD-Sales and Distribution Module

Library of Congress Catalog Number: 98-85891

ISBN: 0-7897-1755-7

Printed in the United States of America

01 00 99   5 4 3 2 1

Interpretation of the printing code: the rightmost double-digit number is the year of the book's printing; the rightmost single-digit number is the number of the book's printing. For example, a printing code of 99-1 shows that the first printing of the book occurred in 1999.

"SAP" is a trademark of SAP Aktiengesellschaft, Systems, Applications and Products in Data Processing, Neurottstrasse 16, 69190 Walldorf, Germany. The publisher gratefully acknowledges SAP's kind permission to use its trademark in this publication. SAP AG is not the publisher of this book and is not responsible for it under any aspect of press law.

Warning and Disclaimer

This book is sold as is, without warranty of any kind, either express or implied. While every precaution has been taken in the preparation of this book, the authors and Que Corporation assume no responsibility for errors or omissions. Neither is any liability assumed for damages resulting from the use of the information or instructions contained herein. It is further stated that the publisher and authors are not responsible for any damage or loss to your data or your equipment that results directly or indirectly from your use of this book.

Trademark Acknowledgments

All terms mentioned in this book that are known to be trademarks or services marks have been appropriately capitalized. Que Corporation cannot attest to the accuracy of this information. Use of a term in this book should not be regarded as affecting the validity of any trademark or service mark.

PUBLISHER
Joseph B. Wikert

EXECUTIVE EDITOR
Bryan Gambrel

MANAGING EDITOR
Patrick Kanouse

ACQUISITIONS EDITOR
Angela Kozlowski

DEVELOPMENT EDITOR
Nancy D. Warner

TECH EDITORS
David Knittle
Brian Bokanyi

SENIOR EDITOR
Elizabeth Bruns

COPY EDITOR
Tonya Maddox

TEAM COORDINATOR
Michelle Newcomb

COVER DESIGNER
Dan Armstrong

BOOK DESIGNER
Ruth Harvey

PROOFREADERS
Kim Cofer
Gene Redding

LAYOUT TECHNICIANS
Michael Dietsch
Ayanna Lacey

INDEXER
Joy Dean Lee

Contents at a Glance

Table of Contents

II Satisfying the Customer

4 Billing   75

6 Trading Worldwide 175

I dedicate this book to my dear wife, Jennifer, and our beautiful daughter, Kezia.
—Jonathan Blain

About the Authors

ASAP World Consultancy is an international SAP consulting company and is part of the ASAP International Group. The ASAP International Group comprises of the following:

ASAP World Consultancy—SAP/Enterprise Transformation Consultancy

ASAP Worldwide—Recruitment and Resourcing

ASAP Institute—Education, Training, and Research and Membership Services

ASAP Standards and Assessment Board—Quality Standards and Assessment Services

ASAP World Consultancy is in the business of selling high-quality products and services relating to SAP and other enterprise applications, computing systems, and implementations. The company specializes in "Enterprise Transformation Management," delivering integrated business solutions.

ASAP International Group operates globally and its activities include the following:

- Introductory SAP courses for corporate clients globally
- SAP implementation consultancy
- SAP permanent, temporary, and contract recruitment
- Business process re-engineering, renewal, change management, and transformation consultancy
- SAP human issues consultancy
- SAP internal and external communications consultancy
- SAP project and resource planning consultancy
- SAP skills transfer to your employees
- SAP education and training
- SAP system testing consultancy and resourcing
- SAP documentation consultancy
- SAP procurement consultancy
- SAP access and security consultancy
- Hardware and installation consultancy
- Development of SAP complementary solutions
- SAP market research
- SAP product and services acquisitions, mergers, and joint ventures

The company is known for:

- Accelerated skills transfer
- Maximizing retained value
- Transformation management
- ASAP world consultancy implementation methodology
- ASAP Institute—comprehensive education and training

The company prides itself on the quality of its people. It uses a combination of its own employees, international sovereigns, and associates, who bring a wealth of experience and skills to meet the needs of its customers.

ASAP has a commitment to quality and is focused on meeting the business objectives of its clients through a number of highly specialized divisions and companies.

The ASAP Institute's mission is "To set and maintain standards of professionalism and effectiveness for those working in the field of Enterprise Transformation, where ERP/Integrated Business Systems are used as the driving force."

The Institute will champion the interests of "End User" customers (potential and existing) within the market and those of its members who aspire to raise the level of provision to them.

The Institute will support the achievement of these standards, through accreditation of desired performance and through career flight path development, and the provision of relevant quality training.

The Institute's main role is to achieve the outcomes required by end user customers and the standards themselves will reflect the best practices and highest levels of performance considered "effective" by the customer. Its additional role is to help members in their working lives.

ASAP International Group can be contacted at the following address:

ASAP House
P.O. Box 4463
Henley on Thames
Oxfordshire
RG9 1YW

Phone: +44 (0)1491 414411
Fax: +44 (0)1491 414412
Email: enquiry@asap-consultancy.co.uk
Author comments: info@asap-consultancy.co.uk
Web site: http://www.asap-consultancy.co.uk/

ASAP 24-Hour Virtual Office
New York City, NY, U.S.A.
Phone: 212-253-4180
Fax: 212-253-4180

Australia—Sydney
Phone: +61 (0) 2 9475 0551
Fax: +61 (0) 2 9475 0551

Europe—Brussels
Phone: +32 (0) 2 706 50 04
Fax: +32 (0) 2 706 50 04

See the advertisements at the back of this book for more details.

Jonathan Blain is the founder of the ASAP group of companies. He has been working with SAP products since 1991. He has a strong business background, having spent 10 years in the oil industry working in a variety of different roles in the downstream sector for the Mobil Corporation. He has specialist knowledge of large-scale SAP implementations, project management, human issues, planning, communications, security, training, documentation, and SAP recruitment. He has benefited from professional business training with the Henley Management College and other institutions.

As a management consultant, he has specialized in matching corporate business strategies to IT strategies. He has a special interest in business engineering and the effective management of change when implementing large-scale IT systems.

Coming from a business rather than a systems background, he is focused on providing business solutions. He believes that the implementation of SAP can improve the way companies do business, and that provided common sense and logical thinking are applied, SAP implementations need not be daunting.

Jonathan is a keen yachtsman and is the vice-chairman of the Yacht Owners Association in the U.K. He has been instrumental in the development of the Hy-Tech Sprint yacht, a revolutionary 43-foot light displacement, water-ballasted ocean cruiser.

Bernard Dodd, after graduating in psychology at Aberdeen University, built and directed an industrial training research unit over a period of nine years at the Department of Psychology, University of Sheffield. Two years with an international business consultancy led to an open competition direct entry to the specialist Civil Service, where he served the Royal Navy for 17 years to become the senior psychological advisor to the Second Sea Lord.

Since 1990, he has specialized in technical interviewing of experts and the writing of system documentation and user handbooks for computer-intensive industries.

Contributions by:

Maggie Fitzgibbon is a certified SAP consultant and trainer who has been working with SAP systems for over six years and has a specialist knowledge of the SD module.

Acknowledgments

In writing this book, we have benefited from the help and support of many people. There is not space here to acknowledge everyone. They have each given their time and effort freely to make this book thorough, accurate, and useful to readers. Equally, there are many companies who have given us much of their valuable time and shared their thoughts and opinions.

Our heartfelt thanks go to everyone who has helped. The writing of this book has been a team effort, and just praise should go to each and every team member.

Introducing the SAP R/3 Sales and Distribution Application

In this chapter

Getting a computer system to work for your company is partly a matter of nature—how the system is built—and partly a matter of nurture—how the system has been brought up and educated. SAP R/3 is endowed with a splendid set of genetically coded genotypes that are called *standard business processes*. Each has the capability to be taught via a process called *customizing*.

This book points out the ways in which your SAP R/3 system can be educated to work with you and for you in the businesses of sales and distribution.

However, a computer system has to interact with people at many stages because it has to be told what is required. At the same time, the people have to learn how to talk to the system.

The way to a skill is intelligent practice, not of every possible activity, but of those activities that lead to the intended capability. One of this book's functions is to prepare a user to get the biggest benefits from hands-on experience and to make all practice intelligent. With a system as complex and comprehensive as R/3, very few individuals would claim to be knowledgeable in all business functions. Every user has to specialize in a narrow range of functions.

This book is about the SAP R/3 SD-Sales and Distribution application, which includes the standard business programs that are needed to support all aspects of sales and distribution for almost every type of business. The emphasis of the application's design is on the individual person at a user-interface terminal that represents his or her company to the prospects and customers. The module is designed for easy use, yet comprehensive in its capability to pull together, rapidly and with clarity, all the information that the customer needs to make an informed purchase and have it delivered promptly and in good condition.

This module's design puts the emphasis on using a sales strategy that is sensitive to the market. Setting up a data structure that can record, analyze, and control the activities that will satisfy your customers and yield adequate profit over the next accounting period and into the future should be a customizing priority.

The SD-Sales and Distribution System provides a set of master data records and a system of documented business transactions. The module's standard business programs are organized around the following five functions:

- SD-MD Master Data
- SD-CAS Sales Support
- SD-SLS Sales
- SD-SHP Shipping
- SD-BIL Billing

These activities represent value-adding processes because your company will lose value, in terms of reputation and in financial terms, if any of these things is allowed to perform badly.

Two other functions are available from the R/3 system and are used by the SD-Sales and Distribution module. They are important because they control the flow of information between the parts of a sales and distribution organization and the other SAP applications in the R/3 system.

They also provide the links between the system itself and its users, wherever they might be:

- SD-SAP EDI Electronic Data Interchange
- SD-SIS Sales Information System

Electronic Data Interchange (EDI) refers to the electronic channels of communication that, in modern business practice, have replaced the messenger systems carrying printed documents. The term *document* is used for both an electronic and a paper record. Similarly, *printing* may in fact refer to the transmission by electronic means of information that could be printed if required.

The SIS Sales Information System will allow you to gain insight on all matters concerning prospecting, sales, and delivery. This system of displays and analytical processes is provided to access the master records and the transaction data in a flexible manner that allows you to conduct statistical analyses and evaluations in support of decision-making and strategic planning.

Aims and Scope of this Book

This book is designed to give you an in-depth appreciation of the SAP R/3 SD-Sales and Distribution application, so that you may be aware of the facilities available when the SAP R/3 Basis system is integrated with the SD module. If you are fully aware of what can be achieved using these standard functions, then you will be in a better position to design the best sales and distribution system for your company. When you have a good design that is in accord with the SD module's facilities, you will be able to direct the customizing process so that the result is a comprehensive system that suits your company and the way your company is expected to develop in the future.

Assessing the Sales and Distribution Marketplace

It is probably true that accounting was the first area of business to see advantages in using computers, although the first mechanical information-processing device to have a significant effect was probably the punched-card processors that compiled early population census data. This data would have had an effect because it portrayed the extent of the marketplace and the resources available to it.

Another first for information-processing technology was the iterative solution to the infamous transportation problem that is still with us—how to route a fleet of trucks between several warehouses and many delivery points.

All the time the information processors were tackling the grand problems, there were catalog compilers at work with index cards and snapshot photographs; these people were making it easier for prospective purchasers to see something they liked and simply mail a form to have it delivered as quickly as possible.

Pressing demands from consumer communities for up-to-date information about what is for sale is not a recent phenomenon—but if you take seriously the concept of a market, there has to be a recognition of two aspects of a physical street market. You can see several products of interest and compare their prices and quality; you can also come to a decision and complete your purchase immediately. You pay your money, ownership is transferred, and the goods are transported.

The designers of the SAP R/3 SD application obviously recognized all this about marketplaces. They have set up the standard programs to support all the usual ways of presenting opportunities to buy at attractive prices, and they have ensured that the back office accounting functions are fully in touch with the sales functions, which are the initiators of all that movement of materials and value that have to be indexed in the annual accounts.

Introducing the Chapters

Chapter 1, "Understanding the Sales Order," looks at the document from which all else in sales could be said to originate. That is probably not true, but much of the SAP R/3 SD application's business data processing can be readily linked with the sales order that documents one of the most significant occasions in the business life of a company: the establishment of a contract between supplier and customer for some goods or services in return for payment.

You might argue that what follows is just a matter of making sure that the customer gets what he ordered and pays for it.

Chapter 2, "Processing Sales Orders Efficiently," points out that there are good and better ways of processing sales orders. There are SD functions that can increase the efficiency of sales order processing and even add value by providing the customer with a backup service that wastes no time in providing sensible responses to inquiries and can deliver reasonable quotations with panache.

Some of the best customers may be those who are partners in scheduling agreements and other arrangements that are of mutual benefit to you and your customer.

Chapter 3, "Pricing Products and Services to Improve Sales," is devoted to the delicate art of pricing. Is this not a technique used in managing products in order to improve sales?

Chapter 4, "Billing," is a walk through the procedures for letting the customer know what is owed. The good news is that rebates and discounts figure prominently in this journey.

Chapter 5, "Arranging Shipping and Transportation," goes into picking, packaging, shipping, and delivering with due attention to the necessary paperwork or electronic messaging. The task is to keep track of the goods in transit as well as keeping track of the documents that represent them in the SD-Shipping module.

Chapter 6, "Trading Worldwide," recognizes that a business data processing system that does not tackle the complexities of conducting trade across the world is not really worth installing. There is no doubt that the subject is complex, but it has to be done properly if the frontiers of export control are to be crossed with commercial benefit.

Chapter 7, "Managing the SD Communications," is really about lists, like shopping lists, that remind you what has to be done, and perhaps the sequence in which they should be tackled (if you intend to carry out the most important actions first). There are so many cunning plans for assembling the list that a modern sales and distribution specialist would be advised to become an expert and subtle list processor. The complementary skill to list processing is the use of output control to see that the SD communications reach its destination in the desired format.

Chapter 8, "Using Modern Sales Systems," is about being nice to customers and prospective customers by dealing neatly with some of the elaborate arrangements that seem to accompany very large orders. This leads naturally to keeping tabs on customers so that you can discern their every need and decide which to satisfy in advance of your competitors, on whom you must also keep tabs. The system name for this kind of function is Sales Support, under whose umbrella there will be multifarious sales activities, even perhaps an Internet product catalog, all destined to keep up good relations with your customers and those who might join them.

Chapter 9, "Using Internet Applications," braces you for grappling with the fact that many organizations are dispersed but cannot afford to be disjointed. You will learn about the mechanisms that are now available for building the commercial networks that include very large numbers of customers as direct users with immediate worldwide access to parts of your SAP R/3 system.

Chapter 10, "Operating the WebRFC Gateway Interface," shows how the remote calling of an R/3 function in a distant installation can now take place and can connect dispersed business units.

Chapter 11, "Programming the Internet Transaction Server," is about something that perhaps you had never thought of doing. This really is about something we have all been waiting for— significant and profitable business over the Internet.

Chapter 12, "Interpreting SD Organizational Structures," is a view of SD as seen by a consultant who is in daily contact with it.

Finally, Chapter 13 is a glossary that gives useful information that you should be prepared to use when addressing managers and consultants.

Taking a View of the SAP Product Range

You can view the SAP R/3 product range as a series of modules comprising standard business processes that have to be expertly coded to ensure that the various modules will successfully interact. It is not quite true that the user will find a working system ready to support his company business, but the bulk of the work when introducing a company to the standard business programs is a matter of setting out which functions shall be active and what data they will have at their disposal.

Your senior management will be all too aware that the more SAP R/3 modules they install, the higher the license costs will be and the more extensive the specialist advice needed to customize the components to represent the company's business. Nevertheless, a company will probably become interested in SAP R/3 because of a particular application or application area.

Recognizing the SAP R/3 Business Application Areas

Applications or modules are usually identified by a two-letter code. The details of how these components are marketed change from time to time, and this may entail groupings that are represented in the components' ID codes. However, the following lists the IDs of many of the modules currently in use and indicates the relevant business application area in which they are usually maintained.

R/3 Component Business Application Area ID Codes

CA	Cross-Application Functions
AC	Accounting—General
FI	Financial Accounting
TR	Treasury
CO	Controlling
IM	Investment Management
EC	Enterprise Controlling
LO	Logistics—General
SD	Sales and Distribution
MM	Materials Management
QM	Quality Management
PM	Plant Maintenance
PP	Production Planning
PS	Project System
PD	Personnel Planning and Development
PA	Personnel Administration and Payroll Accounting
BC	Basis Components
IN	International Development

Anticipating R/3 Release 4.0

SAP R/3 4.0 has a much-improved user interface and two marketing themes to differentiate it from earlier releases:

- Improving value chain management
- Reducing the time it takes users to develop their products

There are additional features, such as full support for companies that want to deal in the European markets, including automatically reconciling differences caused by rounding up values after currency conversion. Dual currency displays are configurable.

Two industrial sectors have received special attention from the version 4.0 software developers, namely hazardous goods management for chemical companies and flow processing support for the automotive industry.

It is expected that there will be a shortage of R/3 release 4.0 specialists for some time and SAP is not pressing existing clients to update unless they need the extra functions. It may make sense to wait for any millennium problems to emerge and be cured in the new release.

Implementing Industry Solutions

Some of the major new developments in release 4.0 are also available as modular components that can be integrated with existing systems or used as standalone systems. The following industry sectors can take advantage of enhanced standalone applications developed for them:

- Human resources management, which is particularly versatile in adapting to rapid changes in human resource laws and their differences across the range of user communities identified by their "region of legal force."

- Supply chain management, which is rapidly utilizing e-commerce site server technologies for business-to-business transactions, using intranet or Internet pathways and extending to sales to the public.

- Aerospace and defense manufacturing, with a particular emphasis on maintaining technical information and production documentation on the wide range of materials used.

The SAP R/3 family of products is increasing with the addition of complete implementations, virtually preconfigured, designed as industry-specific solutions. SAP Retail and SAP Banking, both independent products, illustrate the trend.

For the time being, the R/3 Financial and Manufacturing applications are not expected to appear as independent systems. Nevertheless, there are several banking components that have been released.

The SAP Industry Specific Solution for Banking and Business Management can be configured from the following range of components:

- Financial Accounting
- Purchasing
- Fixed Assets
- Real Estate
- Human Resources
- Projects

- Profitability
- Market Risk Analysis
- Performance Measurement and Analysis
- Credit Risk
- Asset and Liability Management
- Banking Information Warehouse

Accelerating R/3 Implementation

Accelerating R/3 is a theme addressed to the smaller and medium-sized companies that are reluctant to install the full R/3 system because of the reputedly high customizing cost. However, the license fees for these condensed R/3 systems do not make them particularly competitive with other suppliers when the user base is small. Accelerated SAP (ASAP) is an implementation tool that provides many tools and templates and a lot of prewritten user documentation to shorten the implementation, regardless of the functionality set installed. If your company expands its scope of operations, the R/3 system can expand with it—this makes the initial license cost less significant.

Extending the Scope of R/3

A development with a slightly different emphasis comprises a range of cooperative ventures in which SAP is working with other software developers; SAP works with these people to provide ways to rapidly build applications that will be fully integrated with R/3 and eventually become a general-purpose development environment to extend the ABAP/4 systems currently in use. As you would expect, these developments are focused on applications that are amenable to use over the Internet.

Warehousing Data

The data store is a concept from the earliest days of computing when the program logic could be distinguished from the information it was intended to process. A good storekeeper knows where to find anything in the store, but a modern warehouse may contain more items than a human storekeeper could reliably locate. The warehouse concept has the added idea that the required items can be fetched for use very quickly. The data warehouse has the characteristics of a warehouse, but the objects retrieved are, hopefully, meaningful and useful parcels of data.

Data warehousing has been of interest to SAP R/3 users in the form of the Open Information Warehouse as a methodology that is applied to the internal workings of R/3, but which can also be used to develop large stores of readily-accessible information. Loyalty cards in retailing seem to have promoted developments in this technique because it is easy to collect information but not quite as easy to extract and collate it in a way that can add value to the enterprise (via analyzing customer purchasing habits).

The SAP Business Information Warehouse is in operation in the form of three components:

- Extracting, which are functions to copy data from existing R/3 sources
- Staging, which are holding and consolidating functions that allow you to splice in data from mainframe sources and feeds from external database systems
- The Business Explorer, which is an online analytical processing engine optimized to run "what if" scenarios using the combined data

This warehouse is able to operate with R/3 releases 3.0 and 4.0.

Anticipating Enhancements in SD Release 4.0

Users of the Sales and Distribution application can expect to be able to implement additional functions if they update to SAP R/3 release 4.0. The following are examples of these additions:

- Rebates in Kind, which manages those occasions when additional *on-top* goods are delivered *free of charge* or when part of the quantity sold is omitted from the invoice.
- A.E.S., Automated Export System, is a central medium for holding the foreign trade data needed by different authorities and sending it electronically to customs authorities in the U.S. A corresponding Automated Import System is under development.
- Documentary Credits are used to control foreign trade transactions because they are handed over only against proof of payment or acceptance. Letters of credit are managed as a form of payment.
- Cancel Goods Issue for Deliveries is a function that allows you to release stock in transit by reversing the goods issue if, for example, a mistake has been made in the delivery.
- Delivery Interface is a function for rationalizing the movement of EDI and ALE messages such as shipping notifications between internal and external departments.
- Down Payments in Customer Orders are to be incorporated as part of the customer agreement and stored in the sales order.
- Value Contracts are outline agreements in which materials will be released in a specified time period up to a certain total value.
- MAIS Material Information System is being used as a replacement for rolling just-in-time (JIT) delivery schedules. The quantities and dates are fixed in a MAIS Pick Up Sheet.
- Freight Charge Processing is an enhancement of release 3.1's transportation planning and optimizing functions for inbound and outbound shipments.
- Payment Card Processing in SD is designed to extend the range of acceptable payment cards and increase the number of partners in the payment card process. Card data is included in the sales order and carried through to financial accounting. Procurement card processing is included in this function.
- Material Service Numbers as Reference Objects in Service Management is a function that allows you to refer to serial numbers in services such as preventive maintenance contracts.

The Sales and Distribution Marketplace

Understanding the Sales Order

Using Master Data in Sales Orders

A *sales order* is a business transaction that includes a promise to supply some goods or services in exchange for an agreed amount of money. This contract is represented in the SAP R/3 system by a data structure that includes fields to which the detailed information may be assigned. This structure is also referred to as a sales order.

A great deal of information can be attached to a printed sales order, and likewise, many other data structures can be linked to the SAP R/3 sales order in the database. You can regard the sales order as an instrument for controlling and accounting for the business transaction that it represents. This chapter reminds you of how these ideas have been represented in the Sales and Distribution application.

Documenting Customers and Prospective Customers

The persons or companies who have bought from you in the past or are accorded the status of prospective customer are each represented by a master record. The customer master record stores the following types of data:

- General data about the customer and the contact person
- Sales-specific data about pricing, deliveries, and output documents
- Company code data, which includes banking and posting details or payment data for that part of the customer corporation that is trading with you

If a customer is unlikely to deal with you more than once, you do not need to create a full master record. Such a transaction can be recorded on a one-time customer record or a CpD (Contra Pro Diverse) customer record.

Representing Account Groups

Your customer's company might have a complex organizational structure that prevents you from entering a simple sold-to party record for the requirement. The customer master record can be used to represent any of these account groups:

- Sold-to party
- Ship-to party
- Bill-to party
- Payer

Each of the account groups can be assigned a specific selection from the available transaction data. Their documents will then be automatically tailor-made for them by the system. The SD-Sales and Distribution module is provided with definitions and models for the common types of customer relationships. You can also define your own account groups and specify which elements of transaction data are to be included in documents assigned to these groups.

Establishing a Contact Person

All the information you need to carry out sales support is held in the contact person records that are part of the customer master.

Building Carrier and Supplier Master Records

A business partner who is also a carrier and supplier would have a master record maintained in the MM-Materials Management module, as well as in the FI-Financial Accounting module. If the supplier is also a customer from time to time, you can enter its supplier number in its customer record in the SD-Sales and Distribution system, which will automatically create a link. That link ensures that the two records always share exactly the same data in all the fields they have in common.

Using the Additional Data Function

You can predefine additional data in customer master records. You can invoke an Additional Data Screen at either the header or the item level in a sales document.

Additional data for the header is composed of five fields named Customer Group 1–5. The items can have additional data named Material Pricing Group 1–5.

These additional data fields do not alter functionality in standard R/3, although you can supply default entries for them in customer master records and in material master records for header and item fields, respectively. If this additional data is available in inquiries or quotations, it will be transferred to sales orders and then copied into delivery and billing documents.

The following sequence gives access to the master records for the purpose of maintaining additional customer data:

1. Select a sales area screen such as Sales or Shipping.
2. Select Environment>Additional Data.
3. Use the Additional Customer Data (Sales and Distribution) dialog box to edit the data.

N O T E Additional data can be different for each sales area assigned to the customer. The appropriate default data for the sales area will be proposed in the sales documents. ■

When you have a sales document on your screen, you can enter additional data by using either of the following sequences:

■ Select Header>Additional Data.
■ Select Item>Additional Data.

Identifying a Person on the HR-Human Resources Records

If you create a personnel record, for one of your customer sales representatives for instance, the master will be managed by the HR-Human Resources module. You will therefore be able to refer to a member of your staff by entering his or her personnel master record number. This will make available to you any other details about the person you are authorized to see.

Using Material Masters for Products and Services

The SAP R/3 system is quite happy to manage products and services as if they were all materials. If you are in the recruiting business, for instance, you can even maintain material masters for the people you are interviewing and employing.

The *material master* is a standard master record that can store all the information necessary for the management of a material and its stocks. The material master also holds data on how the material is used, purchased, and stored, and how it is to be managed in the sales and distribution processes.

The important point is that every time a material is identified in a sales document (or in any other SAP document for that matter), the system will automatically consult the material master. Although they may need different selections of data, processing any of the following sales-related documents will entail consulting one or more material masters:

- Inquiry
- Quotation
- Sales order
- Shipping document
- Delivery note
- Billing document
- Rebate agreement

Creating a Material Master Record

The material management section is normally responsible for creating new material masters. The section has two basic procedures:

- Create a new master either by copying and editing a reference document or by entering all the data directly.
- Add new information to an existing material master record.

The following sequence is used to add a view to an existing material master record classified under trading goods:

1. Select Logistics>Sales/Distribution>Master Data.
2. Select Products>Material>Trading Goods>Create.
3. Enter the material's number.

N O T E You will be able to access only the screens that have been assigned to SD for maintenance according to the material type that has been assigned to the material during customizing. ■

A message will report that the industry sector has automatically been transferred from the master record. You accept this by pressing Enter and you will be offered a dialog box from which you can select the views you intend to maintain. This choice of views will define a screen sequence that will be recapitulated whenever your ID is associated with the process.

If you accept again, you will be invited to specify the organizational level at which you want to carry out the change. What you have to do is enter a combination of plant, sales organization, and distribution channel that is accepted as valid by the system. You can then step through the sequence, editing the data screens to suit.

Changing a Material Master Record   You cannot change a material master unless the view you are interested in already exists. The following procedure for trading goods works for all material types:

1. Select Logistics>Sales/Distribution>Master Data.
2. Select Products>Material>Trading Goods>Change.
3. Enter the number of the material you want to change.
4. Select the Sales 1 view from the dialog box if, for example, you want to alter the base unit of measure for this material.
5. You must define the organizational level you intend the change to operate from as a valid combination of plant, sales organization, and distribution channel.
6. Enter the new data when you reach the relevant screen; save it. A successful save will be confirmed.

Although you can view changes by displaying all the screen views in turn, it is often more convenient to explicitly ask for a display of the changes in the material you are interested in. After establishing the material and the view you require, you can select Environment>Display Changes. You see a list of all the change documents that have been created for this material, with the user, time, and date the changes took effect. If you want to see what sort of change took place, select Actions>Choose to focus on a particular item in the list.

Deleting a Material Master Record   If your company ceases to offer a material as a product or service, the material master has to be marked for deletion. This will effectively block sales order entry or delivery processing.

You have to select Change>Material>Set Deletion Flag>Immediately.

At the screen titled Flag Material for Deletion: Initial Screen (1), you mark the material number and signify the organizational level at which you want the change to take effect.

A deletion flag cannot be canceled. However, a material master is not actually deleted until archiving takes place, and then only if no business transactions are still open that depend on it.

If you do not want to delete a material, you can block it. For example, it may have technical defects that you expect to be only temporary. Your company may want to discontinue the product for the time being. You can set various types of blocks that prevent sales processing or allow it only with warning messages on all the documents. A block is an example of a master record change.

Defining Defaults for a Material Master Record   If you are in a Sales department, you may want to use the same views of the material masters all the time. What you can do is set up your organizational level data as defaults that are applied to a material master whenever your user ID is recognized. Every user can have a different set of defaults.

The following sequence is suitable:

1. Select Logistics>Sales/Distribution>Master Data.
2. Select Products>Material>Trading Goods>Change.
3. Select Defaults from the menu bar.
4. Select Views and mark the views you want to work with.
5. Mark the field to signify that you want to view only the selections you have made.

These choices are now associated with your user ID when you access material masters, and you will see only the views you have defined.

You can wipe out your default setting by unchecking the View Selection Only field.

Understanding Automatic Material Determination

The idea behind material determination is to provide a mechanism that will rapidly communicate to all sales representatives. When any of them nominates a material, the system will automatically substitute a better choice if one exists. A typical example might be a consumer goods item that has become available in promotional packaging as part of a sales campaign. The substitution may well have a time limit so that the system reverts to the original material after the campaign.

Another automatic material determination function can be to substitute one material number for another under such circumstances as the following:

- An obsolete product has been replaced by an improved equivalent.
- An order arrives with customer product numbers that have to be replaced with your own material numbers.
- The customer may specify materials using the International Article Numbers (EANs), which you prefer to replace with your own material numbers.

The system is able to make substitutions in material determination because it can refer to a set of records that specifies which materials are to be substituted, the replacement material in each case, and the time period or other logical condition that determines when substitution shall be allowed.

Using Product Selection   Some products may be available in alternative packaging arrangements. Your customer may prefer one to another. The packaging arrangement may be seasonal or include coupons from a sales promotion.

You can configure the product selection to be manual or automatic. For instance, you can allow your order entry screens to offer a selection of alternative products so that the order entry representative matches the option to the customer's preference.

Automatic product selection will have the system make the choice on the basis of availability and a system of priorities that you have specified in advance. The priorities system is in the form of condition records that refer to the product's attributes.

Restricting Sales Order Items by Material Listing and Exclusion   You can build a shopping list for an individual customer and have it enforced so that no order will be accepted unless the items all appear on the material listing. If there are only a few materials you are not prepared to sell to a particular customer, you can assemble a customer exclusion list of materials.

Material listing or exclusion can be applied to either or both of the following business partner functions:

- Sold-to party
- Payer

The standard logic applied when the sold-to party is not the payer is to check only the material listing of the sold-to party, if there is one. If not, the payer is checked for a listing. The payer is not checked first because the sold-to party listing may include some rarely ordered or exceptional items that do not appear in the payer listing. If neither has a listing, the customer may order any material.

Creating a Material Listing or Exclusion Master Record   The following sequence sets up a material listing:

1. Select Logistics>Sales/Distribution>Master Data.
2. Select Products>Listing/Exclusion>Create.
3. Enter a value in either the List/excl.type field of A001 for material listing or in B001 for material exclusion.
4. Select Key Combination>Customer/Material.
5. Enter a customer number.
6. Enter a validity period.
7. Enter the material numbers to be listed or excluded.

If you are lucky, your supervisor will have prepared such details in advance and you will not need to enter them each time they are needed.

Accepting Product Proposals

In order to facilitate order entry, frequently occurring material combinations and common delivery quantities can be predefined as product proposals. An item can be proposed by referring to a product proposal, which you can locate using a matchcode. Items provided by a product proposal can be changed in the sales order.

You can define a product proposal composed of the items a customer usually orders. Any order being entered for this customer will then be displayed with this product proposal as a suggestion. A bill of material can be incorporated in a product proposal to specify a configurable material item, provided you do not need to configure the BoM (Bill of Materials).

The following sequence will create a product proposal:

1. Select Logistics>Sales/Distribution>Master Data.

2. Select Products>Product Proposals>Create.

3. Edit the data screen.

N O T E You have to supply data to the Product Proposal Type, Sales Organization, Distribution Channel, and Division fields in the Edit Data screen. ▪

4. Optionally, supply an entry for the Search Term field, which you can later use as a matchcode to retrieve the product proposal.

You complete the product proposal by entering the materials and the quantities. If you are using a bill of material, the details will be identified and copied to the sales document when the proposal transfers there. You need to enter an item category that has been configured in Customizing in the Structure Scope field to allow BoM explosion.

When you save it, the product proposal will be assigned a product proposal number.

Listing Product Proposals by Material

You may need to examine all product proposals that include a particular material. The following sequence will list them:

1. Select Logistics>Sales/Distribution>Master Data.

2. Select Products>Product Proposals>Display.

3. Enter the number of the material in which you are interested.

You will get a list of product proposals that include the material. You can ask for a display of the product proposal.

Contributing to the Materials Database

The products and services represented and managed by the MM-Materials Management system can also be created and referred to from the SD-Sales and Distribution module. For example, a sales representative might acquire information about a new supplier of a material that is already represented by a materials master record. The details can be posted to the MM-Materials Management system, where they will be verified and incorporated into the database. If a prospective customer inquires about a material that he has not previously purchased from your company, the details available in the material masters can be used to provide accurate, up-to-date information. If there is no relevant material master, the MM-Materials Management system will record this inquiry and alert the material controller. The material masters are provided with a range of data fields that may be of interest to the SD functions.

A material type is created during customizing for each of the main product types your company trades in. When a material master is created for a particular product, it is identified as an example of one of these types and is therefore assigned an appropriate material master data structure. This will ensure that the data fields that are irrelevant to a specific type of material will be suppressed when the record is displayed on the screen.

The sectors of industry that you find in your business and that should be given deferential treatment in one or more aspects of SD-Sales and Distribution can be defined during customizing. You can then make sure that products for each sector of industry are assigned the corresponding type of master data structures, which will allow the system to maintain particular information and use it to be responsive to the needs of that sector. For example, the difference between one industry sector and another may be in the matter of distribution lot size, or in the way billing takes place. In this instance, you may decide that some of your products will be sold and packaged in two or more different ways: single units for the retail industry sector, and pallets for the wholesale industry sector. Each sector will have a different cost and billing procedure.

There are four attributes that serve to format the material master data into clusters:

- General data
- Data specific to a particular sales area
- Plant-specific data
- Storage location and inventory management data

The SAP term for a cluster of associated data elements is an *attribute*. These attributes combine to form a *data structure*.

Any characteristic of a material that is always going to be the same is stored in the general data attribute and will be made available every time the material takes part in a transaction. For example, a specific type of steel will have a unique material number and a particular description or specification.

The units of measurement may be a function of the manufacture method, such as a roll of spring steel, or they may be decided on the basis of the most economical unit for procuring this material, such as a pallet.

The following are examples of data that may be stored as general data because it is invariant across all sources and uses of this material:

- Material number
- Description
- Units of measure
- Weight
- Volume
- Material division

Each sales area may be supplied from a particular warehouse or manufacturing plant. Even though the material number is the same, the division of the supply between delivery plants will entail a relevant record on the material master. If, for example, the same material can be obtained from another sales area if necessary, the material master records should show this, even though each sales area normally uses a separate source.

The following are examples of data that may be specific to each sales area:

- Delivering plant
- Sales text
- Units of measure
- Product hierarchy information
- Shipping data

Whether the supplying plant is a warehouse or a manufacturing unit, the costs of storing a material there and the Material Requirements Planning procedures will need to be known in order to plan, cost, and schedule a sales order. This information also finds its place in the appropriate attribute of the materials master, from which it can be accessed by the SD-Sales and Distribution module.

MRP profile, production costs, and export data are examples of data that may be specific to each plant.

A warehouse may have storage locations that are designed for particular materials. If a material has to be stored in such a location, this information is stored in the material master records.

The following examples illustrate the material data that may have to be kept in the storage location and inventory management attribute:

- Temperature conditions
- No other material to be stored in the location reserved for this material
- Storage conditions, such as dust and humidity control; special handling facilities essential

Relationships to the particular sales organizations and distribution channels may affect some or all of the entries. Any particulars that have been determined by the master records of a superior level in the organizational structure will be inherited by a data object in a lower level, unless the record at the lower level carries specific instructions to the contrary. For example, a material that has to be stored in a cooled warehouse will show this requirement in its material master data record. If a particular method of packaging has been determined for a whole class of materials, any material belonging to this class will be packed in this way unless the individual material master record carries contrary instructions.

Working with a Bill of Materials

When a product is made up of several components, the details are documented in a BoM. If additional information is required about any of these components, a *BoM explosion* may be used to call in the extra documentation. If several products differ by only a few components, the technique of *BoM variants* may be employed.

Interpreting Material Status

You can adopt the standard status indicators of the MM-Materials Management system or define indicators of your own to serve the purpose of exercising control over sales activities.

For example, you may want to block the taking of orders for a batch of defective material but permit inquiries about the product in anticipation that a future batch will not be defective.

A discontinued product can be the subject of status control so that future orders will be blocked even though the product is still being shipped to satisfy existing orders.

Making Stock and Inventory Inquiries

Flexible display facilities permit you to assess the various plant stocks and summarize them in the form of overviews. Special stocks can be identified for different treatments. Special stock destined for only one customer would be an example.

Maintaining Customer Material Info Records

If a customer needs special sales and delivery requirements that would not be met by the information stored in the customer master or the relevant material masters, you can set up a customer material info record; this record takes precedence over the rules established elsewhere. The info record contains the following kinds of information:

- Customer, sales organization, and distribution channel
- Your material number and description
- The customer's material number and description
- Shipping data
- Partial delivery arrangements

The system will use the customer material info record to prepare a sales proposal ready to be placed in the sales order if you approve it.

The SD-Sales and Distribution module will operate material determination and material substitution procedures if they have been established. For example, you can define a set of criteria to select a suitable material automatically. You may also have set up the criteria for a material to be substituted automatically in orders for a particular customer. The material listing and material exclusion rules are valid for a certain period of time and serve the purpose of restricting the choice of options presented by the system when preparing a sales proposal.

Understanding the Condition Technique

The SAP R/3 condition technique gets its name from the discipline of formal logic and, in particular, from the conditional proposition form that can be expressed as follows:

```
If {a certain set of conditions are all, in fact, true}
Then {certain actions can be taken}.
```

The logical if...then condition technique is used extensively in the SAP R/3 system to enable the computer to carry out specified actions automatically if—and only if—the proper conditions have been satisfied by the necessary data.

The choice of price information and the imposition of discounts or surcharges are matters that vary from business to business. You can use any data in a document as the condition or trigger for the application of your pricing structure.

Price lists can be standard, based on the material used, customer-specific, and so on. Discounts or surcharges can be allocated by customer, material, price group, material group, and any combination of such criteria.

Each condition master record has a specified time validity and can be constrained so as to permit or forbid manual changes during this period.

Conditions can also be used to define the circumstances when the system may be allowed to handle sales taxes as surcharges. The standard SD-Sales and Distribution system is provided with sales tax formulas for most parts of the world, and you can add your own.

Linking Sales and Accounting

The functionality of the SD-SLS Sales component of the SD-Sales and Distribution system concentrates on the processing of sales transaction data in the wide variety of modes and contexts characteristic of the sales and distribution sector of business. There are many varieties of sales orders and many uses to which the resulting documents can be put.

The variety of business transactions in the Sales and Distribution departments is discussed in this book's Introduction. The intention here is to concentrate on some of the unique, functional enhancements provided by the SAP R/3 system.

Documenting Sales from Inquiries and Quotations

One of the links between Sales and Accounting that often appeals to the potential customer is demonstrated when your company seems to know everything that has gone on previously in relation to a product or service. The inquiry or quotation will be handled by the system as the beginning of a sales order into which it will be converted if a sale is forthcoming. The quotation will carry a date marking the end of its validity period, which you can use to monitor inquiries and quotations and to determine the order in which they should receive your attention.

You will have identified the material required by the inquirer, perhaps by its material number, or perhaps because you have used a previous quotation or order for this customer. You can also enter the material in text form, which the system will interpret using the SAP R/3 Classification System, and then find a material number to consider entering at a later date yourself or have the system enter automatically.

There may be several alternative materials that could possibly interest the customer. You can quote for these as well as for the material requested. If the customer places an order, the system will work on the material the customer chose from your quotation.

Using the Functionality of the SD-SLS Sales Component

The philosophy behind the functionality of the SD-SLS Sales component is to minimize the work you have to do to complete an order. The standard approach is to find what is required and propose it to the user for adjustment and confirmation.

If you simply enter a list of items, the system will try to find those items in a previous order for this customer. If there are none, it will look for the items in the master records and offer you the default values it finds there. For instance, it will suggest business partners to deliver the material if that has happened before; it will propose that you use the lot size and packaging customary for this material.

Much of the information will be in material and customer master records, the following data in particular:

- Pricing
- Tax determination
- Weight and volume determination
- Delivery scheduling
- Payment methods

The system will offer textual materials to be included in the sales order if this is customary, and it will have detailed proposals for creating the commercial papers.

Should you have to save a sales document before it has been fully serviced with appropriate and valid information, the system will accord it the status of an incomplete document and remind you with a list of the missing items.

When you return to the work, the system can show you all the incomplete documents in your task list and the list of defects for each.

Recognizing Outline Agreements

Contracts and scheduling agreements are two types of outline agreements you make with a customer to supply goods and services over a specified period of time.

A *contract* is an outline agreement to supply goods and services in the future, but the delivery date and shipping arrangements are not specified until the customer requests delivery of the goods in the contract. At this time, a *release order* is issued and processed the same way a sales order is. The quantities and general data of each release order are noted in the contract, and the quantities remaining to be delivered are updated there accordingly.

The quantities and dates are specified from the beginning in a *scheduling agreement*, which is otherwise processed much like a series of contracts, using the dates and quantities specified in the outline schedule.

Updating Backorders

If you call for a list of backorders, you will see the order items that could not be confirmed because something was unavailable. The availability will be checked again automatically, and you will see the current situation. If some of the orders can now be satisfied, you can use the update function to have the sales orders confirmed directly.

Understanding the Tasks of the Accounting and Controlling Modules

The SD module forwards billing data from invoices, credit memos, and debit memos to the Financial Accounting-Accounts Receivable (FI-AR) and Controlling (CO) application modules.

The system will automatically generate the necessary accounting documents that are used by the following accounting and controlling components:

- General Ledger
- Profit Center Accounting
- Profitability Analysis
- Cost Accounting
- Accounting

Various actions take place automatically:

- The system posts offsetting entries to the appropriate accounts, defined by account assignment codes.
- Reference numbers are added to ensure that the FI system will associate all billing documents that belong to the same transaction. For instance, a credit memo will be given the same reference number as the invoice to which it pertains.
- The requirements of the CO-Controlling module have to be met by assigning costs and revenues to the appropriate subledgers.

If you are working in the SD module, you may be authorized to display all accounting documents associated with a particular billing document and block billing documents for Accounting, if necessary.

Assigning Costs and Revenue to Different Accounts

A code set is provided to enable you or the system to direct the posting of costs and revenue to the correct selection of the following accounts:

- Customer Accounts Receivable
- General Ledger, such as a cash clearing account
- Revenue
- Sales Deduction
- Accruals for rebate agreements
- Accrual Account
- Accrual Clearing Account

Setting Up a Business Area

A business area can be defined in geographical terms or in terms of particular products. This is another link between Sales and Accounting. During the Customizing for Sales procedure, business areas can be defined to correspond to sales areas or to plants within divisions if the accounts are managed on a product basis.

The system will then post costs and revenues to the accounts assigned for the business area.

Forwarding Billing Data to the Controlling Subledgers

To continue the theme of linking Sales and Accounting, any number of the following subledgers may be set up to receive postings of costs and revenues so as to give meaningful summaries of the value flows:

- Profit Center
- Cost Center
- Extended General Ledger
- Projects
- Make-to-Order Sales Orders
- Plant Maintenance Orders
- Profitability Analysis
- Cost Collector

N O T E If your system has profitability analysis installed and configured for make-to-order sales orders and projects, the costs will not be assigned to profitability analysis until the make-to-order sales order or project is settled.

See Chapter 4, "Billing," for information on assigning costs for a plant maintenance order according to a resource-related billing document.

Taking Advantage of Account Assignment Links

If your system is to post entries in the billing documents automatically to the relevant accounts, it must be able to refer to a source of information that indicates which accounts to target. There are several possible sources:

- Chart of accounts of the company code
- Sales organization
- Customer's account assignment group

N O T E Find the customer's account assignment group in the customer master record. It's in the Billing screen's Account Group field.

- Material's account assignment group

N O T E Find the material's account assignment group in the material master record; it's in the Sales 2 screen's Account Assignment Group field.

- Account key copied from the pricing procedure

The method used is defined in logical terms by the condition technique, in which condition records are consulted to make the account assignments. The account assignment process has to determine the revenue accounts to which prices are posted and the sales deduction accounts to which surcharges and discounts are posted.

It is an automatic process in the standard version of the SAP R/3 system for an offsetting entry to be made to the customer account for all billing types. If you should want the offsetting entry to be made to a G/L account (such as a cash clearing account), your system administrator must define an extra billing type that contains the cash clearing key EVV.

Locating Errors in Account Assignment

One of the account assignment analysis function's tasks is to find out where errors have occurred in account assignment if the system is unable to forward the billing data to Accounting. The general reasons for this type of error are as follows:

- The account assignment group in the payer's customer master record is absent or wrong.

N O T E   Check the CustAcctAssgnmtGroup field in the Header Billing Data section of the payer's customer master record.

- The account assignment group in the material master record of an item on a billing document is absent or wrong.

N O T E   Check the MatAcctAssignGroup field in the Header Pricing and Taxes sections of the material master record.

- The account assignment has not been set up correctly in Customizing.

You can release the billing document once you have manually entered a correct account assignment code.

Linking the Reference Number and Allocation Number

You can find an incoming payment document by searching for its reference number, which may be, for example, the customer's purchase order number or a transaction number.

There may have been cancellations or credit memos created that the FI system needs to associate with the relevant invoice. Two numbers in the billing document header can be passed to the accounting document:

- The reference number in the accounting document header.
- The allocation number in the customer line item. The account line items are sorted and displayed according to the allocation number.

Either of these numbers is accepted in business correspondence.

You can specify how reference numbers shall be allocated at the stage of Customizing for Sales. The following codes are used:

- A—Customer's purchase order number
- B—Sales order number
- C—Delivery number
- D—External delivery number
- E—Invoice's billing document number
- F—External delivery number if available; the delivery number if not available (used mainly in the component supply industry)

If you have to manually enter a reference number or allocation number in a sales order, the following sequence is appropriate:

1. Select Header>Business Data.
2. Edit>Billing Details>Field>Reference.

   Your system may have been customized to enter a reference number automatically in a billing document or to copy it from the sales order. You can examine the automatic data as follows:

   Select Header>Details>Field>Allocat.no.

Hopefully, your system will be working perfectly all the time and you will not have to go into any troubleshooting procedure.

Operating on Sales Orders

In the case of a simple sales order with several items, you can probably complete the entry in a single screen. As you do so, your system will automatically propose relevant data taken from the master records, as follows:

- From the customer master record of the sold-to party, the system will extract sales, shipping, pricing, and billing data. If there is any customer-specific master data concerning relevant texts, partners, and contact people at the customer site, this too will be copied.
- Each material mentioned in the sales order will be automatically identified with specific material master records, which carry information on pricing, delivery scheduling, availability checking, tax determination, and the procedure for determining the weight and volume of the delivery.

The information gathered automatically by the system is used merely to construct a proposal—you can amend or supplement it. You can decide to modify the value of discounts within a permitted range, or perhaps you are authorized to modify the terms of payment or delivery arrangements.

One of the easiest ways to create a new sales order is by referring to an existing document. Your customer may identify a quotation you sent previously, so you can allow the system to copy all the details.

Benefiting from Standard Functions During Sales Order Processing

When your sales order is submitted for processing, the standard SAP R/3 will automatically carry out the basic functions. These functions can be customized to include the following:

- Pricing
- Availability checking if this is defined in the material master record
- Transmitting item details to Material Requirements Planning (MRP)
- Delivery scheduling
- Shipping point and route determination
- Credit-limit checking

There are also special sales order types, of which the rush order and the cash sales order are examples.

Creating a Sales Order

The following procedure will generate a sales order:

1. Select Logistics>Sales/Distribution>Sales.
2. Select Sales Order>Create.
3. Enter the order type.

You may also enter the organizational data, although values for sales organization (as well as sales office and sales group) and values for the distribution channel and division are usually suggested from user-defined parameters.

You must also enter, or select from a list offered by the system, the following data:

- Customer number of the sold-to party
- Customer's purchase order number
- Material numbers
- Order quantities for the materials

Your sales area may include several predefined unloading points or several ship-to parties in the sold-to party's customer master record. In these circumstances the system will offer you the options in a dialog box. The same technique is applied to alternative payers and bill-to parties if they are possibilities.

As you build up the sales order items, you will be shown the material data so that you can check that you have specified correctly. If an availability check reveals insufficient stock for the intended delivery date, you will be automatically shown a screen of substitute delivery proposals.

You can add further information to the header by selecting from the menu. To add data to individual items, you should mark the items before signifying your choice in the menu.

To specify a packing proposal in the sales order, you should select Edit>Packing Proposal.

Linking to a Reference   The following sequence links to a reference: Create Sales Order>Sales Document>Create w/Reference>To Quotation. This will copy both the item data and the header data from the quotation into the sales order.

N O T E   The header data will not be copied unless you leave the Sold-to Party field blank.

A dialog box will offer you the following choices when creating a sales order with reference to another document:

- Copy all items into the new document.
- Copy only some of the items into the new document.

If your system supervisor has authorized partial selection, you can select Selection List and then individually deselect the items not to be copied. You can change the quantities of the items as necessary before they are copied. The system will not allow you to copy from incomplete sales documents. However, you can copy from more than one complete document into a single new document.

If your supervisor has allowed partial document copying, you can make copies into more than one new document.

Creating a Rebate in Kind Item   If you agree to deliver some goods free of charge, the system will account for this as a rebate in kind and handle it as a discount. You can make this rebate a main item or enter it as a sub-item. If the material has the item category group NORM, a standard sales order will assume that a sub-item is a rebate in kind.

1. In the Sales Order screen, select Overview>Double-Line Entry.
2. Enter the material number of the rebate in kind as a new line item directly under the higher-level item.
3. Enter the item number of the higher-level item in the HgLvIt field of the second entry line. Doing so makes it a rebate in kind subordinate to the line item directly above.

You might be challenged by some dialog boxes when you attempt to create a rebate in kind. For example, the system may have difficulties if your customer master record for the sold-to party includes definitions of several ship-to parties or unloading points. Availability may be a problem, in which case you will be offered some alternative delivery proposals.

If you satisfy the system's needs for information, the double-line overview screen will be shown in which the rebate in kind item has been given the item category TANN.

It may happen that you decide to award a discount in the form of a rebate in kind after the sales order has been completed. However, if you subsequently call up Sales Document>Change, you will be able to insert a new item to represent the rebate in kind if you assign it an item number that will cause it to be placed below the item to which it is to be subordinate. If you alter the quantity of a main item, a subordinate rebate in kind item will be automatically changed in proportion unless you deliberately forestall this by the following sequence:

1. In the overview screen, mark the rebate in kind item.
2. Select Item>Structure>Components.
3. Mark the Fix indicator next to the UoM field.

Thereafter, changes to the quantity of the main item will not bring about any changes in the rebate in kind item.

Once you have generated a rebate in kind item as a subordinate that has been accepted by the system and therefore assigned as item type TAN, you can change this indicator to TANN to elevate it to a main item.

Creating a Sales Order with Service Items   The process of entering services is similar to the procedure for generating a rebate in kind item. Services are defined in the material master records with item category group DIEN and item category TAX. If you want the service to be a sub-item, you must call the double-line entry screen and identify a higher-order item to which it is to be subordinate. Like rebate in kind items, changes in a main item are normally matched by proportionate changes in the subordinate item representing the associated service. You can stop this adjustment by using the Fix field.

Changing a Sales Order

You may want to change a few individual items or a large number of items. There is a fast change function for this occasion.

The following procedure is used for individual item changes:

1. Select Logistics>Sales/Distribution>Sales.
2. Select Sales Order>Change.

N O T E   If you merely want to inspect a sales order, select Sales Order>Display, rather than Sales Order>Change. ▪

You may have to locate the relevant sales order. The system will try to be helpful by assuming that you are going to want to change the order you were previously working on in the current session. You can overwrite this and enter a particular sales order number, the number of the relevant purchase order, or even the number of the delivery.

Blocking a Sales Order   A sales order block can stop the shipping function or the billing function. If you place a block for shipping, the system will not allow anyone to create a delivery based on this sales order. If you block a sales order for billing, you will not be able to bill any of the individual items in it. If you are operating the collective processing of billing documents, a billing block on a sales order will prevent any delivery being included in the billing due list.

It is also possible to block particular sales document types for individual customers. You could block sales order creation for a specific customer, for example.

The scope of a delivery block will be controlled by where it is placed. A block in the header will apply to all items. A block in an item will be limited to that item. A block in an item's schedule line will apply only to that schedule line.

The procedure for setting a header delivery block is as follows:

1. Select Header>Business Data.
2. Locate the Shipping section.
3. Mark the Deliver Block field.

Item delivery blocks are set through the fast change function.

If you mark a schedule line that you want to block for delivery on the Schedule Line screen of the item, you can then select Edit and mark the Delivery Block field in the Shipping details.

You can always block an item for delivery at the schedule line level, but your Customizing table TVLSP will control whether you are able to place a block at header level in the business data, where it will stop shipping across the whole sales order. There has to be an explicit assignment of blocking to each delivery type for it to be allowed at the header level.

Deleting a Sales Order   Whether you can delete a sales order item or the entire order depends on how far processing has gotten. The status indicates this progress and reveals whether any subsequent documents, such as deliveries, have been posted.

Deleting an order is a change and follows this sequence:

1. Select Logistics>Sales/Distribution>Sales.
2. Select Sales Order>Change.
3. Accept the sales order proposed or identify the sales order you want to delete.
4. Select Sales Document>Delete>Confirm the Deletion.

If you only want to delete an item or two, mark the items and select Edit>Delete Item>Confirm the Deletion. You would, of course, save the sales order from which you deleted an item.

Rejecting Items in a Sales Order   Rejecting an item in a sales order means that it will not be subsequently copied to any other sales document. The following sequence is effective:

1. Select Logistics>Sales/Distribution>Sales.
2. Select Sales Order>Change.
3. Enter or select the document number for the Sales Order field.
   or
   Select Edit>Select Items>Select All.

4. Select Edit>Fast Change Of>Reason for Rejection.

5. Enter a predefined value in the Reason for Rejection field.

6. Select Copy>Save.

You can also use fast change having selected several items for rejection, perhaps assigning a different reason to each.

Handling Special Sales Orders

Cash sales and rush orders are examples of special sales orders.

A cash sales transaction is defined as a situation where the customer picks up and pays for the goods when the sales order is placed. The system automatically proposes the current date as the date for delivery and billing; then, when the sales order is posted, the system automatically creates a delivery. The system will print out a cash sale invoice as soon as the sales order is confirmed.

By this time the customer may already have the goods, in which case picking is irrelevant. If the customer is going to pick up the goods from a warehouse, the delivery may be needed as proof that a purchase has been made and as a guide to the warehouse for picking.

If the goods from a cash sale are to be sent later, the delivery document will be processed via the warehouse in the usual way, except that payment has already been made.

The main difference between a cash sale and a rush order is that although the customer picks up the goods (or you deliver them) the same day as the order is placed, the invoice is created later.

Processing Orders with Standard Functions

When you enter a sales order, the system can automatically carry out basic functions, such as the following:

- Pricing
- Availability check (if this function is specified in the material master records)
- Transferring requirements to Material Requirements Planning (MRP)
- Delivery scheduling
- Shipping point and route determination
- Credit-limit check

These tasks are carried out with the help of functions selected from standard SAP R/3 programs customized to suit your particular implementation. A strict regime of data structure definition is imposed so that the SAP R/3 system may be applicable to most types of business data processing arrangements. If you follow this scheme, your system will accept your entries and process them efficiently and without error. If you do not structure your data according to the defined arrangements, often you will not be allowed to enter it. If you do succeed in entering incorrect data, the result will not be interpreted along the SAP standard lines.

Setting Up Your Sales and Distribution Organization

One of the most important data structures SAP R/3 uses is the hierarchical structure that defines the relationships between the departments and levels of management responsibility in your company. This structure is adopted in any application module that is integrated with your R/3 basis. For example, the SD module adopts the basic organizational structure and extends it so that all the entities of importance to the business of sales and distribution in your company are represented by a unique master record in the database.

The SD module's purpose is to support the tasks of selling and sending products to business partners. The module will also support performing services for them. Therefore, the system has to have access to data about the products and services and about the business partners who purchase them.

Your company's Accounting and Materials Management departments also need access to this master data. The material master data is stored in a specific way so that all those who need to use it may do so efficiently.

When you are conducting a sale, the SAP R/3 system will become aware of what you are doing only when you successfully enter a business transaction. For example, you will not be able to promise to dispatch a material item that is not on the list of materials. Therefore, your intended transaction will not be accepted until you enter or choose from a list one or more of the materials or services recorded in your database.

Of course there are many more details associated with a business transaction—quantities and destination, for instance. All this essential information is recorded in the system as a transaction document when all possible checks have been carried out; this ensures that you are not entering information that cannot be successfully processed.

Business is made as easy as possible. If you have identified one of your regular customers, you system will probably have suggested the address for delivery. It may even be suggesting the sales items most likely to be required for this customer, based on his purchasing history. The account to which the sale should be posted will also be suggested if the customer is recognized.

In all this transaction work, the system is trying to make data entry as easy and as error free as possible. For instance, your system will have been customized so that your product's quantities will be accepted only in certain units of measure. You enter the number of units, but the system will offer you only those units of measure that have been assigned to the product or service you are dealing with.

If you have to send a message to a colleague or to the customer, there will probably be a set of standard phrases that your company has authorized and from which you can make a simple choice. The system will fill in the details and offer the result for your inspection and approval. Should you find that you cannot achieve the result you intend with the standard messages, there will usually be an arrangement for you to append a free text message. However, if your messages need to be translated into another language, you will be encouraged to use the standard message elements for which the translations have already been entered as standards.

The SAP R/3 system is efficient and reliable because it uses these predefined data structures.

Setting Up Master Data for Sales and Distribution

The master data needed by an integrated sales, distribution, and accounting system can be extensive and elaborate in its structures. However, SAP R/3 uses a logical arrangement of entity types. These types identify the purpose of an item of information by associating it with at least one other entity that is part of a structure's hierarchy. At the top of the hierarchy is the grouping of R/3 services that is defined in systems terms as the *instance* because all the necessary components are started and stopped at the same time. A central R/3 unit is defined by an instance profile, which nominates all the components that are to be active together. When the instance is functioning, it will recognize a code that stands for the very top level of responsibility in organizational terms. In SAP R/3 terminology, this is referred to as the *client level*. There may be one or more affiliated companies, subordinate to the company at the client level, represented by company codes.

The client company may have a number of departments or sections that carry out duties such as the following:

- Sales
- Sales support
- Shipping
- Billing
- Data warehousing

Each of these departments can be defined as a separate entity so that its costs and revenues can be attributed to these functions separately. All these departments will have to post their data to a central accounting facility at least once each financial year. If you are using SAP R/3, this posting will probably take place either daily or in real time as soon as you complete a transaction entry.

Recognizing the Purpose of Master Data

In a SAP system, information that is needed in several places or at different times is entered only once. It resides in master records, where it may be kept up-to-date.

Each master data record has a unique number, and you can arrange to confine certain ranges of these numbers to specific sales areas.

The Sales department will make use of this master information in its business transactions. Here are some of the ways the Sales department will use the master data record:

- General details about business partners
- Information specific to particular customers

- Materials, including services, objects, and assemblies
- Text about materials and sales conditions
- Prices from collected cost data, standard calculations, direct entries, and planning processes
- Surcharges and discounts
- Taxes applied according to local rules
- New product proposals to be offered during the sales process

It is clearly important to have accurate information available. It is fundamental to the design of all SAP systems that a database of master records is held and maintained under strict conditions that ensure that any user who uses this information can be informed of the date it was entered or last amended, as well as the identification of the person responsible for the change. It is also a principle of design that any automatic function that is operating in support of the user will also use the master records. For example, if a sales representative is compiling an order for a customer, that customer's address will be accessed from the master record. The master will be changed—not a local record held by the person who was first informed of the change—if the customer changes his address.

Such a strict system of data maintenance can succeed only if it is also flexible in the ways in which the stored information can be presented to the user and applied to the business processes. The next few sections illustrate the range of options open to the user in relation to the master data records.

Changing Master Data Records in SD

You can copy master records and change them via a variety of standard functions, but the system will record and time stamp every change.

In order to find a master record speedily, you can use any part of any data field as a matchcode.

Appreciating Organizational Structures

SAP R/3's general organizational units relevant to SD-Sales and Distribution are taken from the SAP R/3 Enterprise Data Model (EDM):

- *Client* is the highest level in SAP R/3. The transaction data of one client may not be accessed from another client. There is often a training client and a testing client, in addition to the client code that represents your group or corporate identity and under which the SAP system runs normal business. Some data is managed at the client level because everyone in the corporate group of companies will want to refer to exactly the same information and be certain that it is up to date and correct. Vendor addresses are an example of data managed at the client level.
- *Company Code* signifies a legal unit under the client level that produces its own financial documents, balance sheet, and profit and loss statement, and may well maintain them as continuously reconciled.

- *Plant* can be a production facility or a group of storage locations where stocks are kept. This term is also used in the context of "transportation plant" in the SD-Sales and Distribution system. The vehicle is treated as a temporary storage location. Planning and inventory management take place at the level of the plant, and it is the focus of materials management. It can supply its material stocks to more than one sales organization.

- *Sales Organization* has a legal connotation in that it represents the unit responsible for selling, and is therefore responsible for product liability and rights of legal recourse. All business transactions in SD-Sales and Distribution have to be processed financially within a sales organization. A sales organization can draw its materials from more than one plant.

- *Distribution Channel* defines how different materials reach the customer. Examples of distribution channels include wholesale trade, retail trade, industrial customers, and direct sales from the plant. A customer can be supplied through several distribution channels within a sales organization. Each sales organization may maintain its own material masters. By this means, it might hold different data for these materials from other sales organizations and perhaps separate sets for different distribution channels. Thus, prices, minimum order quantity, minimum quantity to be delivered, and delivering plant can differ for each sales organization and distribution channel.

- *Sales Division* is a subdivision of a distribution channel. The division may have been assigned only some of the total product range, and there may be customer-specific agreements for each division on such matters as partial deliveries, pricing, and terms of payment. You can carry out statistical analyses or set up separate marketing within a division. You can define a division-specific sales organization and freely nominate the products that form product groups, each handled by a separate division.

- *Sales Area* defines a combination of not more than one division, distribution channel, and sales organization. Thus, if there are two divisions using the same distribution channel, each division will belong to a different sales area. An individual customer can be assigned to more than one sales area if there are differing requirements and agreements to be considered. Prices, minimum order, and delivery quantities are the sort of factors that may have to be recognized by creating unique sales areas for them, always in the SAP R/3 structural context of a sales organization, and perhaps a sales division and distribution channel as well.

- *Sales Office* is a method of representing the internal organization. It is a division under the client level.

- *Sales Group* is a further internal subdivision of the people in a particular sales office.

- *Salesperson* is the subject of a unique personnel master record.

- *Shipping Point* is a location within a plant where deliveries are processed. Each delivery is assigned to and processed by one—and only one—shipping point. The shipping point is also an independent organizational entity responsible for scheduling and processing deliveries to customers, as well as to your own warehouses. The shipping point can be specialized with respect to delivering plant, type of shipping vehicle or method, and the loading equipment required.

■ *Loading Point* is a part of a shipping point that is able to offer a capacity to handle deliveries. There may be several similar loading points, and there may be different equipment at some loading points that makes them more suitable for particular types of deliveries—forklift trucks for pallets, for example.

The flexibility of the SAP R/3 system to represent complex and company-specific shipping structures depends on the combination of the various types of organizational units.

Some companies prefer to structure their SAP R/3 system from an accounting point of view; they focus on the various ledgers. Other companies concentrate on the variety and complexity of the products they handle and see their central function as materials management. Still others focus on sales and distribution. Of course, all companies will, from time to time, concentrate on each of these aspects. The SAP R/3 system implementers will seek to build a structure from the standard components that can represent all these points of view.

Defining Business Partners   A *business partner* is any person or organization involved in some way with a business transaction in SD-Sales and Distribution. For example, the customer, your sales representative, the carrier—each of these can be represented by business partner functions in the system. A separate master record is maintained for each business partner.

Defining Customers   The SAP R/3 organizational structure refers to customers and prospective customers as *customers*. A *vendor* is a business partner who carries out a delivery or a service for your company.

A business partner can be a customer and a vendor. If that is the case, you must maintain both a customer master record and a vendor master record for this business partner. You can associate the master records by entering the vendor number in the customer master record and the customer number in the vendor master record.

Documenting Your Sales Personnel   A numbered personnel master record stores data on each employee in your company. This master record resides in the HR-Human Resources module and access to it is strictly controlled by the Personnel department. If your company does not have the HR application installed, you can create a personnel master record in the SD application.

Serving Customers and Business Partners

If your company has business contacts, it will create and maintain a customer master record that contains all the data necessary for processing the business transactions. The accounting department shares the customer master records with the SD departments.

Each customer master record comprises separate data areas for the following purposes:

■ General data about your customer company that might be needed by anyone is stored in a shared area and is identified only by customer number. Maintaining the data can be done using both the master data's accounting view and the sales and distribution view.

- Data that is applicable to only one of the company code level members of your enterprise is stored in a separate area for each company code and is identified by customer number and company code.

- Data needed only for sales and distribution purposes is stored in a separate area for each sales organization and is identified by customer number, company code, and sales organization code.

Creating a Customer Master Record from the Center

The Accounting department is usually in the center of an organization. It may be a prudent policy for this authority to be responsible for creating customer master records that can then be used by affiliated company codes. In particular, customer master records can be created centrally for the payer and the sold-to party, who may also be the payer on some occasions.

There are two similar procedures, as follows:

1. Select Logistics>Sales/Distribution>Master Data.
2. Select Business Partners>Payer>Create>Create Centrally.

   or

   Select Business Partners>Sold-To Party>Create>Create Centrally.

The account group for the payer or sold-to party will be proposed automatically, and you will have to enter the rest of the data. When you enter this data you get access to all the customer master record's SD and Accounting screens. You will have function key links to some of them, and certain fields may have to be provided with special data input.

Creating a Customer Master Record for One-Time Customers

If your sales desk handles many customers who are unlikely to make additional purchases at a later date, it is probably not worthwhile to generate a separate customer master record for each of them. This is where the customer master record for a one-time customer is used. All one-time customers are added to the same master.

The following sequence will set this up:

1. Select Logistics>Sales/Distribution>Master Data.
2. Select Business Partners>One-Time Customers>Create.
3. You have to declare your position in the sales structure by sales organization, distribution channel, and division.

The system will automatically propose CpD as the account group for a one-time account and then assign an internal number for each one-time customer. You accept this by pressing Enter.

The Address screen that you see composes only those fields that can be identical for all one-time customers—they will all be stored on the single master. You should enter a generic title that you want to use for all one-time customers on the master's In the Name field. You might use a geographical region, or you could lump them together on the basis of their inquiries' sources.

After a successful creation of a one-time customer master, you will get a message of the following form:

```
Account <customer number>
Created for SlsOrg. <sales organization>
DistCh <distribution channel>
Div. <division>
```

After you have created suitable one-time customer masters for the various ways in which you want to group them, the system will identify a new customer that can be added. As you are creating a sales order for a customer whose data fits, you will be automatically shown a new customer number and invited to complete the Address screen, as well as add other relevant information according to the one-time customer master's format.

Using a Reference for Customer Master Record Creation

Entering an existing customer number in the Customer field is a quick way to create a customer master record. You might choose as a model a customer you expect to have similar characteristics. The system will copy general data into a new customer master record.

If you also enter data that identifies a sales area, the sales and distribution data that can be shared will also be copied. Country, language, and account group will be copied by default. Unique data, such as the address and unloading points, is not copied. You can change any data that has been copied from a model or reference customer master.

Your customer may already be the subject of a customer master record in another sales area. The general data will therefore not need to be entered again.

Grouping Master Data

Grouping master data records is a means of allowing them to be used elsewhere. Customer master records, material master records, and price master records can all be created and edited in one sales organization and assigned groups for use in other distribution channels or divisions. These sharing arrangements are set in Customizing.

Understanding Customer Hierarchies

Many of your customers may work in hierarchies that are at least as complex as your own. They may have a structured buying organization, for example, or a complex set of outlets to which you may have to assign deliveries.

In spite of this complexity, a customer may rightly expect to enjoy price rebates on the basis of the combined purchases—and the billing structure may be no less complex.

Manipulating Customer Hierarchies

You must expect a customer hierarchy to evolve and change. SAP R/3 handles this scenario by maintaining representations of customers in the form of hierarchical structures in which the nodal elements can be moved and changed.

If you reassign a node in a customer hierarchy, the system will automatically reassign any elements subordinate to this node. If you assign a new customer to a node, all the pricing agreements and other arrangements will be inherited by default from the parent node. If the object you are assigning is itself a hierarchy, all the subordinate elements will also inherit characteristics from the new point of attachment.

By this use of hierarchical objects, the master record system can keep track of any changes in your customers' structures. If they reorganize assets that are potential customers already in your database, your records will be automatically changed to record the newly inherited properties. If a customer acquires a new company with whom you have already done business, your customer master structure can be updated and this will update all the subordinate records.

Assigning Customer Hierarchy Types

If you have a number of customers that are structured in a particular way, you can define a new hierarchy type in Customizing for Sales. The standard default is hierarchy type A.

You can associate each hierarchy type with a particular business purpose and allow only certain account groups to be used in that hierarchy type. You may also have reason to permit only certain types of organizational data to be associated with a specific hierarchy type.

A customer delivery location is typically located at the lowest node of a hierarchy. Above this level may come a customer master record representing a regional office with its own purchasing capability. Above this may come a head office level, again with a customer master record because it can place orders with you. At a still higher level you may have a customer master record to represent the global enterprise that associates all your complex customer's affiliated companies.

The concept of "hierarchy path" refers to the chain of responsibility that links one node in a hierarchy to another at a different level. These paths are used to aggregate quantities and values when calculating customer rebates, for instance.

Hierarchies are designed to represent complicated entities that are prone to modification and rearrangement. You can rapidly reform clusters of nodes and your system will do its best to fill in all the changed details for you—but there can be anomalies. One level of a customer hierarchy may be enjoying a different rebate validity period from another with which it has become merged. Such inconsistencies are detected and reported as errors, which you can interpret by asking for Edit>Error Analysis when the problem node is highlighted in the error message.

From Here

Part
I
Ch
1

This chapter covers sales orders from customers and how your company can efficiently identify the goods and services they require. How can you keep up to date with your customers' restructuring movements? You might like to move on to one of the following:

- Chapter 2, "Processing Sales Orders Efficiently"
- Chapter 3, "Pricing Products and Services to Improve Sales"
- Chapter 4, "Billing"
- Chapter 5, "Arranging Shipping and Transportation"

Processing Sales Orders Efficiently

Automating Business Processes

Although the SD application is optimized to progress routine sales order processing, you can also implement more specialized business processes. For example, the SD application can control the processing of make-to-order items, service contracts, and configurable products.

Predefined texts can form an important resource that can be called upon to facilitate sales and distribution. Methods for maintaining and utilizing texts are an important component of this chapter.

Establishing Pricing Agreements

The SD-Sales and Distribution System will carry out pricing automatically using predefined prices, surcharges, and discounts. You can change the data proposed by the system for computing prices, and you can also change the price for a particular business transaction.

This pricing method is applied to quotations, sales orders, and billing documents. You can call for pricing analysis at any time so that you can inspect the figures and the procedures used to arrive at the price proposal.

The price charged for each particular material or service is what has to be found. The system looks first for a customer-specific material price and uses that if it finds one. If it does not find it, it seeks a price-list price valid for a business segment or some other sector of the market that includes this customer. Only if there is no valid price list will the system use the basic price for the material.

This logical sequence of methods for determining a material's price is set out in the form of a *condition*, which is stored as a condition master record. There is no limit to the complexity of a condition because it must control how the system assembles the cost data and other factors that go into the calculation of a price.

For example, a material might have a base price and a price for the duration of a sales promotion. The material may be a member of a price group that specifies that it shall be subject to a certain surcharge or discount. There may be a surcharge if less than a specified quantity is ordered. Some materials have to be priced to reflect the changes in the currency exchange rate of its country of origin to its point of sale. A particular customer may be allowed a particular price discount; the quantity ordered may attract further discounts. If the customer agrees to pay in advance, there may be a rebate to be taken into the price calculation.

Any of these factors that can affect pricing may be computed according to specific formulas and logical conditions that control when and how the contributing elements are to be taken into the calculation.

Although the calculation will take place automatically, the user and the customer can be shown the details of the calculation under certain conditions that will appear as data in the relevant condition master.

Sales taxes are handled in a similar manner—using logical conditions and formulas appropriate to the pertinent legal system in force.

When the system has arrived at a price to charge for the specific material, it then looks to see if a discount has been defined for this material, this customer, or this material only if bought by this customer. Thus, the system ends up with a price to charge for each item in the sales order.

A further check is then made to see if the total value or total quantity should attract further surcharges or discounts.

Only when the system has arrived at an appropriate material price for each item, applied the discounts and surcharges, reviewed the totals for further surcharges and discounts, and allowed for any sales tax will it copy the price into the quotation, sales order, or billing document.

Understanding Promotional Pricing Agreements

As of release 2.1, SAP R/3 has allowed you to create and maintain groups of condition records for the express purpose of rebate processing. The type of rebate agreement your business requires can be represented as a set of different condition types and condition tables. Release 2.2 enhanced this facility to serve the consumer packaged goods industry and other situations in which marketing programs with extensive discount structures are the norm.

Promotion agreements are differentiated from sales deals.

Master pricing data is maintained as areas of pricing elements:

- Prices
- Surcharges and discounts
- Freight
- Sales tax

You may get a price by consulting a price list and multiplying the material unit price by the quantity, or you may have a price agreement with the customer. The surcharges may be specific to a customer and they may be associated with particular materials.

These pricing elements will normally have only a limited validity period. A price list may go out of date each year; a sales discount will vanish as soon as the sales promotion is over.

Establishing Standard Price Agreements

The standard SAP R/3 is provided with the price agreements commonly used already predefined. These price agreements will be associated with a particular sales organization and distribution channel. The following price agreement types are standard:

- Material
- Customer
- Combination of customer and material
- Combination of customer and product hierarchy

- Combination of customer group and material
- Combination of customer group and product hierarchy

Your system supervisor can add to this set of standard price agreements if you are able to select suitable fields in an SD document that can be used to set up the condition records to compute the price agreement details. The values in a pricing element have to be associated with a currency, although a set of scale points can be used instead of a continuous numerical relationship.

Analyzing Sales Information

In addition to the standard functions for finding and altering individual sales documents online with a customer, sales managers have a choice of reports for displaying and analyzing sales data; this functionality is available as the Sales Information System (SIS). You can customize the reports to suit your requirements. Many companies use this system to build work lists of items selected. What follows is an example:

- Orders with incomplete data
- Credit holds
- Backorders

Exchanging Information Using Texts in SD

In the SD system, business communication between partners in the logistic chain is supported by texts in master records and documents. It is your choice whether you build a text for a single customer or set up information panels that can be used in a variety of situations. Texts are set up in Customizing as follows:

- Sales notes for customers
- Sales texts for materials
- Explanations in order confirmations
- Shipping instructions in deliveries

The system allows you to store texts in the customer master record, the material master record, and the sales and distribution documents. You are also provided with the following services:

- If you have set the control, texts from the customer masters will be offered as proposals in the sales and distribution documents.
- You can arrange for texts to be copied from a reference sales and distribution document into another sales and distribution document (from an order into a delivery, for example).
- The automatic copying of texts can be made dependent on language.

■ Copied texts can be changed even if the references have been canceled.

■ Standard texts can be inserted into sales and distribution documents.

Accessing Text Screens

The customer master record has fields you can edit by choosing Extras>Texts from the screens for general data, sales and distribution, and the contact person.

Material master records may include sales and purchasing texts that you can access by choosing Create or Change and then choosing Select View(s). Other texts are available via the following sequences:

■ Extras>Short Texts

■ Extras>Texts>Inspection Text

■ Extras>Texts>Basic Data Text

■ Extras>Texts>Internal Note

If you want to alter a header or item text in an SD document, you can't do so if it was originated by copying from master records or reference documents—unless you apply the Edit>Unblock sequence to a text you have marked. This has the effect of canceling the reference for text, which allows it to be altered and reused.

It may happen that you want to edit more text than the text screen has space for. You must mark the text in the customer master record and then select Edit>Text>Details. If you are working in a material master record, the sequence is Edit>Long Text>Long Text Screen. In all of these cases, you will be taken to the SAPscript editor to continue editing the long text.

The X indicator appears after a short text if there is a long text associated with it.

Entering Texts in Different Languages

If you want to create a text that already exists in a language other than the original text's language, you have to select the original and follow the Edit>Create procedure until extra lines appear above the original. You have to indicate which language it is in the Language column by identifying it with a matchcode.

Responding to Sales Queries, Inquiries, and Quotations

SAP R/3 has documents specifically for sales queries because your sales representative may need to capture important information before a sales order is formally placed. The system will later be able to refer to this information if necessary, perhaps for a firm quote or for subsequent sales analysis.

Separating Types of Sales Queries

There are three types of standard document types available for sales queries:

- Inquiries
- Quotations
- Sales Information

You can define extra types in Customizing for Sales. For example, you may want to develop a Competitive Quotation type with which you can associate particular competitive information.

Using an Inquiry   A general sales query can be processed as an inquiry. A prospective customer asks about a brochure, but you may be able to glean additional information. That extra information enables you to take the query a little further, allowing you to

- Enter specific products.
- Enter descriptions of products to be researched.
- Carry out automatic pricing.
- Manually check the availability of some items that might be of interest.

Using a Quotation   If your prospective customer has already arrived at some relevant information, you may be able to initiate any of the following actions by creating a quotation:

- Enter specific products.
- Enter descriptions of products to be researched.
- Carry out automatic pricing.
- Manually check availability.
- Check order probability.
- Offer the customer alternative items.

The advantage of using a quotation is that you respond in writing with a binding offer to the prospective customer.

Identifying Sales Information   Your customer may not want a firm quotation at this stage. What you do in this circumstance is identify the document as sales information. It can later be used as a reference for a sales order or for sales analysis.

If you are going to maintain data to support a system of sales queries, you should be sure that the extra work is justified. A system that would benefit from adopting sales query documents has the following characteristics:

- You make few sales of high value.
- You make many sales of low value, but you can negotiate better purchase deals if you have information analyzed from sales queries.
- You operate in a context where customers usually invite bids and tenders from many suppliers, and you want to track how your organization is responding, whether you are successful or not.

■ You want to compare the value of quotations with the value of subsequent sales to see if quotations can be made more predictive.

■ The number of quotations issued is to be compared with the number of successful conversions for each salesperson or group.

Calculating Order Probability

The system can calculate the percentage of probability that a customer for whom a sales query is generated will place an order. This can be inferred from cumulated data stored for the sales document type and for specific customers. From this probability, an expected order value can be computed and displayed on the overview screen. You can then inspect your queries, sorted by order value.

You may have several alternative products or packaging arrangements that could be offered to the customer. Again, the system can cumulate a customer's most probable choices and present them as alternative material determinations.

Building a Quotation from Scratch

If you have no available reference, the following sequence will generate a quotation:

1. Select Logistics>SD>Sales.
2. Select Quotation>Create.
3. Enter the quotation type.
4. Enter the organizational data as necessary.
5. Press Enter to complete the first stage.

You must then enter the following data:

■ Sold-to party's customer number

■ Start and end validity dates for the quotation

■ Material numbers or text for the Description field

■ Quantities

You can mark item data and edit it, and you can supply extra data for the header.

Changing a Quotation

If one of your customers wants to accept some of the items in your quotation but not others, you have to update the quotation. Any items you want to reject on behalf of your customer have to be marked with a standard reason for rejection.

Offering the Customer Alternative Items

You can offer a customer alternatives for an item in a quotation by the following procedure. Use the quotation's double-line entry screen:

1. Enter as the main item what you think the customer is most likely to choose (if you know it).

2. Enter the information for the alternative item directly under the main item.

You have to enter the material number of the alternative in the Material field, and in the AltItm field you have to point out the material for which it is a possible substitute; you do this by entering the material number assigned in the main item. You can repeat the process to accumulate several alternatives to the one main item.

Of course, you may be using a reference that already includes alternatives. In that circumstance, the system will routinely copy only the main items. If it is an alternative that you want copied, you can mark it in the Selection List dialog box that automatically appears whenever you are building a document by copying items selected from a reference.

User Techniques in Sales Order Management

There are some facilities available to all sales documents that can be particularly useful in sales order processing. In particular, the user should be familiar with the following techniques:

- Fast change is a method of changing one field in many documents simultaneously.

- The incompletion log provides an automatic reminder when you save a document if the system discovers that essential information is missing.

- Many routes are allowed for copying information from one sales document to another by citing the source as a reference document. Your administrator may well prevent you from copying out-of-date information. There may be partial copying and later copying of items not previously referenced. A reference item that is assigned the status Complete cannot be subsequently copied.

- Product proposals can be suggested using the most likely order from each customer based on previous sales.

- Checking can be undertaken before any copy is made (to ensure that the customer does not receive any irrelevant information in the quotation, for example).

Entering Dunning Data in a Sales Document

Different business cultures adopt their own terminology and approach to the (often essential) task of pressing a customer to pay for the goods and services already delivered. This section refers to *dunning* as the range of reminders that are presented according to the dunning policy your company has set up for a particular customer.

Dunning can be initiated by a dunning key or blocked at the header or item level in a sales document. The dunning key comes into operation in sales processing. It specifies the maximum number of dunning levels. The key can be chosen to apply other conditions, such as authorizing only one dunning document for a specific line item, even though a multilevel dunning procedure is generally in force.

You may want to hold up dunning on certain line items. For example, your customer may have been in touch with you about the reason for withholding payment. You can place a dunning block on the items in question until the issue is resolved.

Whatever dunning keys or blocks are in a sales document are automatically copied to sales orders. That's where they will be sent from during billing by the Accounting department, which controls dunning.

Perform the following steps to enter a dunning key or a dunning block at the header level so as to make it applicable to the entire list of line items:

1. Select Header>Business Data.

2. Select Edit>Billing Details.

All the items will then carry the header dunning key or block. To single out an individual line item, select Item>Business Data.

Displaying Changes Made in a Sales Document

It can often be useful to review all the changes made in a sales document. A listing will display the situation before and after changes are made, the date of the changes, and the name of the user who made them.

You will also be given statistical information and told which fields and tables have been affected by the changes. The following are the procedures:

1. Enter the number of the document you are interested in from within either the Change Mode Environment or the Display Environment.

2. Select Environment>History>Changes from the initial document screen.

3. Enter criteria that will narrow the search to the type of changes you are looking for.

4. Select Document Changes>Choose.

N O T E If you have marked a line with your cursor, the Choose function will give you further information about the change. ■

What you will see next is the Changes in Sales Order<Sales Order Number> dialog box. You can go on to dig deeper for information:

- Select List>All to see all changes made to this document.
- Select List>Additional Info>Insert

  or

  Select List>Additional Info>Mask to control the display of further information about this document.
- Select Goto>Statistics to inspect statistics on the changes made to the document.
- Mark the line with your cursor and select Goto>Technical Info to obtain information on fields and tables affected by the change selected.

Operating with Contracts and Release Orders

You may agree with a customer that they will order a certain quantity from you within a stated time period. This will take the form of a quantity contract that specifies basic quantity and price information. At this stage there will be no schedule for specific delivery dates and quantities.

By contrast, a scheduling agreement will include the details of a quantity contract, with delivery dates and quantities also specified.

When the customer places a sales order against a contract, it is referred to as a *release order* or a *call-off*. When you create a release order, you have to refer to the relevant contract so as to allow the system to automatically update the released quantities in the contract. A release order is otherwise processed like a standard sales order.

Creating a Quantity Contract

The following procedure will create a quantity contract:

1. Select Logistics>SD>Sales.
2. Select Outline Agreement>Contract>Create.
3. Enter the contract type and the organizational data, if necessary.

N O T E The values for sales organization, distribution channel, and division may be proposed automatically from your user parameters. Entries for the sales office and the sales group are optional. ▨

You have to supply the particulars:

- ▨ Sold-to party's customer number
- ▨ Purchase order number of the customer for this document
- ▨ Dates for the validity period
- ▨ Material numbers
- ▨ Target quantities for the materials totals in the contract

Before you save the contract, you can supply or edit header or item details.

Creating a Release Order for a Quantity Contract

Unlike a scheduling agreement, a quantity contract does not stipulate delivery dates and quantities; you have to enter these with release orders.

1. Select Logistics>SD>Sales.
2. Select Order>Create.
3. Enter the order type and the organizational data, if necessary.
4. Select Sales Document>Create w/Reference>To Contract.

5. Enter the contract number.

6. Select Selection List.

N O T E   When the system can determine the relevant contract, it will display the quantities not yet released for each contract item. ■

7. Change the quantities for the release order, or deselect any contract item not wanted on this release order.

8. Select Copy.

9. Enter the customer's purchase order number.

You can amend any header or item data before you save the release order. You may want to accept proposals when building a release order, and you can make packing arrangements at this time.

N O T E   You may be restricted in the order types you are allowed to use for release orders. ■

Completing a Quantity Contract

If you want to close a quantity contract before all the items have been delivered, you have to assign a reason for rejection to each of the outstanding items, just as you might do in a sales order. When all the items have been delivered or rejected, the system will mark the status of the contract as Complete.

Processing Scheduling Agreements with Component Suppliers

It sometimes occurs that a number of suppliers are under scheduling agreements to deliver components that are subsequently sold in various aggregations. You have to prepare careful plans for release orders against these scheduling agreements. This is normally done as background processing under control of workflow management. It is prearranged in Customizing to accept supplier-provided information through EDI via the IDoc (Intermediate document technique).

However, you can operate the planning function online, so that you may make corrections and adjustments to the plans. For example, you can create new forecast or JIT delivery schedules that automatically replace those already there.

N O T E   A JIT delivery schedule will normally take precedence over a forecast delivery schedule regarding material requirements planning. There is a comprehensive system of planning indicators for setting up this type of logic. ■

Part
I

Ch
2

Defining General Data for Agreement Condition Records

If you record general data, it will apply to all subsequent condition records that you create for the agreement. Each agreement that you create is identified by a unique 10-digit number, which can be assigned by you or automatically by the system.

The following data fields can be predefined for an agreement and subsequently edited if necessary:

- Short text description
- Validity period
- Special terms of payment
- Special fixed value date
- Special additional value days

If you do not define special payment data, the normal default values will be adopted.

Managing Engineering Changes in Scheduling Agreement Releases

If you work in the component supply industry, you can expect changes to individual materials to take place from time to time. The customer will expect the material number assigned to a component to stay the same, even if improvements are made to the actual component. However, all engineering changes have to be subject to engineering change status methodology and have the change status associated with the material number as a supplement.

The engineering change status for a component in a delivery may have to change on a certain date or after a specified cumulative quantity is reached. What you must not do when copying materials data is allow the engineering change status to be copied if it is or will become invalid. For instance, you cannot make a production order that includes a copy of serial numbers from a previous order.

The following procedure is designed to manage the engineering change status of the line items in scheduling agreements with scheduling agreement releases:

1. From the scheduling agreement's overview screen, identify and mark the item for which you may have to create a change of status.
2. Select Item>Schedule Lines>Eng. Change Status.

You can specify either an engineering change status controlled by delivery date or one controlled by the planned cumulative delivery quantity, but not both. You will have to enter the details as agreed with the customer.

Correcting Deliveries for Scheduling Agreement Releases

If your R/3 implementation comes into use in the middle of a scheduling agreement, you may have to alter the values stored for the cumulative quantities. If a deviation arises between your records and your customer's, again, you may have to correct the quantities by posting a correction delivery.

The following sequence is appropriate when you are in the relevant delivery schedule or JIT delivery schedule screen:

1. Select Edit>Correction Delivery.

N O T E In the Correction Delivery screen, you may find it helpful to select Display in order to first inspect the delivery history list, and then locate the delivery to be corrected using the Change function. ▪

2. Enter the correction date and correction quantity into the dialog box.
3. Place a minus symbol after the quantity to enter a negative correction.
4. Select Post Delivery>Enter.

Entering Packing Proposals

In scheduling agreements with scheduling agreement releases, you may have to comply with regulations on how and in what quantity a material is to be packed.

You have to enter a packing proposal:

1. Enter the quantity of each item to be packed as a shipping unit in the Rounding Quantity field in the double-line overview display.

   If packing quantities do not have to be rounded up to complete units for shipping, the rounding quantity for the respective scheduling agreement item must be reset to 0 in the double-line overview screen.

2. Select Edit>Packing Proposal>Packing Items screen.

   If you have entered a non-zero value, it will appear in the Partial Quantity field and be copied as a packing proposal in shipping.

Managing Returns for Scheduling Agreements with Scheduling Agreement Releases

Standard SAP R/3 will create a rush delivery automatically in the background when you save a return with sales document type RZ; RZ is the instrument for recording returns covered by a scheduling agreement with scheduling agreement releases.

This rush delivery is created so that your company can arrange an immediate collection of the materials not required. If you do not need to pick up returns immediately, you can have a new sales document type created in Customizing that is a copy of RZ, but with the immediate delivery indicator switched off. Delivery returns will then be created and appear for normal processing in a work list.

Part
I
Ch
2

Performing Analyses in Scheduling Agreements with Releases

There are three main types of analyses that you can call for regarding scheduling agreement releases. If you select Edit>Analysis from the Forecast Delivery Schedule/JIT Delivery Schedule screen, the following possibilities can be accessed:

- Compare scheduling agreement releases/scheduling agreement release histories
- Display schedule lines in a scheduling agreement release
- Display go-ahead quantities

The Agreement Release Histories function gives the means to make any of the following comparisons:

- Forecast delivery schedule with forecast delivery schedule
- Forecast delivery schedule with JIT delivery schedule
- JIT delivery schedule with JIT delivery schedule

A graphical display of any comparison is available.

If you mark a scheduling agreement release in the Analysis screen and select Goto>Choose, you will be able to inspect the scheduling agreement release's schedule lines. A graphical display is available.

You can select Goto>Display Releases from the Analysis screen to see the cumulative material go-ahead, production go-ahead, and delivery quantities. A graphical display is available.

From Here

This chapter focuses on scheduling agreements. You might like to move on to one of the following:

- Chapter 3, "Pricing Products and Services to Improve Sales"
- Chapter 7, "Managing the SD Communications"
- Chapter 8, "Using Modern Sales Systems"

Pricing Products and Services to Improve Sales

Understanding Service Management

The SM-Service Management component is a system of functions assembled from the following application modules:

- PM-Plant Maintenance
- MM-Materials Management
- SD-Sales and Distribution

Service notifications, warranties, service orders, and service contracts are the principal instruments managed by SM.

The scope of SM can thus include the planning and processing of external maintenance and repair services. The component can support the management of calls, logging, planning, procuring, call completion, and billing.

The plant or equipment that is the object of a service contract can be represented in the SAP R/3 standard hierarchical structure of master records and the Change Management functions can be applied to keep track of any changes the customer might make in the target plant.

A service contract may well involve internal staff and contract partners, all of which can be represented with the HR-Human Resources data structures.

Building a Service Contract

Two standard contract types are available as SD document types: maintenance and rental. They provide fields to store the following data:

- Start and end dates
- Cancellation terms
- Price agreements
- Follow-up actions

These documents can be customized.

Routine costs can be placed in the invoice via a billing plan. Replacement parts and unforeseen costs may be covered by the original warranty agreement. The details will be determined by reference to the original contract, and the SM system will automatically generate a billing request to be forwarded to SD for final billing. A service contract is treated as an outline agreement and managed as a quantity contract.

One way of starting a service contract is to copy data from preceding sales documents, such as inquiries and quotations. Although some goods may have to be moved, the items in a contract represent services and price agreements rather than deliveries. When goods movement takes place during service contract processing, the goods movement is always recorded in the corresponding sales order.

The costs to be collected in service orders are assigned by settlement rules to collectors such as the following:

- Cost center
- Project
- Sales order
- Service contract

A service contract will always bear status indicators, which show what stage it has reached and whether it is actively under control of a particular user.

Data regarding a service contract (such as validity dates and cancellation information) can be stored at the header level and against individual items, as appropriate.

Assigning Service Contract Texts

The following text types are available for use in service contracts:

- V001 General terms of contract
- V002 Sales text
- V003 Field service note
- V004 Note for person responsible
- V005 Extension note
- V006 Cancellation note
- 0014 Warranties

You can identify which of these text types will take part in the text determination procedure for service contracts during Customizing for Sales.

Interpreting Date Determination for Validity Periods

Every contract has a basic validity period, but there are variants:

- Early cancellation
- Extension
- End date automatically determined by the system
- End date entered manually
- Open-ended contract with a start date plus a period after which the contract may be canceled or automatically extended in accordance with the contract.

N O T E Indirect validity dates may be computed from a baseline date.

The following specifications exemplify baseline dates:

- Current date
- Start date

- End date
- Billing date
- Start date plus contract duration
- Installation date
- Assembly date
- Acceptance date when the customer officially accepts the installation
- Contract signature date

Specifying Cancellation Formalities

The following cancellation data may appear at header or item level:

- Cancellation procedure
- Cancellation reason
- Customer's cancellation document number
- Requested cancellation date
- Date cancellation received
- Follow-up action
- Date of follow-up action
- Cancellation party
- Date of customer's document

Understanding Service Contract Items

A service item can be used to represent any of the following aspects:

- Service to perform a particular task
- Material such as a replacement part
- Time spent by a technician
- Response time obligated by contract
- Warranty, represented as the agreed duration and replacements coverage

Creating the Master Data for Service Contracts

A service can be recorded using a master of the type Standard Product—Configurable. The Configuration Editor will be offered as you enter each item in the service contract.

If many of your service contracts are similar, you may decide to create a standard service product with most of the values defined in advance.

The items in a service contract may be composed of some rented items and some purchased items. However, they may only be combined as a multiple item if the same service contract conditions apply. Pricing follows the standard procedure and may apply variants according to the sales area, customer, and sales document. Extra items, such as spares, are added independently to the invoice.

Billing and Service Processing

You may need to bill the various costs of a service in different ways. The following are examples:

- Monthly fee for a maintenance contract, invoiced monthly by a billing plan assigned to the item
- Costs such as labor and parts incurred during service calls, billed using resource-related billing
- Cost determination by reference to a price agreement

The following sequence is suitable:

1. Select Logistics>Sales/Distribution>Sales.
2. Select Outline Agreement>Contract>Create.
3. Enter **WV** for a maintenance contract type

   or

   Enter **MV** for a rental contract.

N O T E The letter codes may have been customized to suit your particular implementation.

You may add organizational data in the form of values for sales organization, distribution channel, and division. The sales office and the sales group may also be identified in the contract; enter the following data:

- Customer number of the sold-to party in the Sold-To Party field
- Purchase order number of the customer for this document
- Start and end dates
- Material number as a standard product or configured product
- Target quantity for the material

If you identified a standard product, the system will automatically display the Configuration Editor; this allows you to enter the values for the characteristics defined in the standard product. If you identified a configured product with predefined values, the system automatically copies these values into the contract.

The following sequence will allow you to complete the header data:

1. Select Header>Contract>Contract Data.
2. Select Enter Run Time>Enter Cancellation Data.

Processing Follow-Up Actions for Service Contracts

In order to prepare for when a contract ends or is canceled, you can enter a follow-up action and a date when the activity should be carried out. You have the following options:

- Create a service contract.
- Create a sales activity.
- Create a quotation.
- Send an electronic mail message to another employee.

You can selectively display the follow-up actions for a range of contracts and have the system prompt you to execute them by offering the specified document for action.

Operating Pricing with Conditions

A pricing element is defined as a condition type. The following are predefined in standard SAP R/3 SD:

- Prices
- Surcharges
- Discounts
- Freight charges
- Sales taxes

The following sequence occurs automatically during sales order entry:

1. Find a gross price.
2. Subtract all relevant discounts.
3. Add any surcharges, such as freight and sales tax.
4. Calculate a net price for the sales order.

PR00 is the condition type that represents the price of a material. However, the price can be derived from various pricing records, as follows:

- Price for a specific customer
- Price list
- Basic material price

Each of the other pricing elements has its particular condition type: discount, surcharge, freight charge, and tax, for example.

Selecting from Competing Pricing Records

Your system may contain more than one price record for a material or service you are using in a sales document. There may be a gross material price used for most customers, but a special price for a particular customer.

The system automatically starts with a simple rule of seeking out the most specific price record, which will be a customer-specific price if one exists.

The next priority is to look for a price-list type that is valid for the particular customer. You may have a wholesale price list, for example.

If all else fails, the system adopts the basic material price.

This sequence of searching out the price is referred to as an *access sequence* and the details are set up during Customizing for Sales.

Setting the Validity of Material Prices

A material price is customized with two attributes:

- A price or a pricing scale for the specific material
- A combination of sales organization and distribution channel for which the material price is valid

Classifying Price List Types

There are no restrictions on how you define your pricing policies because you are allowed to define price-list types and associate them with customers in whatever system you prefer.

For example, you may have identified customer groups, such as wholesale, retail, or direct sales. The system will then choose the price list as soon as it can identify the customer group to which a prospective customer belongs.

Creating Customer-Specific Prices

When you want to allow a customer a special price, as a matter of policy you have to create a pricing record that is assigned to a specific combination of this customer and this material.

It may be useful to apply one of the standard computations for special discounts and surcharges or define formulae of your own during Customizing for Sales.

The following are examples of standard discount types:

- Customer, percentage discount (K007)
- Material, absolute discount (K004)
- Price group, percentage discount (K020)
- Material group, absolute discount by weight (K029)
- Customer/material, absolute discount (K005)
- Customer/material group, percentage discount (K030)
- Price group/material, absolute discount (K032)
- Price group/material group, percentage discount (K031)
- Rebate processing, group percentage rebate (BO01)
- Rebate processing, fixed material rebate (BO02)

- Rebate processing, customer percentage rebate (BO03)
- Inter-company processing, inter-company fixed discount (PI01)
- Inter-company processing, inter-company percentage discount (PI02)
- Invoice lists, factoring discount (RL00)
- Invoice lists, factoring discount, tax (MW15)

Any of these discount record types can be set up with particular values and thereafter referred to by their codes in condition records that control when they are used.

Understanding the Condition Technique in Pricing

The price is an amount used externally by customers and vendors. Pricing is also used to compute costs for internal purposes, such as cost accounting.

Conditions are the circumstances that should apply when a price is calculated in a particular way.

A *condition record* is a data store that can be consulted in pricing. The following standard functions are used to interpret condition records in the process of pricing:

- Validity Periods
- Pricing Scales
- Condition Supplements
- Condition Exclusion
- Upper and Lower Limits
- Reference Conditions

The idea of condition records in the SAP R/3 system is to have in the database a set of logical conditions that can be used when required, either singly or in any logical, valid combination. Pricing is controlled by such condition records because the price charged may well be affected by any or all of the following factors:

- The customer
- The product
- The order quantity
- The date

There will be various activities going on in the background when you are processing a sales order:

- Consult the sales document type and the customer master record to determine which pricing procedure to adopt.
- Identify, from the pricing procedure, the condition types that might be applicable and the sequence in which they are to be considered.

- Follow the associated access sequence (if there is one) for each condition type in order to identify the next key to use in searching for pricing records.

- When a valid pricing record is found, carry out the pricing procedure for the item and repeat the process until all condition types have been processed.

Summarizing the Condition Technique

The system includes standard pricing elements and surcharges, such as freight and sales taxes. If you need other variants, you can either modify the standard version or create entirely new pricing procedures.

To summarize, the elements used in the condition technique are as follows:

- Condition Types to define pricing calculations
- Condition Tables to define how pricing records are to be located in the database using search keys
- Access Sequences to specify the sequence of searches in terms of priority
- Pricing Procedures to control what appears on the sales documents and what control may be exercised by the sales representatives

Processing Promotional Pricing Agreements

The following procedure is used to create both promotions and sales deals:

1. Select Logistics>Sales/Distribution>Master Data.
2. Select Agreements>Sales Deal>Create.
3. Enter a sales deal type code and press Enter.
4. In the Overview Agreement screen, inspect the validity period proposed by the system.

At this stage you can record optional data:

- A short description of the sales deal
- An external reference from the customer
- The number of the promotion of which the sales deal is a part (if any)
- Special payment terms, which will be proposed automatically if the sales deal is assigned to a promotion where they have been specified

N O T E You can save the promotion or sales deal data at the overview agreement stage without generating any condition records.

Generating Condition Records for a Sales Deal

There are four ways to assemble the condition records for a sales deal:

- Create the condition records when you enter the master data for the sales deal.
- Create a new sales deal with reference to an existing sales deal and copy some or all of the condition records.
- Add new condition records to an existing sales deal.
- Copy existing condition records into a sales deal you have already created.

Selecting Variable Views of Condition Record Data

A view has a static part that displays the condition type and the fields that form the condition table key. There is a dynamic part that changes according to the view you select. The display of dynamic pushbuttons will change according to the customizing settings.

The following sequence enables you to work with condition records:

1. Select Logistics>Sales/Distribution>Master Data.
2. Select Pricing.
3. Select the change or display mode for the type of condition record (price, discount, surcharge) you want to work with.
4. Enter your selection data.
5. Select Execute.
6. Select Overview.
7. Choose one of the dynamic pushbuttons at the bottom of the screen to identify the view you require.

The following views are standard:

- Sales deal
- Administrative data (condition creator and creation date)
- Condition rate
- Terms of payment
- Validity period

You can also define what you want to see and create your own variable screen in Customizing. It will be added, as a view, to the set of pushbuttons.

Using the Customer-Expected Price to Avoid Disputed Invoices

Customers in some industries will deduct disputed invoices from payments. This entails extra staff effort to resolve disputes. It may be helpful to record the customer-expected price in all sales documents.

You can use the double-line overview screen of the sales order to manually record the expected price during order entry.

As an alternative, you can set up one of the following condition types:

- Customer-expected price (EDI1)
- Customer-expected value (EDI2)

You have to specify, in the pricing procedure's Alternative Calculation field, a formula that will be used to detect when there is a significant difference between the customer-expected price and the actual price.

If the system detects a difference during order entry, the sales order will be assigned the status of Incomplete, which will block it for delivery or billing until the discrepancy is cleared up and the block released.

In order to use the expected price condition types in the sales order, you first have to select Overview>Double-Line Entry when you are in the Sales Order screen.

If you intend the customer-expected price to refer to the net price per item, enter EDI1 in the Condition Type field and the price in the Rate field.

If the customer-expected price refers to the value of the item as net price times quantity, enter EDI2 in the Condition Type field and the value in the Rate field.

These additional data elements will appear as a new line in the Pricing screen.

The system will automatically mark the sales order as Incomplete if there is a discrepancy greater than that specified in the formula. You may be able to clear the problem before you save the sales order.

Some companies assign specific staff to the processing of sales orders lists marked as incomplete because of discrepancies in the customer-expected price.

Understanding Condition Exclusion

More than one condition record can satisfy the conditions to become applicable to a particular sales or billing document. *Condition exclusion* is a technique for dealing with this eventuality.

What you have to do is create some *exclusion groups,* which are lists of condition types defined in Customizing for Sales with an explanatory text appended. If you assign such groups to a pricing procedure, you can arrange for condition exclusion to operate when necessary.

For example, you can set up exclusion groups so as to accept the best price or discount on behalf of the customer. Examples of results achieved by exclusion group logic follow:

- Choose from the best condition records within an exclusion group.
- Choose from the best condition records within one condition type.
- Choose from the best conditions from different exclusion groups.

- Exclude the conditions within one exclusion group with the condition type from another exclusion group.

When you examine the Pricing screen on the sales order, you can still see any condition records that are valid, even if they have not been taken into account because of the condition exclusion technique.

It may happen that two discounts are applicable, one on the basis of the material and the other a customer-specific discount. The system determines which condition record yields the most favorable discount for the customer. Should the Exclusive Access indicator be set, the system will accept the first one it finds. In these circumstances, the system cannot determine a best price.

If the system is operating the Excluding the Conditions in an Exclusion Group procedure, the discovery of any applicable condition in the first exclusion group will automatically rule out all the conditions within the second exclusion group.

Using Configurable Products in Sales Order Processing

You can define a configurable product as an assembly of components that can be variable, both in terms of which components are included and in the nature of the components themselves. A particular boat may have exactly one of several engines, a mainsail, a foresail, and any number of additional sails from a variety of sailmakers. You can choose any color for the hull, provided it is white!

Such a product is represented in the system by a BoM. Several variants may be configured as standard price-list items, or you may combine variants for a particular customer using a Configuration Editor as you build the sales order. This editor will be presented automatically if you specify a configurable product, so that you can select from the available ranges of characteristics. This type of product will be identified in the classification system and this can be used to assemble a listing.

Understanding Products Managed in Batches

The following types of document enable you to enter individual batch numbers if the material is to be managed in batches:

- A sales query, such as an inquiry or quotation
- A sales order
- A delivery

If you make a manual entry of a batch number in a sales document, the system will check that the quantity you require is available and that the batch you have asked for has not exceeded its expiration date. Once you have declared batch numbers in a sales query, they are copied automatically if you use the query to make a sales order.

There may be a problem here—the batch numbers copied from a preceding document may not be altered. If you make a sales order without referring to a preceding sales document, you can alter batch numbers right up to the creation of a delivery.

The material master has an indicator in the Purchasing and Storage views to show that the material is managed in batches. It is also possible to create a material master for an individual batch.

The availability of a batch material is checked in two stages. The system looks first at the stock position at the batch level and then at plant level.

If you are going to specify a batch number, the system must be able to identify the delivering plant. Use the following sequence:

1. In the initial Order Entry screen, select a batch-relevant item and select Item>Business Data.
2. Either enter the batch number or select from the possible batches.

The system will review the availability of the batch entered and confirm the available quantity.

Batch determination can be carried out automatically in the delivery if an item contains a material that is managed by batch and there is no batch number specified in the sales order.

Understanding Sales Taxes

Country-specific sales taxes are set out as condition types. For example, Value-Added Tax (VAT), for use in some European countries, entails different parameters from tax-determination condition types for use in the U.S., where the standard version includes condition types for state, county, and city sales taxes, as well as taxes based on tax jurisdiction codes.

If the system is to conduct automatic calculation of sales taxes per item, the following parameters must be considered:

- Whether the business being transacted is domestic or foreign
- The tax classification of the customer's ship-to party
- The tax classification of the material

You can signify a Pricing Reference Material so that the system can consult all the condition records that apply to the reference material.

Conducting Manual Pricing

If you are working with condition types that allow it, you can manipulate pricing at both the header and item level during sales order processing. For example, you may be allowed to enter freight costs or apply a header-pricing condition that allows a discount over the entire order.

Manual entries could have been assigned priority over the results of automatic pricing, or the automatic may have been given absolute precedence.

When you are allowed, the following changes are possible:

- Changing a condition amount
- Deleting a pricing element
- Entering additional pricing elements

You cannot add pricing elements unless the corresponding condition types have been defined already. They must also be marked as open for manual processing.

The possibilities for changing automatically determined prices in the Pricing screen may include the following, depending on the configuration of the condition type:

- The rate, such as the amount of a price or the percentage of a discount
- The currency in which the amount is calculated
- The units of measure used to calculate the amount

The condition types for sales taxes and cash discount do not usually permit manual alterations.

You may be allowed to delete a pricing element completely. If so, the system will recalculate the total.

From Here

This chapter tells you about the ways condition records are consulted to conduct pricing in a versatile system that can provide an automatic pricing function, no matter how complex your pricing policies.

You might like to move on to one of the following:

- Chapter 4, "Billing"
- Chapter 5, "Arranging Shipping and Transportation"
- Chapter 6, "Trading Worldwide"

Satisfying the Customer

Billing

Understanding the Billing Module SD-BIL

The task of billing is to create the billing document and transfer the data to FI-Financial Accounting and profitability analysis.

SD-SLS Sales and SD-SHP Shipping are the source systems that provide the information used by SD-BIL Billing in the form of quantity and price data from the reference documents of the inquiry, quote, or sales order, for example. In their turn, these documents will have called upon the MM-Materials Management system to supply materials data.

The functions of SD-BIL Billing are designed to support the following operations:

- Create invoices for deliveries or services rendered.
- Respond to debit memo requests by creating debit memos.
- Respond to credit memo requests by creating credit memos.
- Cancel billing document.
- Transfer posting data to FI-Financial Accounting.

Differentiating Standard Billing Types

The system will interpret the billing document type and use it to control how the billing document is processed. For example, the following billing types are recognized by a standard SAP R/3 system:

- F1 Order-related invoice
- F2 Delivery-related invoice
- F5 Pro forma invoice for sales order
- F8 Pro forma invoice for delivery
- G2 Credit memo
- L2 Debit memo
- RE Credit for returns
- S1 Cancellation invoice
- S2 Cancellation credit memo

Your system administrator can set the control elements of each billing document type so that it is processed in exactly the manner needed by your company procedures. If the standard billing types don't meet all your requirements, you can define new billing types that do.

The following list suggests the kinds of variations that can be manipulated by the control elements of billing document types:

- The number range from which a new document of this type should be taken
- The partner functions permitted at header level
- The partner functions permitted at item level
- The billing type to be used to cancel a billing document

- The posting procedure:

    Transfer to Financial Accounting immediately

    Block for transfer first

    Not transfer at all

- Method of account assignment for Financial Accounting
- Choice of output allowed for the business transaction
- Procedure for proposing the output

Creating Billing Documents

A billing document can be created for a single delivery or sales order by entering the number of the delivery or sales order.

If there are several deliveries or sales orders awaiting billing, you have to direct your attention to the items on the billing due list.

Processing the Billing Due List   The work list of documents due for billing can be processed as a collective. You may prefer to restrict the selection of items from this billing due list by defining selection criteria, such as the billing date for a particular sold-to party.

As the system collects the details of the documents due for billing, it will compile a log showing the defects of any that are incorrect or incomplete, insofar as the system can check on these matters. You can examine this log and perhaps supply the information needed to correct the defective or incomplete items.

For all the items that are correct in the billing due list or the subset of it that you have defined, the system will automatically generate the billing documents and carry out the posting necessary to the accounts of the FI-Financial Accounting system.

Choosing the Pricing and Tax Determination Sources   When you are about to create a billing document, you have to decide whether to carry out pricing and tax determination again, using the latest figures, or to copy the prices, surcharges, and discounts from the sales order on which the billing document will be based. You can also change the price manually right up until the document is forwarded to the FI-Financial Accounting system by posting the completed billing document.

Creating the Billing Documents   When you create a billing document, you will not be allowed to enter the transaction unless you have referred to an existing sales order, delivery, or another billing document.

Your choices are as follows:

- Explicitly specify the documents to be billed by entering their numbers or searching for them by selecting a matchcode
- Process a billing due list

Part

II

Ch

4

In practice, you will probably use these methods in various combinations. You could enter some selection criteria and have the system select all the documents matching these criteria and enter them in a billing due list, perhaps as a background task. You can also arrange to combine several deliveries in one invoice.

If you specify a billing schedule for a particular customer, the system will automatically select the documents to be billed by the date defined in the billing schedule.

Using the Billing Methods

The choice of which of the several billing methods to use is determined by looking at the calendar that contains the billing schedule for the particular customer.

There are three main options:

- A separate invoice is created for each delivery.
- All deliveries within a particular user-defined period are combined to form a collective invoice.
- Several invoices are created for different parts of a delivery according to the criteria defined by the customer, such as material pricing group.

Making an Invoice List   If there is one payer responsible for several invoices, they can be combined in an invoice list. This list can be compiled by a collective run and can include both single and collective invoices.

There may be an advantage to the payer in this, because you can total the invoices on the list and apply discounts on the total value. You can grant factoring commissions, for example.

Either the individual invoices on the invoice list or the total of the list can be posted to FI-Financial Accounting.

Defining Billing Methods Rules   You can define the rules to be used to decide when and how to combine deliveries in a collective invoice or invoice list. You also have control over the rules that affect the splitting of invoices for each customer or for each type of business transaction.

Here are two examples of billing methods rules:

- The sales order has to be completely delivered and the goods issue has to be posted before a delivery can be invoiced.
- Deliveries or invoices cannot be combined if there is more than one payer.

Using Volume-Based Rebate Processing

After a specified period of time has passed, the sales to a specific customer in that period may qualify for the grant of a volume-based rebate. You may have arranged for invoices to be combined to assist in reaching the rebate level.

The rebate is a payment subsequent to the settlement of all the individual orders. It is arranged in the form of a credit memo posted to the account of the customer to whom it has been granted.

Setting Up Rebate Conditions   In the SD-Sales and Distribution system, the rules for automatically granting volume-based rebates are set up in the form of logical conditions that have to be met. During customizing, you can define the criteria and the critical values making up the conditions for a rebate agreement.

For example, you can agree to grant a rebate rate based on the overall volume of sales to a specific customer in a certain period. You can grant an additional rebate for sales in a defined product group. And you can offer yet another rebate if the volume of sales of certain specific materials reaches a predefined value.

Any bill-to party can enjoy a rebate. This facility allows you to use rebate agreements to control the payment of licensing fees or commission payments.

Accruals in FI-Financial Accounting for volume-based rebate processing are created automatically. In every invoice, the rebate rate is recognized as an accruals rate, and the amount is posted to the appropriate account.

Calculating a Rebate   Rebate settlement begins with a run to compile a list of credit memo requests. This will be based on the sales and the accruals. You may wish to edit this list manually.

When the credit memo request list has been released, you can create the credit memos. These will reverse the accruals in the FI-Financial Accounting system. You will thus credit the customer for the rebates you have granted.

Part

II

Ch

4

Simulating the Billing Due List

You may find it useful to try out the processing of a billing due list without making any financial postings. The simulation option is provided for this purpose. Any document marked for billing will be processed, and the system will display a list of the billing documents that would be created. Any simulated billing documents containing errors will be displayed with useful information about their processing status.

During a billing due list simulation run, you can also display the following information:

- Billing items
- Error log
- Data on foreign trade
- Log for the Billing Run, which will tell you which documents were created if this billing due list has been processed on a previous occasion

Processing the Billing Due List   The following sequence is appropriate for processing a billing due list:

1. Select Logistics>Sales/Distribution>Main Menu>Billing.
2. Select Billing Document>Billing Due List.
3. If the billing date is not the current date, enter the billing date in the To field.

You may expect too many billing documents to be created in a single batch by using the full billing due list. You can usefully limit the output according to a single sold-to party or by specifying a particular destination country. Such conditions can be combined to limit the output to suit your requirements.

The defaults proposed by your system may not be exactly what you require. Perhaps you need a different billing document type for certain customers. You can alter the defaults by accessing the Settings menu, where you will be able to edit the default data.

Specifying the Documents to Be Selected   You can arrange for your documents to be grouped for billing according to the following types of characteristics:

- Order-related
- Delivery-related
- Rebate-related
- Intercompany billing document

Checking the Billing Due List   Before the billing documents are actually created, you can inspect the billing due list and make amendments to it if necessary. The following sequence is appropriate:

1. Select Billing Document>Display Billing List.
2. Unmark any documents you do not want to invoice.
3. Select Billing Document>Save.

The next display will be the Log for Billing Run screen, which contains the following information:

- The billing run number in the title bar
- The number of billing documents created
- The number of errors

If you have selected Simulate and subsequently want to save some of the billing documents, the following procedure is appropriate:

1. Mark the relevant documents.
2. Select>Billing Document>Save.

The following procedure will display the billing documents generated from the billing due list:

1. Select Logistics>Sales/Distribution>Billing.
2. Select Billing Document>Billing Log.

The following data has to be entered:

- If known, the number of the billing run should be entered in the Number of Collective Run field.

■ The user who processed the billing due list should be entered in the Started By field.

■ The billing date should be entered in the On field.

The Select>Goto>Notes sequence will display any errors on the billing documents created.

If you are not conducting the billing due list run in simulation mode, and if no errors have been detected, the billing documents are created and the billing data is passed to the Accounting department.

When you are setting up a search specification for billing due lists, you may have targeted more than one. If only one billing due list exists for the chosen selection criteria, you will be shown the screen titled Log of Collective Run *<number of the collective run>*.

If several billing due lists match your search codes, you will see the screen named Existing Collective Runs for Deliveries and Billing Documents. By marking the line with your cursor, you can elect to see any of the following:

■ Notes

■ Billing Documents

■ Document Flow

Processing Billing as a Background Task

Billing can be processed as a set of background tasks to reduce overall processing time. For example, you might decide to divide the work according to the customer or sold-to party. Alternatively, you can divide your runs according to document number ranges. Each run can be started as a separate process that will run in parallel.

Defining Billing Schedules   The typical occasion for using billing schedules is when you have some customers who require invoices to be processed periodically. One collective invoice is issued for all deliveries due for billing by a certain time. You will have to define a billing schedule for these customers.

What you have to create is a factory calendar that is made up of special rules rather than a set of working days. These special rules identify the days on which billing has to be carried out. For example, an invoice can be required every last working day of the month. You have to specify this day as both the Valid From day and the Valid To day. This single day becomes the only working day each month for the purpose of issuing invoices.

You have to quote the ID number of this factory calendar in the Billing Schedule field on the Billing screen of the payer's customer master record.

When a sales document is processed, the system will copy the billing date from the factory calendar to the relevant document as follows:

■ For credit and debit memo requests and returns for which order-related billing is carried out, the system copies the billing date into the sales document.

- For sales documents such as standard orders for which delivery-related billing is carried out, the system copies the billing date into the delivery. However, it is not displayed there.

When the specified next billing date on the factory calendar arrives, the system will select all sales orders and deliveries and assign them to a billing due list. Because the ID number of the factory calendar is defined in the customer master record, all sales orders or deliveries for that customer over a particular period will share the same billing date. They can all be assigned to the one collective invoice.

Canceling Billing Documents The way to cancel a billing document is to create a cancellation document that cites the original billing document. When you post a cancellation document, the system will create the necessary reversal documents in FI-Financial Accounting. You can cancel credit memos and invoices in the same way.

Some errors or changes can be dealt with by editing the billing documents. Other errors cannot be rectified except by canceling the billing document and making a fresh one without any errors. The critical moment is usually when the document is posted for transfer to Financial Accounting. Editing may be possible before then. Canceling may be the only option after posting if, for example, the billing data has been posted to the wrong accounts when it was transferred to the Accounting department.

The act of canceling a billing document is actually one of creating a cancellation document, which entails copying data from the reference document and transferring an offsetting entry to the Accounting department. This offset allows you to bill the reference document once again.

If you find there is a problem because your billing document contains an invalid account assignment, you will not be able to post a straightforward cancellation document, because this will automatically copy the account assignment error, which the system will reject. However, the original data must be passed on so that the billing documents can be reorganized. What you have to do is to post a cancellation document and then complete the original billing document.

N O T E As of release 3.0E, the billing document is completed automatically after it has been canceled. ▦

When you complete the billing document, the system compares it with the corresponding cancellation document and sets the posting indicator in the two documents to "completed." Reorganization to clear the problem can then be carried out for both documents.

The following sequence should be adopted:

1. Select Logistics>Sales/Distribution>Billing.
2. Select Billing Document>Cancel.
3. Enter the billing document to be canceled in the Document column.
4. Select Edit>Execute.

From release 3.0E, the system automatically completes a document after it has created the corresponding cancellation document.

Up to release 3.0D, you have to complete a canceled document manually by using the following sequence:

1. Select Create Billing Document>Billing Document Change.
2. Enter the number of the canceled billing document.
3. Select Billing Document Complete.

N O T E If you need to, you can find the number of the canceled billing document by displaying the document flow in the cancellation document.

4. Enter the number of the cancellation document related to the canceled billing document and press Enter.

Once the "completion" operation on the billing document has been successfully concluded, the posting status in the billing document will be set to E. The corresponding cancellation document will also have a posting status of E. The posting status can be viewed in the Header Details screen for the billing document.

Understanding Invoices

When a sales order is executed, the deliveries and services are invoiced to the customer. The transaction ends there unless complaints are made about the delivery.

There are two main ways of generating an invoice:

- Specifying the document(s) to be billed
- Processing a billing due list

Your reference when creating an invoice can be a sales order or a delivery. For example, you would create an invoice on the basis of the delivery if you wanted to make sure the goods were sent out before the invoice is created. On the other hand, you might want to receive payment before letting the goods leave your warehouse. In this case you would create an invoice on the basis of the sales order. If it is a service you are billing, you would probably refer to a sales order rather than a delivery.

The standard version of SAP R/3 provides the following billing document types for invoices:

- Billing document type F1, which is based on the sales order
- Billing document type F2, which is based on the delivery

Creating Invoices

The following sequence is appropriate for creating an invoice for specific deliveries or sales orders:

Part

II

Ch

4

1. Select Logistics>Sales/Distribution>Billing.
2. Select Billing Document>Create.
3. In the Document column, enter the numbers of the deliveries to be invoiced.

   or

   In the Document column, enter the numbers of the sales orders for order-related invoices.

N O T E   If you need to change the default data proposed by the system, perhaps by referring to another billing document type, use the Select Settings>Default Data sequence. ▪

The following sequence will allow you to review the invoices created and change them if necessary:

1. Select Edit>Execute.

N O T E   If all sales orders or deliveries are correct and complete, the number of the last invoice created is displayed in the Edit screen. ▪

2. You will reach foreground processing, where you can display the notes on any errors in the log by selecting Edit>Log.
3. Select Billing Document>Save to return to background processing having saved the invoices.

N O T E   The invoices that contain errors are blocked for further processing. ▪

If any errors occurred in account assignment when you created a billing document and these can no longer be eliminated, you have to cancel and complete the billing document and inform your system administrator immediately.

Changing Invoices

You can make changes in an invoice before it is dispatched by doing the following:

1. Select Logistics>Sales/Distribution>Billing.
2. Select Billing Document>Change.
3. Enter the number of the invoice.

   or

   Select a matchcode and press Enter when you have located the invoice number.
4. Make the changes and save the billing document.

Before the invoice has been passed to the Accounting department, there are only certain changes you will be allowed to make, as follows:

- Change output and texts.
- Initiate new pricing for individual items.

or

Change the prices manually.

All you can do after the invoice has been passed to the Accounting department is to change the output and texts. Any changes to the rest of the invoice can only be handled by canceling the invoice and making another.

Displaying Invoices

In order to display a single invoice, follow this sequence:

1. Select Logistics>Sales/Distribution>Billing.
2. Select Billing Document>Display.
3. Enter the number of the invoice you wish to inspect or find the number by selecting a matchcode and pressing Enter.

You can also display all invoices that match the search specification you have defined, such as the blocked invoices or those that are for the same sold-to party. The billing due list processing log is also available for your scrutiny.

Displaying Changes to an Invoice

For inspection purposes, it can be very helpful to see only the alterations to an invoice or to the set of invoices that have been changed. The following sequence is appropriate:

1. Select Billing Document>Change.

or

Select Billing Document>Display.

2. Enter the invoice number.
3. Select Environment>Changes.

or

Press Enter and Select Environment>Changes.

Some of the errors may be correctable in time to avoid an adverse reaction from the customer; but there may well come a time when there has to be positive action to record and process an unsatisfactory situation.

Processing Complaints

There are two types of complaints: One can lead to a credit memo, the other to a debit memo. Having goods returned can justify a credit memo; so can a late delivery. On the other hand, if the customer has been undercharged, a debit memo may have to be posted. What you have to

Part
II

Ch
4

do is to decide how to deal with each complaint so the customer and your company are both reasonably satisfied with the outcome.

If a customer makes a complaint about a delivery concerning the quality or the type of goods, you can pick up the goods free of charge from the customer location and generate a returns order in the Sales department, which will lead to a credit memo request and eventually a credit memo posted to the customer's account in FI-Financial Accounting. The returns order will carry information about the complaint in short texts and perhaps free text, both of which can be analyzed later.

A credit memo request can also arise in the Sales department because the customer has complained about a late delivery. This request will be blocked for billing until the amount of the credit has been decided, when the request can be released and a credit memo created. The credit memo is posted to the customer's account in the FI-Financial Accounting system.

If a debit memo request is created in the Sales department, perhaps because a customer has been undercharged, a similar procedure is followed. This time, the result is a debit memo amount, which is posted to Accounts Receivable in FI-Financial Accounting.

Using Credit and Debit Memos

When a credit or debit memo is generated, the reference quantity is the order quantity minus the invoiced quantity. The standard version of R/3 will operate pricing so that pricing elements, including any surcharges and discounts, whether automatically determined or manually entered, are copied from the reference document without alteration.

Your system cannot process credit and debit memos unless a relevant reference document can be identified, such as a credit memo request for a credit memo. For instance, you might want one department to be responsible for deciding whether a credit or debit memo is justifiable, even though the request originated elsewhere.

While such decisions are being made, it is usual to have the system block the intended credit or debit memo or the returns document created for billing. Once a decision has been made, the credit or debit memo or the returns document can be released for financial action or rejected, whichever is decided. When your sales system is being customized, you can specify which billing types will be blocked in this way.

Allocating Billing Document Types

If you need to create a credit memo or a debit memo, the system will suggest a relevant billing document type according to the type of reference document, as follows:

Reference Document	Billing Document	Billing Document Type
Credit Memo Request	Credit Memo	G2
Returns Order	Credit for Returns	RE
Debit Memo Request	Debit Memo	L2

In many ways, credit and debit memos are handled like invoices. You can nominate the documents to be billed or specify them by a matchcode. You can process a billing due list. The system will determine whether a credit or debit memo is to be created from the reference document. However, there is one attribute that you must specify explicitly. This is the date of the sale or the services rendered. A credit or debit memo can refer to a transaction that took place in a previous tax accounting period. The system has to be able to determine how to compute the taxes for this period to propose a correct legal adjustment.

Creating Credit or Debit Memos

The following sequence is used to create credit or debit memos:

1. Select Logistics>Sales/Distribution>Billing.
2. Select Billing Document>Create.
3. Select Settings>Default Data.
4. Enter the date of the services rendered and, if necessary, additional default data.
5. Press Enter to release this data for the billing document.
6. Enter the number of the credit or debit memo request that is the reference document in the Document column.

You can use the Edit>Execute sequence to return to the foreground process where you can inspect the results. If there have been any errors, you can use Select Edit>Log to display the notes on the errors.

When you are satisfied, the sequence Select Billing Document>Save will re-engage background processing and save the invoices. However, the credit and debit memos will now be blocked for further processing because there have been errors.

If all sales orders or deliveries are correct and complete, the number of the last credit or debit memo created will display.

There may be an error in account assignment when you create a billing document. In such cases, you must cancel the document and rebuild another, having notified your supervisor.

Integrating with Financial Accounting

The integration of SD-BIL Billing with the FI-Financial Accounting application allows the system to carry out posting automatically when a billing document is created.

Understanding Pro Forma Invoices

The responsible authorities in a country that is importing goods or services may require advance warning that a shipment is about to be made. The importer may need the same advance notification. The instrument of choice for this purpose is the pro forma invoice. You can create one from a sales order or from a delivery.

Part
II

Ch
4

The reference quantity can be taken as the total order quantity or from the quantity of a particular delivery. The following billing document types are used as appropriate:

- Billing document type F5 is based on the sales order.
- Billing document type F8 is based on the delivery.

You do not have to wait for a goods issue before creating a delivery-based pro forma invoice. You can generate any number of pro forma invoices because they do not affect the billing status in the sales order or the delivery to which they have referred. No data from a pro forma invoice is passed to Financial Accounting.

The following sequence is used to create a pro forma invoice:

1. Select Logistics>Sales/Distribution>Billing.
2. Select Billing Document>Create.
3. In the Document column, enter the numbers of the deliveries.

   or

   In the Document column, enter the numbers of the sales orders you want to invoice.
4. Select Settings>Default Data.
5. In the Billing Type field, enter F5 for order-related pro forma invoices.

   or

   In the Billing Type field, enter F8 for delivery-related pro forma invoices.

You can review the pro forma invoices and alter them by the following sequence: Select Edit>Execute to reach foreground processing.

Pro forma invoices can be changed by following the same procedure for changing an invoice.

Error notes can be inspected in the log by selecting Edit>Log. If you then select Billing Document>Save, you will return to background processing having saved the pro forma invoices. If all sales orders or deliveries are correct and complete, the number of the last invoice created will display.

Building an Invoice List

Each of the documents you want to include in an invoice list must first be billed and transferred to Financial Accounting (FI). They will be blocked for normal dunning procedures until you have entered them on an invoice list and transferred it to FI. The invoice list date will be used by the system to calculate a new dunning date for each invoice.

The system will also copy the appropriate invoice list number to the relevant billing document as a reference number to be associated with incoming payments.

The transaction of saving an invoice list automatically creates an accounting document for the factoring discount and possible taxes. This accounting document is then posted to the corresponding G/L account in FI.

Payments from the customer are monitored from the FI-Financial Accounting system, and any dunning of overdue payments will originate from this system. The dunning key that determines the dunning procedure to be applied is first recorded in the sales order, either on the basis of customer master records or because you have made a manual entry of a dunning key or canceled the default key placed there by the system. This enables you to exclude the dunning of a customer for particular invoices.

Although the procedure is automatic, you can place a posting block on the transfer of invoices and credit or debit memos by an entry on the billing document. The posting will not take place until you release this block.

Your display facilities enable you to list blocked billing documents so you can easily attend to them.

The following sequence will begin the process of building an invoice list:

1. Select Logistics>Sales/Distribution>Billing.
2. Either, Select Invoice List>Create and enter each billing document individually.

   or

   Create a work list.

If you generate a work list of the billing documents that are needed to build an invoice list for processing, this list can be assigned for background processing.

The sequence for creating a work list to build an invoice list is as follows:

1. Select Invoice List>Edit Work List.
2. Enter the selection criteria.
3. Select Invoice List>Display Work List.
4. Select the billing documents you want in the invoice list from the work list.
5. Select Invoice List>Save.

Relating Invoice Lists and Factoring Discounts

An invoice list has the job of telling a particular payer on a specific date what billing documents have matured. The list can include invoices, credit memos, and debit memos. Any of these billing documents can be a collective invoice that combines items from more than one delivery. Standard R/3 provides for two types of invoice lists:

- Invoice list for invoices and debit memos
- Invoice list for credit memos

If you process invoices, debit memos, and credit memos together, the system will automatically create a separate invoice list for the credit memos.

A payer may be the head office of a buying group. This payer may accept all the invoices for goods that are shipped to individual members of the buying group. It is usual for the payer to collect not only the payments due from the individual members, but also a factoring or *del credere* discount.

The payer may be liable to pay taxes on factoring discounts. It depends on the tax regime of the payer's country. The German tax on factoring discounts, for example, is a standard 15%.

When you are setting up invoice list processing, you can reimburse the payer in advance for this tax liability by creating special condition records.

Customizing for Invoice List Processing   The system administrator will set up the following parameters during customizing for sales:

- Condition type RL00 (factoring discount) must be maintained and, if required, condition type MW15 (VAT: factoring discount tax).
- An invoice list type must be assigned to each billing type you want to process in invoice lists.

N O T E   Standard R/3 includes invoice list type LR for invoices and debit memos and type LG for credit memos. ▓

- Copying requirements must be defined to make sure that all documents in an invoice list use identical fields such as Payer and Terms of Payment.
- A customer calendar must be defined in the master data to specify the time intervals or dates on which invoice lists are to be processed.
- The ID of the customer calendar must be entered in the Billing view of the customer master record of the payer in the Inv. List Sched. field.
- Pricing condition master records must exist for condition type RL00 and, if necessary, MW15.
- Output condition master records must exist for condition types LR00 (invoice list) and RD01 (single invoice).

Relating Factoring Discounts to Pricing   The system treats factoring discounts in invoice lists just like other kinds of pricing elements. Factoring discount data is stored in condition records that are accessed during document processing according to a control system of condition types, pricing procedures, and access sequences. This control data is specified during customizing for sales by the system administrator.

Interpreting the Structure of an Invoice List

Like other billing documents, an invoice list is comprised of a header and one or more items. The items represent the billing documents included in the invoice list. The header has an overview of summary information, such as the net value of all documents in the invoice list, the value of the factoring discount, and details of taxes. The header carries information about partners and output.

Changing Header and Item Data

Only some of the header data is amenable to change. The billing date can be changed in the course of processing the invoice list. You can display document details of an individual or collective invoice. But you cannot change any data in a individual billing document once it has been entered as part of an invoice list.

One of the few global changes you can specify for all items in an invoice list is the form of output.

Selecting a Revenue Account by the Condition Technique

When you post a billing document to the FI-Financial Accounting system, the appropriate revenue accounts and sales deduction accounts will be determined automatically by the system by using the condition technique.

A condition is a set of criteria used to make a decision. The standard account determination condition is to use defined ranges of values over the following criteria to determine the appropriate accounts for posting:

- The material
- The payer
- The business transaction type
- The condition type of the prices, surcharges, and discounts in the billing document

You have control over the critical values in each criterion, and you may want to define other criteria and their critical values during customizing.

Calling for Revenue Account Determination Analysis   During billing processing, you can call for Revenue Account Determination Analysis, which will show you a listing of the FI-GL General Ledger accounts being used for prices, surcharges, and discounts for the particular business transaction on which you are working.

Processing by Business Area   The revenue and sales deduction accounts in FI-Financial Accounting may be segmented according to user-defined business areas to provide a more structured analysis of profit and loss. When you are posting as a result of billing processing, the system will take the data on the deliveries or sales orders to determine the business area segments of the accounts to which posting should take place.

Using CO-Controlling Account Determination   Costs and revenues can be distributed between profit centers, business segments, or projects. These values are used for profitability analysis in the CO-Controlling module. This control account determination is specified in the CO system and in the SAP R/3 PS-Project System.

Cost can also be assigned to the cost centers where they originated, as well as to orders such as production orders. The cost centers are defined and maintained in the CO-Controlling module.

Part

II

Ch

4

Understanding Rebate Agreements

A rebate is a special discount paid retroactively to a customer if a specified volume of sales is achieved in a time period. A rebate agreement is established that includes separate condition records for each product the customer is likely to buy. These condition records specify the rebate amount or percentage for each product, and perhaps also a pricing scale that invites the customer to attract a larger rebate by ordering more.

The system has to keep track of all billing documents, such as invoices and credit and debit memos, if they concern products that can attract a rebate. You can arrange for the system to automatically post rebate accruals so that the accumulated value of a rebate is recorded for accounting purposes.

The end of the rebate processing task is signaled by your issuing a credit memo to the customer for the accumulated rebate total.

Making Rebate Agreements

You have to record the following details for a rebate agreement:

- Who will receive the rebate payment
- How the scope is defined for the amounts that will attract the rebate, for example, customer for any material

    or

    customer per material
- Until what date the rebate agreement is valid

The following types of rebate agreement are available in standard R/3:

- Rebate Based on a Material
- Rebate Based on a Customer
- Rebate Based on a Customer Hierarchy
- Rebate Based on a Group of Materials

Preparing for Processing Rebates   The sales organization in which you are processing sales orders must have been designated for rebate processing by the system administrator in Customizing for Sales.

The payer is usually the customer and must have been designated for rebate processing by marking the Rebates field in the Billing view of the customer master record.

The billing type, such as invoice or credit memo, must have been marked for rebate processing by the system administrator when defining billing types in Customizing for Sales.

You may want to allow a rebate without regard to the material but solely on the basis of the sales to a particular customer. For this purpose you must create a token material master record that is identified as a special material for settlement.

If you plan to create rebates that do not depend on a material but, for example, depend only on the customer, you must create a special material master record for a material for settlement.

Because they are based on sales volume over time and are paid retroactively, rebates are slightly different from other kinds of discounts. Nevertheless, the system processes rebates like other kinds of pricing elements. Rebate data is stored in condition records and rebate processing is under the control of condition types, pricing procedures, and access sequences established during Customizing for Sales.

Exploring a Rebate Agreement A rebate agreement is usually comprised of a number of individual agreements expressed in the form of condition records. A rebate agreement with its condition records is assigned a rebate agreement number. General information and terms that apply to all the individual condition records, such as the method of payment and the rebate recipient, will be recorded in the agreement. For example, the following parameters will apply to all the conditions in a rebate agreement:

- Validity period
- Status, such as whether the agreement is released for settlement
- Rebate recipient who will receive the credit memo
- Currency, which is usually the sales organization currency
- Method of payment, such as check, bank transfer, and so on

When a credit memo is posted, this information will be copied to Financial Accounting.

Exploring a Condition Record Each condition record in a rebate agreement can include its own values for the following parameters:

- Basis for the rebate, such as customer, customer per material, rebate group, and so on
- Validity period

N O T E The validity period for a condition record must be the same as or within the validity period of the rebate agreement of which it forms a part.

- Condition rate as an amount or percentage
- Material for settlement
- Accrual rate
- Other control data, such as the pricing scale type

During Customizing for Sales, the system administrator can specify that certain information is to be taken from corresponding condition types. For example, you might want all condition records of a particular condition type to apply only percentage rebate rates.

Using a Material for Settlement Master Record If you want to pay rebates that are independent of particular materials, you have to refer to a material for settlement master record. For example, you may want rebates to be based on the following:

■ Customer

■ Customer hierarchy

■ A group of materials

Token material for the settlement master record can be created by using any material type and material application type. If you call for a list of material types, this material will appear in the display unless your system administrator has created a special material for settlement type in Customizing for Materials Management. The data for this master record has to be maintained in both the Sales and Accounting views of the material master records. It is customary to assign a distinctive material number and to enter explanatory text in a material for settlement because this will help trace your rebate settlements. The system will ask for the number of the material for settlement when you are creating a condition record for a rebate agreement because this is needed to determine material master data such as the account assignment for the rebate.

Building a Rebate Agreement

Alternatively, you can base a rebate on a particular material that the customer buys from you. The following agreement types are standard:

■ Type 0001, which applies a percentage rebate based on the value of the order and can apply to customers per material or customers per rebate group. It uses condition type B001 for both.

■ Type 0002, which pays a rebate on the quantity ordered. It uses condition type B002.

■ Type 0003, which pays a rebate on all orders from a particular customer. It uses condition type B003.

■ Type 0004, which pays a rebate to your main customer for their orders and the orders from all their subsidiaries defined in their customer hierarchy. It uses condition type B0004 for customers per-material and condition type B005 for customer hierarchy per-material.

■ Type 0005, which pays a rebate on the basis of sales volume independent of material. It uses condition type B0006.

In each of these rebate types, you have to specify a material or material group to which the rebate agreement will apply. However, you can specify a special material for settlement that will award a rebate regardless of any particular material.

Defining a Rebate Group of Materials   You may find it useful to define rebate groups based on materials that will attract the same rate of rebate. These will be established during Customizing for Sales. You can assign a particular material to a rebate group by entering it in the material master record.

Using Rebate Agreement Types   A rebate agreement type enables you to specify how the system will automatically propose data when you nominate the type during the creation of a rebate agreement. The proposed data can include the following:

- Condition types you can use
- The default validity period for the agreement
- The status required before an agreement can be released for payment

Rebate agreement types can be defined in Customizing for Sales if the standard types are not sufficient.

Understanding the Rebate Processing Index for Retroactive Rebate Agreements   The start date of a retroactive rebate agreement is in the past. The system has to take into account all the billing documents that have been created between the validity start date and the date on the retroactive rebate agreement. There are two kinds of situations you might have to handle:

- All the necessary settings have been made in Customizing and to the relevant payer master record.
- The necessary settings have not been made.

The following requirements have to be met:

- The sales organization and the relevant billing types have all been marked as relevant for rebate processing.
- The pricing procedure has been defined with the extra condition types needed for rebate processing.
- The intended payers have been authorized for rebates and so documented in the master records.

If all the requirements have been met, the rebate processing index is correct. This implies that the system will find that all the billing documents it encounters will have been marked for rebate, and the rebate agreement can be settled on the basis of sales volume when the time comes.

The rebate processing index is not correct if the necessary settings have not been made in Customizing and the payer has not been marked for rebate. In such cases, when the rebate agreement is settled, the system will not be able to find all invoices relevant for the rebate agreement and will not be able to determine the correct sales volume on which to base the rebate.

Creating a Retroactive Agreement   You will not be allowed to create a retroactive agreement unless the system is assured of finding the necessary billing information. This assurance is signaled by the rebate processing index being "Correct."

As you begin the normal process of creating a rebate agreement, the system will recognize that the rebate agreement is retroactive. It reads the rebate processing index to access all the billing documents that are relevant for this retroactive rebate agreement. These documents are needed to calculate the rebate amount, which will be used on the credit memo request and on the correction sales document (type S2) that is automatically created.

Understanding Rebate Accruals

The purpose of rebate accruals is to show your Accounting department how much your company owes customers with whom you have rebate agreements. You may not need to use this facility if your rebate agreements all have relatively short validity periods.

You can also use a rebate accrual to make a rebate payment that is not based on sales volume but is perhaps related to sales, such as a single payment to a customer in recognition of the fact that he has made a special display of your products that may well result in a larger order for them from your company.

Posting Accruals Rates Manually

The aim of an accrual rate posted manually to a condition record is to anticipate the rate at which the rebate will be calculated at final settlement.

The accrual can be the same as the condition rate if no pricing scale exists for a rebate condition record. But if you have created a pricing scale for a condition record, the customer's orders may attract different condition rates, depending on the order quantity, volume, and any agreements in force. In such cases, you have to manually enter your best estimate of the accrual rate that will equate to the rate for which the customer will qualify by the time the rebate agreement has run to completion.

Financial Accounting receives an accrual automatically every time a billing document is posted if a rebate agreement in force is relevant to the items on it, whether it be an invoice, a credit memo, or a debit memo. The FI application posts the accrual in two accounts. The sales deduction account is posted, and an accrual account is posted to accumulate the accruals until the rebate agreement is finally settled with a credit memo.

If there is some reason why an accrual posted manually has not been passed to Financial Accounting, the manual accruals and manual payments in the rebate agreement will be blocked.

At the moment when you save a rebate agreement, the system automatically creates a credit memo request, which will be used to create a credit memo. When this credit memo is released, the accruals will be posted to the FI system.

An accrual posted manually can be used to manage lump sum payments as well as to correct accruals previously posted. You have control over the posting time and the amount. It can be convenient to build accruals for a particular condition record or reverse them in part or in full.

The procedure for posting accruals manually is as follows:

1. Select Logistics>Sales/Distribution>Master Data.
2. Select Agreements>Rebate Agreement>Change.
3. Enter the rebate agreement number or find it by using a matchcode; select Goto>Manual Accruals.
4. Against each rebate condition record, enter the accruals to be posted. Enter a negative amount to build accruals, or a positive amount to reverse accruals. Save the rebate agreement.

N O T E It is not possible to reverse more accruals than actually exist for a condition record. ▪

You can inspect accrual information about an individual condition record by marking the condition record and choosing Payment Data. You will see the total accruals posted for the condition record, as well as the accruals that have already been reversed.

Building a Rebate Agreement

Creating a rebate agreement is begun by the following procedure:

1. Select Logistics>Sales/Distribution>Master Data.

2. Select Agreements>Rebate Agreement>Create.

3. Enter the rebate agreement type you intend to create—for example, a customer rebate is type 0003.

If your system was suitably configured in Customizing for Sales, it can automatically propose data such as the validity period, the sales organization, and the division. The currency is always proposed by default.

If you have a suitable model in the form of an existing rebate agreement, you can copy it, even though it may have expired, and edit the data to suit your new requirements. The Create w/Reference command is used for copying.

At this stage you can accept or edit the data proposed by using the overview screen. You must then continue by completing the data that will apply to all the condition records that are going to be created within the rebate agreement, as follows:

▪ The name or number of the rebate recipient

▪ The payment method

▪ The customer's reference for the rebate agreement

Adding Condition Records Within an Agreement

You have to make at least one condition record for a rebate agreement by using the following sequence:

1. Select Logistics>Sales/Distribution>Master Data.

2. Select Agreements>Rebate Agreement>Create.

3. When you have identified the agreement and reached the overview screen, enter the condition data by using the sequence Select>Goto>Conditions.

You have the option of entering a new value for the accrual rate, allowing the system to automatically propose the value you have entered as the default condition rate.

If you want to create a pricing scale for a condition record, you can mark the condition record and press Scales. If you need to alter anything in a condition record, you should mark it and press Details.

It is sometimes convenient to see an overview of condition records that have been previously entered in other rebate agreements. You can initiate a selective search for them on the basis of their key combinations if they correspond with the agreement on which you are working. For example, you could ask for condition records that pertain to the same customer and same material, or that match the customer plus rebate group key combination. If you select Validity Periods, you will be shown the list of the condition records that meet your search specification.

A condition record need not be based on a specific material. A signal for this situation is provided so that the system will prompt you to enter a value in the Material for Settlement field.

Renewing Rebate Agreements

When a rebate agreement becomes invalid, you can renew it by using the following sequence:

1. Select Logistics>Sales/Distribution>Master data.
2. Select Agreements>Rebate Agreement>Extend.
3. Enter the relevant selection criteria, and then select Program>Execute.

The system will display a list of all the rebate agreements that were able to be renewed automatically. Any rebate agreements that could not be renewed are noted in the log.

You system administrator can use the Customizing for Agreement Types function to establish a calendar for extending rebate agreements by a half year or full year. At the times suggested by the calendar, you can confirm for each rebate agreement, whether it is to be renewed automatically or not. The following sequence is appropriate:

1. Select Extras>Rebate Calendar>Change Rebate.
2. Select Reactivate or Remove, according to whether you wish to permit a rebate agreement to be renewed.

Deleting a Rebate Agreement

If a rebate agreement has to be deleted before the end of its validity period, the system has to create a credit memo request to reverse any accruals that have been posted to Financial Accounting as a result of the rebate agreement. When this has been done, the status of the rebate agreement will be altered to indicate that a credit memo request has been posted.

The following sequence is suitable for deleting a rebate agreement:

1. Select Logistics>Sales/Distribution>Master Data.
2. Select Agreements>Rebate Agreement>Change.
3. Enter the number of the rebate agreement or locate it by selecting a matchcode.
4. Select Agreement>Delete. Confirm the deletion.

Settling Rebate Agreements

The important date in settling a rebate agreement is the services rendered date. If your company is shipping products to your customer, the services rendered date is taken to be the same as the billing date. The system refers to this date to determine whether a billing document qualifies for rebate processing. If a document is to be subject to rebate processing, the services rendered date on it must fall within the validity period of one or more existing rebate agreements. But the billing date for a service, for example, could be later than the services rendered date. Therefore you may have to allow some time after the end of a rebate agreement's validity period before you search for the documents that will be eligible for final rebate processing.

The payment of a rebate amount to a customer does not take place until after the end of the agreement validity period, because all the related billing documents must have been processed and posted to Financial Accounting.

There are two settling possibilities:

- With final settlement
- With partial settlement

These options are discussed in separate sections that follow.

Settling a Rebate Agreement with Final Settlement

The system has two jobs to do before final settlement, namely: calculate the rebate based on the sales volume statistics or the lump sum, and deduct any rebates previously paid. If any accruals have already been posted on this agreement, the system will reverse them automatically.

A credit memo request is generated with the end date of the agreement validity period proposed as the billing date. If this has been arranged in Customizing, the system will automatically block the credit memo request. If and when the credit memo request is subsequently approved, the person responsible can remove the billing block, which will allow the creation of the final credit memo.

Credit memo requests generated for rebate processing will be marked with the matchcode F, Credit Memo Request for Rebate. You can use this when searching for rebate credit memo requests during order processing.

There are three ways of carrying out final settlement of rebate agreements:

- Automatically
- Manually
- In batch mode as a background task

If you want to settle a single rebate agreement, you can do this from within the rebate agreement before you save it. You can manually round up the value of the credit memo request. If an error is detected during settlement, you can cancel the credit memo request. Canceling can also be used to simulate what would happen in settlement, although there will be no posting of amounts to Financial Accounting as a result of the simulation.

Settling Rebate Agreements as a Background Task

There are two standard report functions that allow your system administrator to settle high volumes of sales rebates in batch mode as a background task, if necessary, after the close of the regular accounting periods.

RV15C001 and RV15C002 can be called to assemble lists of rebate agreements according to search specifications that can include agreement status and specific recipients. The lists can be analyzed and edited before being released for payment.

Organizing Final Settlement of Rebate Agreements

Final settlement will not be successful unless all credit memo requests and credit memos have been closed.

The following sequence is suitable for final settlement of rebate agreements:

1. Select Logistics>Sales/Distribution>Master Data.
2. Select Agreements>Rebate Agreement>Change.
3. Enter or select the number of the rebate agreement you want to settle.

NOTE According to your custom settings for rebate agreement types, you may have to manually release an agreement before you can process it for settlement by editing the Status field. ▣

4. To effect settlement as a background task, select Payment>Execute>Settlement>Background. The system confirms that a credit memo request has been created.
5. If you need to change the credit memo request, select Payment>Credit Memo Request>Change.
6. If you have to cancel a credit memo request, select Payment>Credit Memo Request>Reset.
7. If you need to make minor changes to the final settlement amounts, select Payment>Execute>Settlement>Using Payment Screen.

You will be able to inspect the final settlement amount in the Amount to be Paid field beside each condition record. The system will allow you to make any changes before you save the rebate agreement. After you have saved the rebate agreement, however, you can only change or cancel a credit memo request by calling it up as a sales document by using the following sequence:

1. Select Logistics>Sales/Distribution>Sales.
2. Select Sales Order>Change.

Carrying Out Final Settlement as a Background Task

The background task of rebate final settlement is managed by report RV15C001.

The following sequence is suitable:

1. Select Logistics>Sales/Distribution>Billing.
2. Select Rebates>Rebate Settlement.
3. Make a selection and mark at least one field under the Rebate Settlement Status section.
4. Mark the Carry out Final Settl. field under the Action to be Taken section.
5. Select Execute.

If you omit the command to carry out the final settlement action, this procedure will list rebate agreements without actually carrying out final settlement.

Making Changes After Final Settlement

When you see the outcome of a final settlement, you may decide that a particular condition record has been left out of the rebate agreement. Perhaps you will decide not to pay the amount calculated by the final settlement.

The possibilities open to you depend on whether or not the relevant credit memo has been posted to Financial Accounting.

If the credit memo has not been posted, you could change the amount in the credit memo request, or you could delete it altogether, like you would delete a sales order. What happens is that the rebate agreement is reopened so you can change it as required and then initiate final settlement again.

If the credit memo has already been posted to Financial Accounting, you have no choice but to cancel the credit memo by using a cancellation document. Once you have done this there are two options:

- For a minor change, alter the credit memo request and then post it to create a new credit memo.
- For a major change, copy the existing rebate agreement and make any alterations to it as a new rebate agreement. Because you will have canceled the existing rebate agreement, you can perform final settlement again using the altered copy.

Settling a Rebate Agreement with Partial Settlement

Perhaps you prefer to make a partial payment before waiting for the expiration of a rebate agreement. Your system administrator can establish limits during Customizing for Sales. For example, the following limits can be selectively imposed:

- Limited to the cumulative accruals of the condition record on the date of partial payment
- Limited to the amount that would be paid if final settlement were to be carried out on the date of partial payment
- No limits to partial settlement

The way you carry out partial settlement is to call up the Manual Payment screen within rebate agreement processing. You can specify the amount to be paid for each condition record, and the system will automatically create a credit memo request for each amount.

If your system has been so configured, the accruals will be reversed automatically with the appropriate credit memos. However, the system will not attempt to reverse accruals that are not there, no matter what value of accumulated accrual payment you authorize.

If there are previous partial payments still open, you can still make additional partial settlements in the form of credit memo requests or credit memos. However, the system will always take account of all open documents that are relevant when calculating the maximum amount of partial settlement you are allowed to make.

To make a partial settlement of a rebate agreement, use the following sequence:

1. Select Logistics>Sales/Distribution>Master Data.
2. Select Agreements>Rebate Agreement>Change.
3. Enter or select with a matchcode the number of the rebate agreement you want to settle.
4. Select Payment>Manual Payment.
5. Enter the intended payments in the Amount to be Paid field against each rebate condition record.

N O T E As you enter an intended payment against a rebate condition record, the system will automatically represent each payment as a negative amount.

If your system has been given limits during Customizing, you will be advised of the maximum amount per condition record. You will elicit an error message if you try to make a payment that exceeds this limit. You can automatically assign the maximum for a particular condition record by the following procedure:

1. Mark the condition record with your cursor.
2. Select Edit>Pay Max Amount.
3. Save the rebate agreement.

If you want to display the payment information for an individual condition record, you should mark it and select Payment Data. This will show the amount already paid for the condition record and the amount of accruals posted and reversed.

Authorizing Lump Sum Payments

The typical use for a lump sum payment is to recognize that your customer has made a special promotional effort not necessarily in proportion to the sales volume. The lump sum payment is managed as a special condition record you create with other rebate condition records. You have to specify it as a condition type for lump sum.

There will be no Accruals Rate field because the condition does not relate to sales volume. For the same reason, there can be no automatic posting of accruals for lump sum payments. You have to post them manually. You are allowed to determine the precise time when an accrual for a lump sum should be posted, and you specify the amount. If you want, you can post the accrual as soon as you have created the rebate agreement to which it belongs. On the other hand, you may wish to confirm that your customer actually carried out the special task before you release a lump sum payment to recognize it.

You also have the option of paying a lump sum by partial payments, made during the rebate agreement period, or with final settlement at the end of the rebate agreement period.

Reviewing Current Rebate Agreements

It may be quite useful to conduct a selective review of the rebate agreements that are current. For example, you could compile a list by using any of the following as the basis for selection:

- Agreement number
- Rebate recipient
- Organizational data
- Status

Once you have built such as list, you could carry out such operations as the following:

- Release specific agreements for settlement.
- Display the verification level of an agreement.
- Make changes to a specific agreement if its status allows this.

The system administrator can run a rebate processing report to determine, for example, the progress of retroactive rebate agreements. In particular, the report would point out the proportion of sales that occurred within the validity period both before and after the date the retroactive rebate agreement was actually created.

The following sequence will display rebate agreements:

1. Select Logistics>Sales/Distribution>Billing.
2. Select Rebates>List.
3. Enter your selection criteria.
4. Select Program>Execute.

Reviewing the Payment History of a Rebate Agreement

A payment history is essentially a list of all credit memos and all credit memo requests that are still open. You are allowed to be selective between the following possibilities, provided they are appropriate for the particular rebate agreement you are scrutinizing:

- Final settlement
- Partial settlement
- Statistics corrections
- Manual accrual postings

The list display will be subdivided to show the amount that was paid and the accruals that were reversed for each condition record.

The following sequence is effective:

1. Select Logistics>Sales/Distribution>Billing.
2. Select Rebates>Rebate Agreement>Display.
3. Enter the agreement number or select by using a matchcode.
4. Press Enter.
5. Select Payment>Rebate Documents.

You will be offered a dialog box from which to choose the following rebate document types:

- Final settlement
- Partial payments
- Statistics corrections
- Manual accrual postings

The display of rebate documents will match your specification in so far as there are any.

Developing Billing Plans

There are some types of sales orders for goods and services that are conveniently managed by billing to a specified schedule. A contract for rental of a resource might be billed monthly for as long as the contract is in force, for example. If your company is producing make-to-order items that are controlled as projects, you could bill the customer according to the percentage of the work completed at specified stages or milestones in the project.

A billing plan is a schedule of billing dates for a single item in a sales document, and your system can be customized to build such schedules automatically on the basis of control data maintained in it. As of release 3.0E, you can define a billing plan at the header level that is valid for all items assigned to it.

Two general kinds of billing plan are available:

- Periodic billing, which bills a total amount on each billing date in the plan.
- Milestone billing, which distributes the total amount over several billing dates according to progress through a project. These amounts are calculated as percentages or predefined as fixed values.

The system will determine from the item category when a billing plan has to be created and whether it will be periodic or milestone. This decision is established at Customizing, and you cannot change it from the sales document.

When you create a billing plan, you are allowed to label it with a freely definable search term when you have access to the Details screen of the billing plan in the sales document. As you save this document, the system will automatically assign a unique ID number to the plan that you can later pinpoint by using your search term.

The overview screen for a billing plan for rental contracts will be different from the screen for a project-related milestone billing plan, so you can record any data unique to your plan. For example, you will probably want to assign company names for each milestone.

Exploring the Concepts of a Billing Plan

Billing plan processing has to be able to deal with the following entities and functions:

- Automatic Creation of Billing Plan Dates
- Pricing
- Billing Block
- Billing Index
- Billing Status
- Billing Rule for Milestone Billing
- Fixed Dates in Milestone Billing
- Document Flow
- Creating with Reference

These ideas are discussed in the sections that follow.

To operate the function for automatic creation of billing plan dates, you have to have specified general date information, such as the start and end dates of the period over which the billing plan is to be valid. This information can be copied either from the contract header or from proposals in the billing plan type.

The system has to retrieve pricing information so each sales document item can be billed on the date due according to the billing plan. There may be specific amounts already set down in the condition records for the item. Alternatively, amounts may have been explicitly assigned for particular dates in the billing plan. In milestone billing, there may be actual amounts specified, or particular percentages of the total, for each milestone.

Although you may have set out a schedule of dates in a billing plan, a billing block can be set for any of these dates independently. This will prevent billing unless an authorized person has released the block. For example, you may want to encourage a new customer by not billing at a particular billing date unless a certain volume of sales has been achieved. Other dates in the billing plan need not be affected by a block.

If you are operating a milestone billing plan, the system will automatically set a billing block on each billing date. The only event that will normally allow one of these blocks to be removed will be a satisfactory report from the project system confirming that the corresponding network milestone has been reached.

A billing index is a marker your system attaches to every date in a billing plan. If a billing block is in force, this billing index will include a copy of the relevant information.

The billing status is a key that is assigned by the system to each billing date in the billing plan. The status key can be interpreted to determine how far the billing process has reached for that billing date. For example, if the billing has to be successfully completed by a particular date, the billing status for it will have been set to "C," which stops it from being billed again.

Every date in a milestone billing plan can be associated with an individual billing rule. This is used to control how the amount will be calculated, either percentage or fixed amount.

You are also able to specify that the amount to be billed will be a final settlement that includes billing not yet processed. Price changes may come into force after a billing date in the plan has already been processed. The differences in price can be taken into account during final settlement. You have to manually enter the final settlement because it is not automatically proposed by the system.

An SAP R/3 system will allow you to define milestones in a network and assign to them planned and actual dates for the completion of work. The same dates become the billing plan dates, which are blocked until the Project System confirms the attainment of the relevant milestone.

You can have milestones based on the delivery of certain order items. Billing for these will be calculated on the requested delivery total rather than on the total of confirmed quantities delivered.

Each billing date in a milestone billing plan can be controlled according to the following parameters:

- Fixed date, planned date, or actual date.
- Updated every time with the actual date the milestone is completed.
- The milestone billing date is updated only if the completion date is later than planned.
- The milestone billing date is updated only if the completion date is earlier than planned.

As of release 3.0C, you are allowed to assign milestones to the dates of a billing plan during milestone billing, even if no network plan has been opened. What you have to do is to assign each milestone manually as part of billing plan maintenance by making an entry in the Fixed Date field so it is not left blank, which is used to signify that the date cannot be associated with a milestone.

Integrating Sales Items and the Project System   Any item in a sales document billing schedule can be associated with a project by assigning it to a network in this project. If you want to see the schedule line data concerning the project, proceed as follows:

1. In one of the overview screens of the sales document, select Item>Schedule Lines.
2. Mark the schedule line of interest.
3. Select Procurement>Details.

Interpreting Milestone Billing Document Flow   As each date in a billing plan is processed for billing, the system will update the document flow for the corresponding sales document item so that all the system documents that should be created or updated will be properly processed automatically. Chapter 7, "Managing the SD Communications," elaborates on the document flow concept.

Adopting a Billing Plan by Reference   A billing plan type can be provided with a reference during Customizing for Sales. The number of an existing billing plan can be entered. If the system encounters an item that needs a billing plan, the reference plan will be proposed with fresh dates computed for it if necessary. The system can redetermine the billing dates by consulting the current date rules.

Controlling Billing Plans

The following control elements affect billing plans:

- Billing plan type
- Date description
- Date category
- Proposed date category
- Proposed date

The assignment of billing plan types to sales document items will bring these control elements into use.

The basic control data is held in the billing plan type. For example, the rules for date determination will calculate the beginning and end dates for the schedule of billing dates. The billing plan type will also include a date rule that sets the horizon for the billing plan. The horizon is calculated as the last billing date in the billing plan arrived at by adding a specified time period to the current date.

The billing plan type will be displayed in the sales document but cannot be changed.

Interpreting a Date Description   A date description is an information element that can be assigned to a billing plan. The system will assign a date description automatically on the basis of the date category used in the billing plan. The description explains the purpose of the billing plan and takes no part in billing processing.

Date Category   A date category is a key that defines data for each billing date in the billing plan. For example, the date category controls the following parameters:

- Billing rule
- Date description
- Billing block
- Whether the date is fixed or not
- Billing type proposed for billing, such as invoice or pro forma

Customizing the Proposed Date Category   If your system has been customized with a date category specified in the billing plan type with which you are working, the system will automatically propose this date category and its corresponding data for each billing date in the plan.

The only date category that is not proposed as part of the standard version of the SAP R/3 system is Final Settlement. This you must enter manually during processing.

Using a Proposed Date in Milestone Billing   The date proposal function enables a standard billing plan to be created as a model and used by the system to suggest a predefined schedule of billing dates during processing. You can accept these dates as the basis for an actual billing plan or change any of them if you need to.

Pre-Assigning Billing Plan Types to Sales Document Items   A billing plan is controlled by the item category. Your system administrator can use Customizing for Sales to specify which individual item categories will be supported by order-related billing through a billing plan. At the same time, a billing plan type can be assigned to each item category.

Setting up Periodic Billing

The billing dates in a periodic billing plan can be derived from the start and end dates, the period, and the horizon. These date values can be determined from the following sources:

- Calculation by using control data from the billing plan
- Header data in a rental contract
- Dates entered manually

Defining Start and End Dates   Whenever possible, start and end dates are taken from the corresponding rental contract. Your system can be configured to arrive at these dates indirectly by, for example, using the installation date as the contract start date and adding the length to compute the end date.

Processing the Period   Standard periods are monthly, quarterly, and annually. These control the number of billing dates created for a billing plan. They also govern whether a billing date is processed for billing on the first or last day of the month.

Finding the Billing Horizon   You may not be able to enter an end date for a billing plan. Or the end date may be so far in the future that not all billing dates can established. You have the option of entering a rule for determining the billing horizon.

The horizon for periodic billing determines the last date of the billing plan and is always arrived at by reference to the current date. If the current date is updated during processing, for whatever reason, the system automatically extends the horizon. This effectively extends the schedule of billing dates by the same number of days.

You can have the system calculate dates from the current horizon by a manual entry, or you can have this take place automatically.

If a billing plan is processed without an end date, the invoice will start a process that automatically extends the billing plan to the horizon. The manual initiation procedure is as follows:

1. Select Logistics>Sales/Distribution>Sales.
2. Select Outline Agreements>Contracts>Periodic Billing.

Using the Header Functions in Billing Plans   As a method of controlling the amount of repetitive work needed in billing, the SAP R/3 system provides a range of functionality that can be specified in the header of a billing plan. From there it will be automatically applied to all the schedule line items in the plan.

All the items that belong to the same item category will be assigned the same billing plan type. If this type is specified in the header, it can be applied to all the individual items by default. You can scrutinize this plan after marking the Header Billing Plan field on the Item Billing Plan screen.

If you need to define different billing plans for specific items, you can remove the assignment and maintain each item billing plan separately.

The way to remove or set an item assignment is by editing the assignment indicator. However, once an item has been partially billed, it can be disassociated from the header but you cannot apply the header billing plan to it.

Because you can copy the header billing plan to individual item billing plans, you can make global changes at the header level and be assured that the changes will be applied automatically to all the items assigned to it. Again, however, dates that have already been billed cannot be subjected to changes made at the global header level.

If you are running periodic billing, the system will carry out pricing, determine the billing document value, and control the document status, all at item level, regardless of the information maintained at header level.

Totals and status are dynamically determined at the header level. Any information displayed in the header billing plan will be valid for all the items that refer to that header.

In milestone billing, the header fields for billing document values and status are determined dynamically from all the items assigned to that header billing plan.

The document value displayed at the header level is the sum of all assigned items.

Controlling Displays   The following sequence will move you from the sales order to the header billing plan: Header>Contract>Billing Plan.

If you want to know whether an individual item has been assigned to the header billing plan, the following sequence will lead you to the header billing document field for the item where the assignment will be indicated: Item>Contract>Billing Plan.

You can consult the following fields in the Billing overview screen by selecting Overview>Billing:

- Billing Relevance indicates "I" for each item if the sales order is relevant for an order-related billing document, and a billing plan exists.
- Header Billing Plan indicates "X" if the item billing plan refers to the header billing plan.

Scheduling Milestones   Any item billing plan assigned to the header billing plan will adopt the dates generated in the header billing plan. If you want to set milestones in the header billing plan, the following sequence is suitable: Edit>Generate Dates>Manual Milestones.

These milestones will then be copied to the item billing plans assigned to that header. You may need to insert a milestone in a particular item plan. To do this, you must remove the item from the header billing plan and build up its milestone separately.

If you assign the item to the header billing plan again, your manually set milestones will be deleted and the header billing plan will again be in force.

Using Header Billing Plans in Periodic Billing   A billing document value or status indicator will not appear in a header billing plan for periodic billing because the following functions can only be operated on individual items:

- Pricing
- Determining status
- Determining date-from
- Determining date-to

Manipulating the Billing Validity Period   You can enter the start and end dates manually, or you can have them computed by reference to predetermined rules. If you change the rules at header level or alter the dates you entered manually, the new dates will be copied automatically to all the item billing plans associated with the header billing plan.

If you need different dates for any item, you have to follow a different procedure.

You can specify a validity period manually in the Date-from and Date-to fields in the item billing plan. If you do this, the system will delete the rule for this item and use these manual entries to establish the billing dates.

The item dates you have entered manually will be used, even though you may change the header billing dates. If you delete the manually entered dates from the Date-from and Date-to fields, the rule in the billing header will again determine the billing dates for this item.

Understanding Third-Party Orders

The defining characteristic of third-party orders is that your company is not the one to deliver the items requested by a customer. Your company acts as an intermediary by passing the order over to a third party. You will get billed, but the third party will ship the goods directly to the customer.

Not all of a sales order needs to be third-party items. There may be reason to have a third party deliver items you could deliver yourself. Another variant is for you to order products from a third-party vendor for delivery to your own warehouse for subsequent delivery to the customer by your company.

This arrangement is supported by functions referred to as "individual purchase order processing."

Third-party orders are controlled in two slightly different ways:

- Control by material types
- Control during processing in the Sales and Purchasing systems

These aspects of third-party order processing are discussed in the sections that follow.

Controlling Third-Party Orders Through Material Types

Each material of interest to your company, and this may include services if you want, will be assigned a material type code that identifies where it stands in the following list:

- Material or service produced only internally
- Material or service that is only available from third-party vendors
- Material or service that can be procured externally or produced in-house

The material type is consulted to determine how order processing will take place.

Processing Third-Party Orders in Sales

Whether your system will recognize third-party items automatically is a matter established through Customizing. You may be allowed to change a normal item manually to a third-party item during sales order processing.

What you can do is mark a material as a third-party item in the material master if it is always delivered from one or more third-party vendors. You need to enter BANS in the Item category group field in the Sales 2 screen of the material master record.

If you have done this, the system can automatically assign such items to the TAS category during sales order processing.

It is not uncommon in some industries for third-party vendors to be called upon only very rarely. In such circumstances, you may prefer to manually overwrite the item category NORM during sales order processing on those rare occasions when you need to signal TAS and engage a third party.

Your system will respond to a TAS item in a sales order that has been saved by automatically generating a purchase requisition in the Purchasing module. Each recognized third-party item in the sales order will be matched to a corresponding purchase requisition item. There will be an automatic search for a suitable vendor of each of these requisition items.

It may happen that a sales order item has more than one schedule line. In such cases, the system will create a separate purchase requisition item for each schedule line.

Processing Third-Party Orders in Purchasing

Once a purchase requisition item has been created, the normal procedure for creating purchase orders will be followed, and the system will copy the delivery address of your customer from the sales order so the third-party vendor who receives this purchase order will deliver it appropriately.

Part
II

Ch
4

The sales order format provides a place for you to enter text against any third-party item. These texts are automatically copied onto the corresponding purchase order before it is placed with the third-party vendor. The number of this purchase order will appear in the document flow information of the original sales order.

Just as in normal purchase orders, there may have to be changes when a third-party vendor is engaged. Dates and delivered quantities may not be exactly to your original requirements. Whatever alterations are made in the purchase order will be automatically reflected in the sales order.

Using a third party can affect automatic delivery scheduling. The Purchasing department will usually specify lead times for deliveries from a third party. The system will consult this information and may also customize it to allow time for the Purchasing department to process these third-party orders.

Luckily, you can consult lists of sales orders for which there are purchase requisitions and purchase orders that contain discrepancies from the sales order. This process is called "Monitoring the External Environment."

Creating a Third-Party Sales Order

The only different task you have to perform for a third-party sales order is to overwrite the TAN item category with the TAS entry. Otherwise, the process is the same as for normal sales order processing.

Displaying Purchase Requisitions for Third-Party Items

Once you have saved a sales order that includes third-party items, you will find that the system has automatically recorded the numbers of the corresponding purchase requisitions in the sales document.

To find a third-party purchase requisition number, do the following:

1. Mark the item in the initial data entry screen of the sales order.
2. Select Schedule Line.
3. Place your cursor on the schedule line in which you are interested.
4. Select Edit>Procurement.

You will now be shown the purchase requisition number for the schedule line item.

If you need to see the purchase requisition item that is generated for a schedule line, proceed as follows:

1. Mark the item in the initial data entry screen of the sales order.
2. Select Schedule Line.
3. Place your cursor on the schedule line in which you are interested.
4. Select Edit>Purchase Requisition.

Constructing Installment Plans

The system manages an installment plan by creating just the one invoice from which you can list or print the amounts and dates of the installment payments.

These installment amounts are calculated by the system as percentages of the total invoice amount and entered as separate customer line items. Your system administrator will normally define the sequence of percentages by referring to a key that identifies one of a set of standard payment terms. The system will automatically allow for rounding differences in the final payment.

The payment terms key can be maintained by the system administrator by using the following parameter set:

- Down payment
- Number of installments
- Payment dates
- Percentage of the invoice value

You have the facility to record a default payment terms key in the customer master record on the Billing screen for the sales area. Another possibility is to overwrite the payment terms key in the sales order header or item.

If you want to print explanatory text on the order confirmation, you can refer to the payment terms key, where such text is provided as standard.

Part
II

Ch
4

Understanding Resource-Related Billing

There are some products and services that do not easily submit to the disciplines of fixed or standard pricing. For example, your first instance of make-to-order production may be difficult to estimate. Some service tasks, such as building maintenance, can uncover defects that entail unforeseen expenses. Consulting is another service that is difficult to quantify and price because there are seldom any useful reference quantities to act as guidelines.

Resource-related billing is a method of assembling a billing document on the basis of the individual materials, the internal company services needed, and the costs that will be passed on to the customer.

What sets off the creation of resource-related billing documents is a billing request. You can create billing requests for any of the following:

- Customer orders
- Customer projects
- Service orders without reference to a customer order

The items that appear in the billing request document are developed from information on the resources to be billed.

A structure with a hierarchical form is made from the sales order items. These are objects that have been valued and can therefore appear in a billing request document. The list of such objects could include any of the following entities:

- Internal orders and service orders with the associated sales order

- WBS (work breakdown structure) elements, transactions, internal orders, and service orders with the associated customer project

Creating a Billing Request

The process of creating a billing request is begun with the following sequence:

1. Select Logistics>Sales/Distribution>Sales>Order>Subsequent Functions> Resource-Rel. Billing.

2. Enter a sales order item or an order number into the Create Billing Request for Resource-Related Billing screen.

You will notice that the system creates two views of billing requests:

- View for the Sales Order, in which all relevant objects are included in a sales order item. By doing this, either one item of a sales order, such as a maintenance order, is billed or the whole billing hierarchy underlying the item is billed.

- View for the Order, in which the resource items for each individual order are identified, such as the associated internal orders or plant maintenance orders.

If you want to restrict the period for which the documents are to be selected to form the billing request, you can make an entry in the Date field.

Next you have to select an indicator to signify your preferences concerning statistical key figures. If you set the indicator for statistical key figures, the system will refer to the appropriate key figures or cost drivers and compute the costs according to a predefined standard procedure. If you do not opt for statistical key figures, the system will locate the documents needed for billing on the basis of cost and services.

Another indicator that must be set is Object Selection. You will set this indicator if you do not want the system to select the objects for billing automatically. What will happen is that you will be shown an overview list of all the objects in the billing hierarchy.

You are allowed to strike out individual objects or branches of the object hierarchy. This creates a partial billing structure, because the resource items contained in the suppressed objects will not be taken into account during billing.

Should you leave both indicators blank, all the objects belonging to the sales order item will appear in the billing request.

When you save the billing request, all the resource items included by the hierarchy of objects you have defined will be copied to become items in the billing request. The system will not make any quantity changes to the resource items.

However, when you see the display of the items in the billing request, you can edit them if you wish and save the edited billing request. You will see a document number assigned by the system for this billing request document.

Changing a Billing Request

If you have to change a billing request at a later date, you can use the following sequence:

1. Select Logistics>Sales/Distribution>Sales>Order>Change.
2. Enter the billing request number.
3. Select the required overview.
4. In the Change Debit Memo Request overview screen, you can edit the items and save the altered billing request.

The kinds of changes you might want to make are, for example, quantity changes in the resource items that have been suggested by the system. You might want to reduce the quantity so the customer is billed for only a partial quantity in the billing request on which you are working. The system will remember the residual value and present it when subsequent billing takes place.

Some resource items are single events or processes that are not associated with a quantity. These will be assigned the quantity 1 automatically.

You can mark a resource item as not relevant for billing if you signify your reason for rejecting it. This item will be treated as if it were completed. It will not be proposed in subsequent billing documents.

There may be some reason for you to allow a customer a grace period or moratorium from certain payments. This you can arrange by marking these items as not relevant for billing until the grace period is over.

When you are ready to reset a resource item to bring it back into the billing process, you can enter a rejection reason key to ensure that it will be included in the billing request for the next billing period.

The conditions for pricing can be changed on an item-by-item basis. If you do this, the system will revalue the resource items you have altered.

Although you can mark a resource item to render it unbilled or partially billed, this item will again be proposed for billing when the next billing request is generated.

N O T E The item quantity determines whether an item can be designated as partially billed.

Once a billing request has been started, you are not permitted to add new resource items. Your only option is to delete the old billing request and create a new one.

Part

II

Ch

4

Canceling a Billing Request

There are two main reasons why you might want to cancel a billing document:

- You have decided not to process the items in a billing request.
- You wish to defer the items and make them available for a new billing request.

You cannot use the Cancel function to cancel a billing document because the accounting functions will have already begun some of the processing. The proper thing to do is to enter a suitable reason for rejection. This means it will not be taken into account in the current billing document, but it will be available for billing in subsequent billing documents.

Changing System Settings for Resource-Related Billing

Your system will be provided with standard reasons for rejection, and these can be edited to suit your company through the online *Implementation Guide*.

Several system settings may have to be set up in this way to suit your company in the matter of resource-related billing. The following are some examples:

- Settings for document types in SD
- Settings for pricing
- Determining activities for billing request items
- Defining reasons for rejection

Some suggestions about these system settings are made in the sections that follow.

Adjusting Settings for Document Types in SD   If you intend to create a billing request for a sales order, you have to specify the document type for the subsequent billing request in the settings for the sales order document type from which the billing request will be generated.

You also have to specify a condition type in the settings for the billing request document type because this condition type will control how the line items will be costed.

The standard proposal for the condition type is EK01.

Adjusting Settings for Pricing in Resource-Related Billing   Your customer is charged for costs such as bills from vendors and hotel costs because these are resources used. You would not expect a general sales price to be specified for these as material items in the billing request. Usually the price of this type of item is determined from the actual costs incurred.

You will probably mark conditions for these kinds of prices as non-mandatory, such as PR00, in the pricing procedure used for pricing in the billing request.

Determining Activities for Billing Request Items   When the system is inserting items in a resource-related billing request, it handles resource items as if they were all activities. Therefore you must have prepared for this by associating all your activities with an appropriate application element. Thus you need to create a "service material"—an activity that can be quantified and priced as if it were a physical material—for each of the entities that could appear in your resource-related billing request.

For example, you might use any or all of the following entities as costing objects:

- Cost elements
- Cost center/activity type combinations
- Statistical key figures

You have to assign each entity to the appropriate application to enable the system to know where to look for the pertinent information needed for the billing process. Thus, you may have your resources associated with any or all of the following types of application billing object:

- Internal orders
- Maintenance orders
- Projects

Specifying Reasons for Rejection   The reasons for rejection have to differentiate between the following situations:

- An item in a billing request is not relevant for billing.
- An irrelevant item in the billing request has to be reset so it can appear in subsequent billing requests.
- An item in a billing request will be canceled if you have to mark the whole billing request as canceled.

The text for an individual reason for rejection can be edited in the online *Implementation Guide*. The system also needs to know how to react to each reason for rejection if the so-marked item is suggested in a subsequent new billing request.

Some of the standard reasons for rejection set the indicator codes that control the item, as in the following:

- VN—Item not relevant for billing, not to be proposed in subsequent billing requests, not forwarded for printing, treated as completed, and cannot be transferred to the billing document.
- VB—Reset item not relevant for billing on this occasion, so the item will not be forwarded for printing, the item is still open, and the item cannot be transferred to the billing document.
- VS—Cancel item. This reason for rejection is used to mark an item that has already been used in a billing request, but that has been subsequently canceled. This reason for rejection can also be used to mark an item that is to be transferred to another billing request.

All these reasons for rejection are used in normal billing. There are no reasons specific to resource-related billing in standard SAP.

Blocking Billing Documents

If a billing block has been set in a billing request, you will have to remove the block before a billing document will be created in response to the request.

Canceling Billing Documents

Once a billing document is canceled, you are free to edit the billing request if you want. You can either edit the billing request ready for a subsequent billing run, or you can mark individual items by using the cancellation key as the reason for rejection.

Exploring Resource-Related Billing Objects

The billing objects that can take part in resource-related billing are the following:

- Sales order items
- Maintenance service orders
- Internal orders assigned to a sales order
- Assembly orders
- Projects

Developing a Billing Hierarchy   The revenue from a sales order is copied to the cost collector for sales order items. The items retain an association in the cost collector with the revenues that they earn. The sales order item need not be wholly self-contained. You can assign the following objects to individual sales order items:

- Internal orders
- Networks or production orders developed during assembly order processing
- Maintenance orders

For example, several different maintenance orders can be combined into a regular maintenance contract.

The only kind of maintenance order that can be billed without the corresponding sales order is a service order of order type SV01.

A sales order item and the order assigned to it constitute a billing hierarchy. There is no limit to the complexity because any object can include subordinate hierarchy objects such as WBS elements, orders networks, or network activities.

There are two main ways for you to assign an order to a sales order item:

- Enter the corresponding sales order item when you are maintaining the order master data for the CO-Controlling application, which handles internal orders.
- In the PM-Plant Maintenance application, you can form the settlement rule correctly for PM orders. For instance, if the settlement is carried out for a sales order, the order is assigned to the sales order item specified.

Resource-Related Billing for Customer Projects   A "customer project" is a sales order linked to one or more projects. However, each revenue element is recorded in the project itself, not in the parent sales order. The revenues are collected in the billing elements assigned for this purpose.

In a sales order, the billing element referenced in the sales order item is, by default, the highest element in a billing hierarchy. A sales order item must not be assigned to more than one WBS element because the system will assign a resource item to the first order item it finds when creating the billing request. This need not be the sales order item to which you want the resource assigned.

Determining Expenditures to Be Billed   A characteristic of resource-related billing is that individual materials, internal company services, and costs are passed on to the customer. "Expenditure" is what a business spends on the goods and services consumed and the taxes due. Expenditure has to be compared with revenue in the profit and loss accounts.

There are various ways for the system to access information on expenditures:

- The CO application has line items for costs and services in the standard settings.
- If you set up the billing request to use statistical key figures when billing, the system will accept measured amounts of resources consumed and calculate costs from them.
- Additional information may be available in other data structures that have been associated with your system or with a particular customer.

Creating Service Activity Materials for Resource-Related Billing   A service material is a device for assigning resource items to sales order items. Internal company services and additional costs incurred are all represented as activities.

These activities are defined for internal orders, maintenance, and project system elements in the *Implementation Guide*. This allows you to specify the following entities:

- Cost elements
- Cost center by activity type combinations
- Statistical key figures that can be used in pricing calculations

The system can only apply resource-related billing for service tasks if you have defined these operations in terms of activity materials that can be assigned values from which costing data can be calculated. If no value is assigned, the system will default to quantity 1, thus converting a price to the total cost.

When you define an activity material, it is usual to enter an explanatory title or other text that can be included in billing documents.

The billing request is assembled by converting the cost centers/activity type combinations contained in all the resource line items for a particular service. An item is created in the billing request for each of the resource items so determined. Exactly how the individual resource items are priced is determined by conditions that are set up in the *Implementation Guide*.

Developing a User Exit for Resource-Related Billing   Although the costs of the resources are normally determined from information that is companywide, you can identify resource items that are to be billed for each customer individually by using a customized program module that is known as a "user exit" because it is a way of producing a result after processing that is an enhancement unique to a particular SAP R/3 user implementation. For example, your company could develop a user exit that performs some or all of the following functions:

Part
II

Ch
4

- Adding resource items that are not selected in the standard for new documents
- Checking items in existing documents
- Updating the document flow

The sequence for creating a user exit for resource-related billing is as follows:

1. Select Tools>Business Engineering>Customizing.
2. Select Controlling>Product Cost Controlling>Cost Object Controlling>Cost Object Controlling for Sales Order Processing.
3. Select Period-End Closing>Resource Related Billing>Define User Exit for Resource Related Billing.

Just as you might need to create a routine for resource-related billing using the mechanism of the user exit, you may need to develop billing based on resources if you provide a service to your customers.

Understanding Resource-Related Billing for Service Orders

If your company is providing a service to a customer, perhaps maintenance of a specific plant item, you could bill that customer a monthly fee by using a billing plan, which could be assigned to a particular item in the service contract you have established with your customer.

Alternatively, you could recover the costs incurred during service calls by billing your customer using resource-related billing.

For example, you may have a maintenance contract in which there are price agreements that control how costs such as labor and parts will be determined. You can install and configure the SAP Service Management application to assist in this.

The resource-related billing process creates a billing request to the Sales and Distribution application, and an invoice is sent to the customer.

Billing the Resources for Service Activities

In the SM-Service Management module, a service call can automatically create a service order. The technician reports the maintenance activities carried out as confirmations in this service order. There may be planned and unplanned usage of materials.

An account assignment object will be assigned to the service order that collects all costs associated with the maintenance activities.

A billing request can be created for the service order directly or for the sales order to which the service belongs. You can also generate a billing request for an individual contract item in a service order.

Price agreements can be stored in the service contract. If so, they are consulted when the billing request is created.

Using Billing Requests

A billing request can usefully include items in addition to those that seek payment. Some items may be free of charges. For instance, you may be working for a contract fee or under a warranty. In such circumstances, you will probably want your customer to see a complete listing of all the work done, especially where the cost of labor and parts is covered by the contract fee or through warranty.

In summary, a billing request can include the following items:

- Grace items or no-charge items
- Items covered by the regular maintenance fees
- Items covered by warranty or guarantee

The system knows when to bill an item because the master records for completion confirmation in Service Management carry indicators.

Building a Service Contract

If you make reference to another document, the system will copy the validity period and cancellation data into a new contract. If you have no reference, you must enter the necessary data. If you can reference a previous inquiry, quotation, or existing contract, the copied data can serve as the basis for editing.

Part II
Ch
4

The items of a service contract can be any combination of the following:

- Materials
- Service materials that represent activities, such as the material type for services DIEN
- Standard configurable products that you will be invited to configure by entering suitable values into the configuration editor
- Standard configured products that already have predefined values that you can inspect by using the configuration editor

The following procedure will create a service contract:

1. Select Logistics>Sales/Distribution>Sales.
2. Select Outline Agreement>Contract>Create.

An alternative way of creating a service contract is as follows:

1. Select Logistics>Service Management>Contracts and Planning.
2. Select Contracts>Contract Create.

The next step in creating a service contract is to select WV for a maintenance contract, or MV for a rental contract.

You have the option of entering organizational data. As a user, you can have a user profile that will suggest your usual values for sales organization, distribution channel, and division. You can also record entries for the sales office and the sales group.

The system also needs the following data:

- Customer number of the sold-to party in the Sold-to Party field
- Purchase order number of the customer for this document
- Start and end dates
- Material number to differentiate standard or configurable product
- Target quantity for the material

If you have entered a standard product, you will have to respond to the configuration editor by entering the values for the characteristics defined in the standard product.

If you entered a configured product with predefined values, the system will automatically copy these values into the contract.

The following sequence will allow you to enter data in the contract header:

1. Select Header>Contract>Contract Data.
2. Enter the relevant run-time and cancellation data, and then return to the overview screen.

N O T E If you select Header>Contract>Price Agreements, you can enter price agreement data in the contract header so that a price agreement can be specific to a particular contract.

If an item type has been so specified in Customizing, the system will automatically create a billing plan for any item of this type that is included in a service contract. The following sequence will display the plan for your inspection:

1. Mark the item.
2. Select Item>Contract>Billing Plan.

Canceling a Service Contract

Either you or the customer can cancel a service contract.

If you do it, the effect is immediate. But if the customer sends in a request to cancel a contract, the system will only cancel the service contract if the requested cancellation date is in accord with the cancellation rules specified in the contract.

The system can find at least one date in the future when a cancellation could be allowed within the rules. This it will propose as the contract end date if the customer's requested date is not allowed. You have to confirm the proposal before it can generate a cancellation.

Processing Intercompany Business

A definition of intercompany business processing in an SAP R/3 system must refer to business transactions between two component companies (company codes) belonging to one organization. The SAP R/3 system recognizes organizational structure by assigning every transaction document a client code that refers to the parent- or highest-level user of the implementation. If there is more than one subsidiary company that needs to maintain separate financial documents, each of these subsidiaries will be assigned a company code in addition to the client code shared by all users of the system. If there is only one company, the client code and the company code will be the same, but they will be formatted in the fields defined for client and company code.

Thus, in SAP R/3 terminology and document identification numbers, intercompany business processing comprises transactions between company codes. Except where the context would otherwise be unclear, these discussions will use "company" to refer to the legal entity that maintains its own financial documents, whether or not it is a member of a corporate group or its parent.

Defining Intercompany Sales Processing

The paradigm of intercompany sales is when a sales organization assigned to the ordering company code creates a sales order for goods from a plant assigned to another company code. The supplying company code then delivers the goods to the customer.

Another example of intercompany sales processing is when an intercompany stock transfer is transacted. In this instance, a purchasing organization assigned to the ordering company code creates a purchase order ordering goods from a plant assigned to another company code.

The supplying plant in the delivering company code delivers the goods to the plant for which the purchasing organization ordered the goods.

It is a legal requirement that each company code balance its accounts independently of other corporate members. Therefore, the delivering company must bill the ordering company for the goods. The instrument for this internal billing transaction is an intercompany billing document.

In general, there are three stages in processing intercompany sales:

- Processing sales orders
- Processing deliveries
- Billing

It is usual for the sales organization and the plant to be assigned to different company codes. Their responsibilities are divided as follows:

- The sales organization processes the sales order and bills the customer.
- The plant delivers the goods to the customer.

As an example, consider an enterprise that includes two subsidiary companies. The enterprise as a whole is represented in SAP R/3 as Client 0000. By definition, the associated companies will return their own financial documents as well as contributing to the consolidated accounts. In the corporate SAP system, all their individual transactions will bear their identification numbers in the field designated Company Code. In SAP parlance, these corporate members are company codes. Table 4.1 illustrates a typical assignment of identification codes.

Table 4.1   Intercompany Transactions Are at Company Code Level

Client Code Organization	Company Code (Warehouse)	Sales	Plant
0001	0001	0001	0001
0001	0002	0002	0002

In this type of enterprise, you can expect to see arrangements for intercompany sales at preferential rates. The mechanism to handle these is the condition record. In a master condition record set up in Customizing, there will be a formulation such as the following:

If plant 0002 is going to bill sales organization 0001 for goods, the price charged will be at 80% of the net invoice value.

The condition record is so named because of the implied "if, then" logical structure of the procedural rule or rules that it specifies.

Now imagine a sales order placed by Customer G with sales organization 0001. Let the detailed items be as follows:

■ Item 1, Product A, 20 pieces (Plant 0001), USD, 200

■ Item 2, Product B, 50 pieces (Plant 0002), USD, 500

From Table 4.1, it is apparent that the second order item has to be procured from a plant that belongs to an affiliated company. Therefore, there must be some intercompany sales processing between the two company code entities. Each plant may well be responsible for its own deliveries, but the billing process will be controlled from company code 0001 because it was sales organization 0001 that received the sales order. The account books must take this into consideration.

The billing process will have the following components:

■ To the customer from sales organization 0001, USD 500 as the sales price on the invoice.

■ To sales organization 0001 with an intercompany billing document from sales organization 0002 for USD 400, which obeys the condition record and charges only 80 percent of the net invoice value.

This illustration shows that intercompany billing is handled the same as other pricing elements. In fact, intercompany pricing data is stored in condition records and is controlled by condition types, pricing procedures, and access sequences according to the control data defined in Customizing for Sales.

Moving Goods by Intercompany Stock Transfer

If one member of a corporate group receives stock from another, the movement of value will be recorded as an intercompany stock transfer. The normal sender and receiver will be a plant in each of the company codes.

The delivery from one plant to another will be controlled by a purchase order in much the same way as a delivery would be conducted in response to a sales order from a customer. The delivering plant will charge the receiving plant.

A standard type NB purchase order can be used for an intercompany stock transfer. The delivering plant will generate a delivery document and an intercompany billing document type IV by using the information on the purchase order. Prices and delivery costs will be shown. When the goods depart, a goods issue will be posted in the vendor plant. When the goods arrive, a goods receipt will be issued against the purchase order, and the system will post values and quantities in the receiving plant. Meanwhile, the dispatching plant will create an intercompany billing document.

The receiver will check the invoice against the purchase order and post an invoice receipt if all is well.

Customizing for Intercompany Business Processing   Your system administrator has to set up condition records for use in intercompany sales processing. For example, condition type PI01, which is used to assign a fixed amount per material unit, must be associated with all the materials or material types for which it is going to be used. Alternatively, or in addition, condition type PI02 must be maintained to identify the materials that are going to be priced as a percentage of the net invoice amount for intercompany sales.

In many circumstances, a particular sales organization will not deal with all possible plants in an enterprise. Therefore you have to establish condition records that define the allowed combinations of plant and sales organization.

Each plant, as a production or storage facility, will typically serve a particular sales area. This can be delineated in various ways by nominating sales organizations, distribution channels, and divisions. Again, the permissible combinations of plant codes and sales area entity codes have to be explicitly preserved in the records before intercompany sales processing can be successful.

Sales master data has to be maintained as follows:

- A "special customer" master record for internal purposes to represent the ordering company code entity that is to be processed as a normal customer with special pricing arrangements.
- Condition records to specify intercompany charges for every permissible combination of plant and sales organization; these may well recognize the different costs of intercompany transportation.

It may be necessary to exercise control over the exchange rate to be applied in intercompany business that entails foreign currency conversion. The Exchange Rate Type field in the Sales view of the customer master record receives a value to specify which type of exchange rate will be used.

Creating a Condition Record for Intercompany Sales Processing   An intercompany condition record can be created by the following sequence:

1. Select Logistics>Sales/Distribution>Master Data.

2. Select Pricing>Prices>Others>Create.

3. Enter PI01 for a fixed amount.

   or

   PI02 for a percentage.

You will have to enter or confirm the following information needed for the condition record:

- The sales organization in the ordering company from which the sales order originates
- The delivering plant that is the source of the material
- The material
- The rate at which the plant will charge the sales organization

N O T E   Either a percentage to be applied to the net invoice value or a fixed amount per sales unit of the material has to be entered as the rate.

There are various ways your system can make an intelligent guess at the delivering plant as soon as you specify a sales organization in the ordering company code affiliate. The following master records can be associated with a sales organization and, if so, can be consulted:

- Customer-material info record
- Customer master record
- Material master record

The search will follow the order listed.

When you are maintaining the delivering plant information in the sales order, there are two possibilities:

- Select Overview>Procurement if you want to enter the same information for the whole sales order.
- Select Item>Business Data if you are going to assign plant information to items individually.

You might want to use a matchcode to list the alternative plants from which the material can be obtained. You can always edit any suggestions that may be offered by the system, although there will be an automatic check to confirm that you have specified one of the permitted combinations of sales organization and delivering plant.

When the system is automatically carrying out pricing, it will refer to pricing master data from the sales organization. The charge arrived at for an intercompany sale will be shown on the Pricing screen of the sales order as a statistical value, because there will have been no effect on the final value of the sales order for the external customer. This intercompany pricing element is not printed out on documents intended for the customer.

Working with Intercompany Deliveries   A single delivery can be created by the following sequence:

1. Select Logistics>Sales/Distribution>Shipping>Delivery>Create.

2. In the Shipping Point field, enter the shipping point assigned to the delivering plant.

If you want to arrange several deliveries, the following procedure is appropriate:

1. Select Logistics>Sales/Distribution>Shipping>Delivery>Process Delivery Due List.

2. Select Settings>Organizational Data.

3. Enter relevant sales area data to define the selection criteria for your delivery due list.

4. Select Settings>Further Selection Screen.

5. Enter further selections, such as the ship-to party or the material number, if these are needed to refine your delivery due list.

If an intercompany business transaction is the basis for the delivery, the goods will be delivered to the customer.

If an intercompany stock transfer is the basis for the delivery, the goods will be delivered to the plant assigned to the company code that placed the purchase order. Goods issue is carried out in the delivering plant.

When you are arranging a delivery as a stock transfer in response to a purchase order, you are not allowed to treat it as a single delivery. What you have to do is process the delivery due list and mark the specific item "Stock Transport."

You will find it useful to identify the purchase order number by searching as follows:

1. Select Settings>Further Selection Screen.

2. Enter the ordering company code sales organization in the Purchase Document From field.

Using Billing Information and Analysis Techniques

Your display of billing documents can include invoices, credit memos, and debit memos.

The following are billing document display functions:

- Incompletion or Error Log
- Document Flow
- Document Status
- List Billing Documents
- Process a List of Billing Documents
- List Incomplete Billing Documents
- List Blocked Billing Documents
- Billing Due List
- Invoice List Work List
- Log for a Billing Run

The following are analysis functions available in connection with billing:

- Performing an Account Assignment Analysis
- Performing a Split Analysis
- Displaying an Accounting Overview for a Billing Document

Operating the General Billing Interface

The general billing interface is an enhancement of SAP R/3 that allows you to bill external business transactions, provided the data from the external system to be used in your billing process has been prepared in a sequential file to a specified format.

If you do not want all the information your system requires for billing to be prepared in this file, you can have data copied from existing master records. The general billing interface has the ability to identify which data fields are essential and which can be transferred, at your discretion. You can elect which data elements will be copied from your existing master.

If you have many one-time customers, you can refer to a CpD customer master record that stores all the data you need for these isolated transactions. This saves processing resources over the standard scheme of maintaining separate customer master records.

The general billing interface allows pricing elements and VAT amounts to be transferred. You can alternatively specify that new pricing will be performed during billing. This can be total pricing or only for taxes.

Your external business partner may use reference numbers. You can enter these in the interface as external delivery or order numbers. Your SAP R/3 system then records document flow by using these reference numbers when you create a billing document.

You will find it useful to spot a relevant billing document by searching for the external reference number. Your system will also prevent double-billing to the same external reference number.

Understanding Credit Management

The credit limit is the maximum allowed for a loan to a particular customer or type of customer. The control area for managing credit can extend over more than one company code, but a single company code is not allowed to exercise control over more than one credit control area.

The SAP R/3 functionality in credit management is designed to facilitate and enhance the control of credit. The following features are considered important by users:

- Your company can specify the criteria to be used for automatic credit checks and ensure that these checks are performed automatically at sensitive moments in the sales and distribution cycle.
- Internal electronic mail can be set up to automatically inform credit controllers if any critical situation should develop.
- If a credit representative needs to review a customer's position, the historical data is readily available.

Setting Up a Credit Policy

You may deem it prudent to monitor a single customer or a defined or nominated group of customers. It may also be necessary to divide your credit control activities to be able to report to the hierarchical organization of your corporate group. There may be sense in controlling credit in a decentralized way, perhaps not. Some of your working environments may be more erratic in a financial sense than others. This can be due to business customs, political realities, international currency markets, or a combination of all of these.

SAP R/3 credit management functions work on a set of master records that are maintained to keep in tune with the changing needs of credit control policies.

The main division of credit control records concerns the credit control areas that are chosen because the customers in each area are likely to be prudently managed by a common credit control policy. For example, you might separate Europe from Asia, and France, Germany, Japan, and Korea at the next level, as appropriate. At each level in such a hierarchy, there will probably be a credit controller who has the task of deciding cases that are not amenable to management by automatic rules.

Credit data for each customer will be assembled at each credit control area to which this customer might be assigned. For example, you might maintain the following fields in a particular credit control area master for each customer:

- Credit Limit
- Risk Category
- Customer Credit Group
- Credit Representative Group
- Date of Next Review
- Text in Explanation of the Policy
- Blocked Status Control Information
- External Credit Data

The information in some of these master record fields is likely to be sensitive, and therefore access and alteration has to be governed by authorization control. Which fields will be so controlled is a matter determined in Customizing for Financial Accounting. The online *Implementation Guide* provides instructions for maintaining this data.

The following fields include the credit data to which only authorized Financial Accounting credit representatives have access for editing:

- The total of the loans represented by all the credit amounts that have been approved over all the credit control areas
- The amount of the highest credit amount so far assigned to a single credit control area
- The total credit limit set for all credit control areas combined
- The maximum limit for any individual credit control area

Automated credit control can be arranged to take place at certain logical moments from order receipt to delivery creation and goods issue.

The essential act is for you to define risk categories according to your credit policy and then assign each customer to one of these categories. As an additional check, you define credit groups of document types. A document credit group combines various types of orders with particular delivery types to create a composite type for credit control purposes. In logical terms, you can combine credit control areas, risk categories, and document credit groups to construct checking rules.

The following monitoring operations can be carried out by standard checking rule structures:

- Static Credit Limit Check
- Dynamic Credit Limit Check with Credit Horizon
- Maximum Document Value
- Changes Made to Critical Fields
- Date of Next Review
- Overdue Open Items
- Oldest Open Item
- Maximum Number of Dunning Levels Allowed
- User-Defined Checks

Responding to a Credit Check Failure

The system response to a warning is to automatically record a specific credit status on the document and save it.

There are various things you can arrange to block if a document is marked with a particular credit status code:

- Creating material reservations
- Creating purchase requisitions
- Creating production orders/planned orders
- Creating delivery due indices
- Printing order confirmations
- Creating deliveries

The credit status can also block the following shipping functions:

- Picking
- Packing
- Posting goods issue
- Printing delivery notes

You can also specify which urgent or serious problems will automatically send electronic mail messages through output control to the responsible credit representative.

For example, a representative can be allowed to process credit holds for customers within a particular risk category whose total credit exposure is below, say, 80% of the allowed credit limit. Anyone with credit exposure near 100% of their credit limit can be referred to a more senior credit representative before a credit hold can be processed to release the credit control block.

Credit Controlling According to Document Value

It may be convenient to define document value classes according to the total value on the document. You can then allow specific credit representatives to process work lists that include only documents in value classes within their range of responsibility. Any document of higher value will be referred automatically to a senior.

As of release 3.0D, all processing of a blocked sales document can be blocked until it is released by credit management.

Working with Other Credit Control Tools

The concept and functionality of the internal mail partner can be implemented to link credit managers and credit representatives for the more rapid handling of credit problems.

Credit controllers will have access to SAPscript word processing and can record their credit decisions as text in the document or in the scratch pad zone of the customer master. These decisions can be communicated by ready access to online credit, financial, and sales information systems.

From Here

This chapter was about the important but not particularly glamorous task of asking for money. SAP R/3 has virtually all known billing mechanisms programmed as standard functions. Your task will be to choose which will be set up, or you may have the job of streamlining the billing process so that no time is wasted and no customer is lost through errors.

You might like to move on to one of the following:

- Chapter 5, "Arranging Shipping and Transportation"
- Chapter 6, "Trading Worldwide"
- Chapter 7, "Managing the SD Communications"
- Chapter 8, "Using Modern Sales Systems"

Part
II

Ch
4

Arranging Shipping and Transportation

Introducing the SD-SHP Shipping Application Module

All the data required to arrange a prompt delivery can be determined in the sales order. By having the system display all the orders due for delivery, you can manage the deadlines. Bottlenecks will be foreseen and the remedies will be at hand. These are the main activities empowered by the SD-SHP Shipping functions:

- Monitoring the deadlines and progress of orders due for delivery
- Creating and processing deliveries
- Planning and monitoring work lists for shipping activities
- Monitoring the availability of goods
- Processing outstanding orders
- Supporting the picking operations, with possible links to the Warehouse Management System
- Supporting packing and loading of deliveries
- Managing transportation and information support for transportation planning
- Supporting foreign trade requirements
- Creating shipping output documents and transmitting them
- Managing decentralized shipping
- Updating data in goods issue
- Posting the goods issue document to FI-Financial Accounting at the time of delivery

Using Decentralized Shipping

When the SD-Sales and Distribution system has reached the point of being able to specify a delivery, it may be convenient to pass this delivery document to another system. For example, there could be several satellite systems working on a decentralized shipping basis, each receiving a subset of the deliveries due from the central system.

These are some of the advantages recognized by companies that adopt the decentralized shipping approach:

- Shipping processing can be carried out continuously, even when the main computing system is unavailable.
- The SD-SHP Shipping module can be used on a satellite computer in conjunction with another sales order processing system, for instance, from the SAP R/2 system. One company can be selling, another delivering, and each can have its own computer system, not necessarily from SAP.
- The system load can be distributed over various computers by relieving the main system of the shipping functions.

The net effect of decentralizing shipping in this manner is to minimize delivery times and improve customer service.

Distributing Functions Under Decentralized Shipping

The sales order is entered on the central host computer system where the stocks are managed. The availability of the order items is checked there, and the scheduling takes place there for the shipping activities of perhaps all the satellite shipping subsystems.

When the due date arrives for a delivery, the satellite initiates the shipping activities and has the delivery data transferred from the host. Data relevant to the materials handled by the satellite will already be held there in the form of copies of the material master records.

A transfer of customer data takes place for every business transaction so the information is up-to-date.

Picking at the satellite can be linked to a MM-WM Warehouse Management system there or in the host. As the batches and quantities are gathered to the picking location, the specifications are confirmed in the delivery document. You can add packaging and other shipping elements at the same time, together with the weights and volumes, for the loading data that will appear on the shipping output documents to be generated locally.

When the delivery is completed, the goods issue for the delivery is automatically confirmed. The data is transferred back to the host, where the status of the sales order is updated.

The satellite system does not post quantities or values to the FI-Financial Accounting system; this is done centrally when the delivery confirmation is returned.

As soon as the delivery has been confirmed, the central host system will release the delivery for billing, and it will appear on the billing due list.

Tracking Document Flow in Decentralized Shipping Processing

It may be useful to trace the way in which sales information gets converted into successful deliveries in a typical situation where a central sales and distribution system creates sales orders used as the references for deliveries.

When a delivery is proposed, an availability check and delivery scheduling take place. If you initiate delivery printing, the delivery data is transferred using the CPI-C protocol to the R/3 Shipping System.

In the R/3 Shipping System, deliveries will be created as a result of the communication documents received. At this stage, however, they will not refer to any sales orders.

At the satellite shipping location, there is an opportunity to edit each delivery before a pro forma goods issue is posted, and the possibly edited delivery data is returned to the central sales and distribution system. If all is well, the central SD office will post a goods issue document. This will inform Materials Management and initiate the sending out of an invoice for the delivery.

Inspecting the Shipping Communication Documents

There are two standard types of display: global overview and selective overview. They can be called as follows:

1. Select Logistics>Sales/Distribution>Shipping.
2. Select Delivery>Decentralized Systems.

N O T E Some menu items may be abbreviated on your delivery screens—"Decentraliz.systems," for example. ■

3. Select Communication>Evaluate Commun.doc.
4. Enter the search criteria to identify the documents you require.
5. Select Program>Execute.

The next screen you will see will tell you how many documents have been identified by your search specification, sorted by communication type and summarized for processing status. If you mark the Delivery line of entries of interest, the following sequence will retrieve a selective overview: Select>Goto>Overview>Commun.doc.

Here you will see the record number of each chosen document together with such information as the following:

■ Record type
■ Time and date of reaching the system
■ Time and date processed
■ Error status

Differentiating the Communication Elements in Shipping

A decentralized system needs formal communication elements to enable data transfer and the checking of transfer transactions. The following sections point out the elements and their different functions.

Defining a Communication Document   A communication document is defined as a chain of data that is transferred in one transaction. Therefore, a communication document is created for each data transfer transaction between the participants in a decentralized shipping system. The communication document is a collection of communication records with the same number. The first and the last record of the communication document are marked appropriately so that the data chain is recognizable as a logical unit.

A communication record is an extract of data in the R/3 format that is to be transferred.

Understanding Communication Record Type   Types of communication records are differentiated according to the sort of data they bear, which can depend on the nature of the transaction and the direction of the communication.

In addition to the type, a communication record has a record number. All communication records with the same number are part of the same communication document, regardless of their types.

A specific table is defined in the R/3 Data Dictionary for each record type and reflects the data structure of that communication record type. Communication records of that type are stored in this table.

Converting to the R/3 Format   A decentralized shipping system can include various partner systems, such as SAP R/2 installations and systems from third-party suppliers.

Transfer of communication records always adheres to the R/3 format, no matter in which direction the communication is taking place, and no matter between which systems. Each participating system is responsible for converting to or from R/3 format as necessary.

Building a Data Chain of Communication Records   Records are given a status indicator to define their roles in a communication chain that forms a communication document during the technical transfer process. The following status codes illustrate the system:

- F—First record
- L—Last record of
- Blank—Other record
- S—Single to indicate that the communication document consists of only one record

Interpreting the Communication Document Number   The system automatically constructs a communication document number according to the intended recipient. The number includes elements to define the technical factors such as the target system, the software application, the client company, and the receiving interface program.

The communication number is also used to determine the key for the queue file. This is an intermediate file from which the communication documents can be transmitted automatically or manually to the partner system.

When you make a data transfer, a send program is called to perform the following functions:

- Create the communication document.
- Write the communication document to the intermediate file.
- Establish a connection to the receiving program in the target system.
- Transfer the communication documents using CPI-C.

A receiving program is called in the target system to perform as follows:

- Write the individual communication records to the tables defined for each of their specific record types.
- Create a status record from which you can check the communication process.
- Test the data contents in the communication records.
- Execute the necessary postings in the receiving system.

Part
II

Ch

5

Monitoring Communication in Decentralized Shipping Processing

If no errors occur in the communication, all you have to do is process the deliveries created by the communication documents. You can monitor the documents received in the R/3 Shipping system because, if any errors occur, you may have to reprocess the communication documents manually.

The global overview listing will give you the following information:

- How many documents have been received
- Which documents have been received
- Where errors occurred during the transfer of the documents
- When a document reached the R/3 shipping system and when it was processed there
- The status of each document as complete, open, or incorrect
- Which data a document contains

By selecting List>Refresh, you can update the global overview of communication document transmission.

If you have invoked the Selective overview screen by specifying which communication documents are of interest, you can mark one and select Goto>Display>Commun.doc to see the header data with the number of the delivery created, the item data, and any texts belonging to the documents selected.

If you know the record number of a communication document, you can access the details by the following sequence:

1. Select Logistics>Sales/Distribution>Shipping.
2. Select Delivery>Decentraliz.Systems.
3. Select Communication>Shipping>Display>Commun.Doc.
4. Complete the Communications Document field by entering the document number you require.
5. Select Program>Execute.

Reposting Communication Documents in Decentralized Shipping Processing   If the status of a communication document in the global overview is Open, it means that no decentralized delivery has been automatically created from it. If the system has detected some inconsistency, the communication document will be marked Incorrect.

If you examine the communication document in the Selective overview, you will have access to text that explains why there is an error.

Reposting can take place in one of the following processing modes:

- A—Always. Reposting is prompted in the foreground, and you are branched to the delivery document to process it manually.

■ E—Exception. Reposting is prompted in the foreground only when an error has occurred during attempted transmission.

N O T E If no error occurs during attempted transmission using the E Exception mode, reposting of Open communication documents is carried out automatically without branching to the document. ■

■ N—Never. Reposting takes place automatically in the background, even if errors occur.

If you are reposting from the Selective overview screen, the following sequence is appropriate:

1. Mark the document of interest.
2. Select Edit>Repost comm.doc.
3. On the Create Decentralized Deliveries from Communications Records screen, enter the indicator code of the processing mode you intend to use.

N O T E A fresh number for the communication record is proposed automatically when you are creating decentralized deliveries from existing communications records. ■

4. Select Program>Execute.

If you chose manual processing, the system will show you the Create Delivery screen with default values in place. If you select Continue, you will be able to create or edit the delivery.

Delivery items from the central Sales and Distribution system cannot be deleted, nor can you change the plant, storage locations, and batches. You can check batches only if they are created manually in the R/3 system.

Confirming Decentralized Deliveries   Once a decentralized delivery has been created in the R/3 shipping system, it must be confirmed in your central Sales and Distribution system by a corresponding posting of a goods issue in the decentralized R/3 shipping system.

Confirmation that the delivery has been fully and successfully processed can occur automatically by using output control. Your system must have arranged for the sending of output in batch to be scheduled.

If confirmation has been carried out successfully, either automatically or manually, the status Completed will appear in the document flow for the decentralized delivery.

Editing Decentralized Deliveries   As in a central R/3 system, you can edit decentralized deliveries in any of the following processing modes:

■ Individual processing
■ Processing using delivery due list
■ Processing by making selections from deliveries in process

Although you can group deliveries and process them together, the communication to the central Sales and Distribution system cannot be by a group data transmission.

Transferring Material Master Records in a Decentralized System

When you create or maintain central material master records of type LgO or Material SD, they can be transferred automatically to the decentralized system by using communication documents that update the decentralized records. To ensure that consistent data is maintained across a decentralized system, you can change material data that has been transferred from the central system only if you are changing the central records and thus promulgating the change throughout the decentralized system.

You can create and maintain local master records that will not be updated from the center if, by so doing, you will not impugn data consistency.

Changing Materials Decentrally   The following procedure will allow a decentralized R/3 system to maintain materials data:

1. Select Logistics>Sales/Distribution>Master Data.

2. Select Products>Material>Decentraliz.Shipping>Change Decentrally.

You will reach the Change Material: Initial screen, where you can take up the different sales views. You will find, however, that many of the fields will not allow you to make local alterations because this could compromise data consistency across the decentralized system.

Maintaining Materials Centrally in the Decentralized System   Although this is not the normal procedure, there is a method for creating and maintaining central records from a decentralized system if the central maintenance function is temporarily unable to do so. Provisions have to be made to confirm that this holding of parallel data is consistent, and you will need to be authorized for this activity.

The following sequence will invoke the procedure:

1. Select Logistics>Sales/Distribution>Master Data.

2. Select Products>Material>Decentraliz.Shipping>Create Centrally.

3. You can create material masters in the standard way from the Create Material: Initial screen.

A similar procedure will enable you to change a material master held centrally from a decentralized R/3 system.

Recognizing and Analyzing Errors in Decentralized Shipping Processing

You might need to use any or all of the following functions if errors are detected in communication documents in a decentralized R/3 shipping system:

- Examine incoming mail regarding data transfer errors and mail the employee responsible for data transfer errors.

- Analyze the system log for items relevant to data transfer.

- Evaluate the communication documents by using the Error Analysis option.

This is the way to begin this troubleshooting process:

1. Select Logistics>Sales/Distribution>Shipping.

2. Select Delivery>Decentraliz.Systems.

3. Select one of the Error Analysis options according to what you want to do.

Understanding the Delivery Document

You can regard the main purpose of a shipping organization as the successful processing of delivery documents and the transfer of goods and value they represent. Certainly, most shipping activities need to refer to the delivery document. The picking and delivery scheduling can begin when it is posted, and monitoring the progress of these activities will also come into force. As a physical delivery moves through various stages, the delivery document is kept posted with data so that it can be regarded as the central means for keeping track of the goods, and hence value, in transit.

A delivery can refer to a sales order or a transportation order. It need refer to no other document. A work list can be used to create deliveries automatically. You also can generate them manually. Orders can be combined into deliveries, and your customer may wish or agree to partial deliveries. Not surprisingly, SAP R/3 provides various overviews for you to monitor created deliveries and outstanding sales activities.

Reading the Shipping Work Lists

For every shipping point under the control of the Shipping department, there can be a work list of sales orders due for delivery. How frequently these work lists are processed will be a matter to be determined by the management and operating staff—all things being equal, the sooner the better.

A shipping point is a facility that offers a separate shipping capacity. It can be one of several identical loading bays, for example, or it may have a special handling capacity such as a forklift truck that is larger than the other shipping points. The shipping point may owe its individuality to the fact that it is dedicated to the orders for one particular customer.

The appropriate shipping point is either automatically determined by the system or entered manually during order creation. The criteria for automatic shipping point determination are as follows:

- Shipping conditions specified for the sold-to party—for example, "as soon as possible" or "normal shipping conditions"
- Loading group of the material—for example, "by crane," "by forklift truck," or "by special staff loading team"
- Delivering plant—for example, "road truck," "rail wagon," or "dedicated transporter"

Each order item has to be assigned a route. Which route is chosen will depend on the following criteria:

Part
II

Ch
5

- The shipping conditions specified for the sold-to party
- The delivery weight of the order item
- The geographical relationship of the destination to the shipping point

Each route will impose certain restrictions in the choice of means of transport and the number and nature of the legs of the journey. If the order item has to change delivery plant en route, there will be extra costs and delays, but to have the whole route executed in one particular means of transport may be unacceptable for other reasons: It may take too long, the atmospheric pollution by the vehicle may be damaging to the reputation of your company, or the vehicle may have to make the return journey without a payload.

You can call up a list at any time to see which deliveries are scheduled to use a particular route or shipping point over a selected time interval. You may be able to effect an improvement in the planning of loading and transportation activities by a manual change to one or more of the parameters assigned by the system.

Creating and Processing Deliveries

To the SAP R/3 system, a delivery is a document. It has to carry all the data necessary for preparing and delivering the material in the sales order.

Creating a Complete Delivery for a Particular Sales Order   The goods specified by material number and quantity can be copied from the sales order to the delivery document. If what you want is a single delivery group comprising all the items, you can set the Complete Delivery indicator. This may have been set already in the Shipping screen of the customer master data or manually in the sales document.

The system will apply the latest possible delivery date among the items to the whole delivery group. There will be a corresponding adjustment to delivery schedule lines and Material Requirements Planning if your system has these as integrated functions.

If you need to set the Complete Delivery indicator, the following sequence is available in order entry: Select Header>Business Data>Proposal From Customer Master Record.

The shipping point can be selected automatically by using the shipping conditions that will be available from the customer master records.

If the shipping conditions have changed, or if there has been no previous specification of the customer shipping conditions, you can correct matters by a manual entry before you post the delivery to have it executed.

Creating All Deliveries Due   From your display of all sales orders due for delivery, you can select, on the basis of a specific shipping point, a particular material, a single ship-to party, and so on, in any combination that leaves you with the selection of deliveries due that you intend to create. You also can refine your list by imposing other restrictions, such as the maximum gross weight your vehicle can carry or the maximum overall dimensions.

The list of sales orders due, perhaps refined by your selection procedures, can then be processed simultaneously to become delivery documents. The system will log for your attention any sales order documents that are not correct or that lack a needed data element. You can return to these later and enter the missing data.

Creating a Delivery Manually It is possible to manually enter all the relevant information needed to create a delivery. You may want to do this if the central system is unable to provide access to the sales order, or if the information you require is not there.

Automatic Checks in Delivery Creation

The system carries out checks to help ensure that the delivery data is complete and correct. When you see the display of the delivery due list in detail, you may find that you have to change some of the data entered by the PP-MRP Material Requirements Planning function because the situation has changed since that planning operation was performed.

The specifications in the material master records in MM-Materials Management will have provided the data for automatically calculating the weights and volumes of the individual delivery items and the totals for the delivery as a whole. The same MM system will be the source of stock data the system will use to check that the material intended for the delivery is indeed going to be available for this purpose.

At this moment, just before a delivery is created, the system will take another look at the scheduling specifications in the sales order: the customer's required delivery date or the standard delivery conditions assigned in the customer's master records. You will get a warning and a proposal if a change in scheduling is needed.

Forming Delivery Groups

When you set the indicator to initiate a complete delivery of a sales order, the system forms the items into a delivery group that is thereafter managed as a single object. However, the formation of a delivery group cannot proceed for any item to which the following conditions apply:

- No order quantity has been confirmed for the item.
- The item has more than one order quantity.

A delivery item may appear with confirmed quantities on more than one schedule line. Under these circumstances the system will propose the date of the latest of these schedule lines as the delivery date on the Delivery Group overview screen. It will also delete the earlier schedule line or lines and carry their confirmed quantities into the single schedule line that remains for this item.

You may want to create a delivery group in a sales document for only some of the items. What you have to do is to use the Overview>Delivery Groups screen to assign the same delivery group number to each of the items you want to be delivered together. The system will create as many delivery groups as you have marked and automatically propose a delivery date for each of them.

If you specify a delivery group number on an item, it will be added to the group. You can remove it by deleting the group number.

You or your customer may not like the proposed delivery date for a delivery group. You can change it, and the system will revise the shipping and transportation dates if necessary.

If you delete a delivery group by deleting the delivery group numbers for every item in the group, or delete the complete delivery indicator, the system will try to recreate the original schedule lines. If there were any items whose original quantity could not be confirmed, there will be a new availability check.

Managing the Delivery Situation of an Item

A delivery situation is the result of taking into account the goods availability position and the agreements in place with the customer or the sold-to party concerning partial deliveries.

If the sold-to party will not accept partial deliveries, you have to see that all the items in the sales order are collected together in one delivery group that then becomes the focus. The availability check and the transfer of requirements have to be adjusted to fit the earliest delivery date possible for the delivery group.

If the sold-to party has agreed to accept partial deliveries, you can, if necessary, create several deliveries from the one sales order. This might suit the availability situation, both of goods and of the shipping facilities.

It might make sense to combine several sales orders into one delivery group, if the customer has agreed to such an arrangement.

In all these procedures, for effectively managing the delivery situations as and when they arise and planning to smooth their passage before the time comes, the SAP R/3 Shipping system can be allowed to act automatically by setting up the appropriate logical conditions and data elements.

The creation of a delivery document, when it is posted and proved to be valid, is the occasion for the system to update automatically the material stocks and the work list of the Shipping department, where the display of the delivery situation of the sales order will show the updated status key.

When the delivery has been posted, the system will offer you a proposal to print or send by electronic mail the shipping output documents mandated during customizing.

Assigning Shipping Elements

A shipping element is an item of material that is managed separately in the SD-Sales and Distribution system because it is used in shipping and is necessary for the purpose of handling and protecting the goods in transit. It may be on loan to the customer for a specified period, and a charge can be raised if it is not returned within that period. The following items can be managed as shipping elements:

- Boxes
- Cartons
- Pallets

- Trucks
- Trailers
- Supporting travel rigs

To protect and handle a particular delivery, it may be necessary to have the item first packed in cartons. A group of cartons, perhaps, can be protected by a box, and several boxes can be loaded into a freight container. All these shipping elements can be treated as a hierarchy of shipping elements that is recognized by the system and specified for use for one or more types of material or one or more customers.

The shipping elements need not be specified as a hierarchical structure; they can be referenced simply as a packing list, which is also recognized by the system as a data object and can be changed under the control of the procedures of change management.

Working with Serial Numbers in Deliveries

Serial numbers assigned to each example of a material or product are used to keep track of the specific physical object for a variety of purposes. If there are individual masters for each serialized item, they can be used in plant maintenance or routine servicing, for example. The word *object* is used to distinguish a documented serialized item.

During Customizing, serial number profiles are defined that specify when serial numbers can be entered and in which transactions. A serial number profile is identified by its profile number and has to include the following control data information:

- The business transactions during which serialization must take place
- The business transactions during which serialization can take place
- The business transactions during which serialization may not take place
- The business transactions during which you can enter new serial numbers
- The business transactions during which you can select from serial numbers already created and stored in the system
- The business transactions during which, if you are using serialization, you must create equipment master records

It is possible to define different business transactions with different parameters for serialization in one serial number profile.

A serial number profile is confined to a single plant and stored in the Basic Data field group of the material master record from which it may be viewed in the Sales/Plant Data screen. If a material has not been assigned a serial number profile, you cannot serialize examples of it.

By definition, a serialized material item is an object and has its own master record. The following data is therefore potentially available about this object:

- Company-specific location in a particular plant
- External location identified as the customer who purchased this item

- The last operation carried out on this object, such as the number of the delivery to the customer

If you need to create a serial number record as part of the sales master data, the procedure is as follows:

1. Select Logistics>Sales/Distribution>Master Data.
2. Select Products>Serial Numbers>Create.
3. Enter the material number.
4. Enter the serial number.
5. Enter reference data if required.
6. Select Edit>Details.

At this stage you can enter master data details.

Whether or not you can or must enter serial numbers for materials in a delivery will depend on the values set in the master data records for each material. When you reach the dialog box, you have to mark the delivery item for which you want to enter serial numbers and select Item>Serial Numbers.

There are three possibilities:

- You can select from serial numbers for which you have already created master records and which you have selectively displayed.
- You can enter new serial numbers manually in the Serial Number field.
- The system can automatically propose new numbers if you choose this option.

When you save the results of this operation, the system will automatically create new master records for each serial number you have assigned.

You can delete a serial number that appears in the dialog box and prevent it being assigned. This will not delete the serial number master record, which can later be assigned elsewhere.

Creating Equipment in Deliveries

Materials for which you carry out plant maintenance are akin to serialized materials because they require individual equipment master records on which their maintenance details can be stored.

The equipment indicator in the Serial Number dialog box is a signal that a separate equipment master record is mandatory for this object. The system will automatically create it when you save the delivery.

It is still possible, however, to set the equipment indicator in the Serial Number dialog box during delivery processing, even if the object is not obliged to have an equipment master record. You have to mark the serial numbers you are going to use and choose Create>Equipment.

You can delete the equipment indicator manually if you have set it, but not if the system set it.

Working with Inspection Lots in Deliveries

Your customer or legal authorities may require you to carry out and give evidence of quality checks for each delivery.

If you need to provide quality checks every time for a specific material, you should set the Quality Check function in the material master and arrange to consult inspection data in the QM-Quality Management module. You may need to specify additional data for deliveries to a particular customer, in which case you should mark this in the customer master record.

If you cannot release a delivery without agreement from the Quality Assurance department, you need to create customer-specific information records in the QM module. The following are the steps you need to perform:

1. Select Logistics>Quality Management>Quality Planning>QM in Sales/Distr.

2. Select Sales/Distribution>Create.

From the Create QM Control Data in SD screen, you can create customer-specific information records.

There are several supporting facilities available in this QM component. For instance, you may have a delivery item that includes a batch of material that has been divided into partial items, each comprising a partial lot that needs inspection certification. The system will calculate an inspection sample for each of the partial lots and append to each the results of the inspection when they become available. There may have to be different usage decisions on any lot that does not come up to standard.

Interpreting Shipping Incoterms as Conditions

Incoterms are shipping terms that establish the respective liabilities of both the shipping party and the recipient. They are recognized internationally and interpreted similarly.

A simple shipping term is "FOB" (Free on board). An Incoterm can be qualified additionally by adding the loading port.

The SAP R/3 Shipping system allows you to create condition records that use one or both parts of a standard Incoterm.

A freight condition is predefined by condition records and is used when the system is applying automatic pricing to a delivery group.

Two freight condition types have been predefined as follows:

- KF00 is a freight condition type that applies to each item in a sales document.
- HD00 is a freight condition type that is applied manually to the header and applies without exception to the entire document.

Your system can have various freight condition records defined using these freight condition types.

Part
II

Ch
5

Controlling Goods Issue

A significant aspect of goods issue is that it signifies the end of the business transaction as far as the shipping function is concerned. The goods have left the plant.

Several consequent actions take place automatically, including the following:

- The stock record of the material held at the plant is reduced by the goods issue quantity.
- The change of stock is represented by a value flow recorded in Accounting by updates to the stock account and the stock changes account.
- The material requirements for the delivery are reduced or eliminated, depending on the quantity.
- The status of the delivery is updated and the system will automatically update the goods issue status on all the associated sales and distribution documents.
- If your company bills immediately after goods issue, the delivery enters the billing work list and invoicing will soon occur.

Because the delivery document provides the data that is copied into the goods issue document for posting, you are not allowed to alter the goods issue document. If you want to change anything, it must be done in the delivery document, essentially before goods issue. If you were allowed to change a goods issue, the customer could be invoiced for a different quantity and type of goods from what was delivered.

Interpreting the Goods Issue Status Indicators

The standard SAP R/3 system provides the following goods issue status indicators:

- Blank indicates that the item is not relevant for goods issue.
- A indicates that goods issue processing has not yet been started for the item.
- C indicates that goods issue has been carried out for the item.

Goods issue is an all-or-nothing matter. You cannot have a partial goods issue for a delivery.

You can find the goods issue status of the entire delivery from the header as follows:

1. Access the Delivery Overview screen.
2. Select Header>General Header Data.
3. Examine the status indicator in the Goods Movement field.

The goods issue status for a delivery is copied to each delivery item where it can be inspected as follows:

1. Access the Delivery Overview screen.
2. Select Item>Status.
3. Examine the status indicator in the Goods Movement Stat. field.

The goods issue status can also be determined from the document flow as follows:

1. Access an overview screen in the sales order or in the delivery.

2. Select Environment>Document Flow.

3. You will see the numbers of all the preceding and subsequent documents related to the sales order or delivery with which you are working.

4. Mark the delivery number of interest.

5. Select Goto>Status Overview.

6. Examine the processing status for the entire delivery in the Goods Movement Status field.

Posting Goods Issue for a Delivery

There are some sensible checks made before you can post a goods issue for a delivery. The following are some examples:

- There must be a complete set of data, including the storage location, the batch, and the valuation type.

- Picking must have been finished for all the items. If the required quantity could not be picked for any reason, the goods issue must refer to the picked rather than the required quantity.

- If you are operating the warehouse management system MM-WM, the item picked must have the status Completed in MM-WM. This status is only assigned if all transfer orders for the delivery have been confirmed.

The procedure for posting a goods issue for a delivery you have created or changed is as follows:

1. Access one of the overview screens.

2. Select Edit>Post Goods Issue.

When the delivery has been successfully saved and the goods issue posted, you will see a message that includes the delivery number. There will be no reference to the goods issue document number, which is not a sales and distribution document.

If you want to see the stock quantities and values, you can access a goods issue document from the MM-Materials Management or FI-Financial Accounting applications. The following procedure is appropriate:

1. Access the overview screen of the delivery of interest.

2. Select Environment>Document Flow.

3. Mark the goods issue document in the list of the document numbers associated with the business transaction.

4. Select Environment>Display Document.

   or

   Select Environment>Display Accounting.

The Display Document command will give you the materials management view that includes the plant, the storage location, the batch data, and the movement type for the delivery item.

The Display Accounting command will show you the financial accounting document that displays the posting key that controls posting to the relevant balance sheet accounts and the value that is posted.

Reversing Goods Issue Posting

You cannot cancel goods posting or subsequently alter a delivery. However, you may discover a mistake, or perhaps the goods are damaged leaving your plant or in transit. In such circumstances, you must cancel the entire business transaction.

The problem will have been detected too late to stop an invoice from being sent for the delivery, so you must post a returns order for the customer and the material using order type RE. You can refer to the original order so the details will be automatically copied to form a proposal. You may wish to alter the quantities proposed if, for example, only some of the goods arrived damaged. The returns order will then appear in the document flow listing.

You have to create a returns delivery for the returns order. The system will propose the delivery type and offer the delivery quantities in the returns delivery to correspond to the goods issue quantities in the original, but incorrect, goods issue document.

When you post this document you post a copy made from a goods issue document as a returns delivery, just as you might post an ordinary delivery. The system will automatically recognize that the returns delivery is a goods receipt and will associate it with the original goods issue document. It will then clear the value flow represented by the original goods issue posting by carrying out a corresponding reverse posting.

The final task in this sequence is to invoice the business transaction with a returns credit memo. Again, the system will propose a billing type. The effect of this invoicing of a returns credit memo is to clear the original billing document for the incorrect goods issue document.

Specifying Goods Issue Dates Manually

One of the few alterations you are allowed to make before posting a goods issue is to specify an actual goods issue date. This does not affect the planned goods issue date. The following sequence is suitable:

1. Access the Quantity overview screen in the delivery.
2. Select Edit>Actual GI Date.
3. Enter the actual goods issue date in the dialog box.
4. Select Post Goods Issue in this dialog box.

The default value will be the current date if you do not specify an actual goods issue date.

Picking and Confirming

A picking list, or pick list, is a document that makes sure that the goods in the warehouse arrive at the shipping point at the right moment to become part of a delivery. Clearly, only the right goods and the right quantities will do. And it is no use getting the goods to the shipping point just before the transport is due to leave if some work has to be done to prepare the goods and protect them with the specified shipping elements. If the goods need special storage conditions, picking will have to make allowances for this.

The typical sequence is as follows:

■ A picking location or loading zone is automatically determined for a delivery by using data on the sales order delivery document that will indicate the shipping point and the storage conditions to be observed.

■ A picking list is printed for each delivery when the delivery is created, or later. The picking list can be sent by electronic means.

■ When the picking has assembled the available quantities at the picking location, the quantities are confirmed to the system. If they are insufficient but stock is available, picking is carried out again for the shortfall, by using the same loading zone. If the quantities required cannot be picked to the picking zone, for whatever reason, the delivery quantity is reduced. The system will make the appropriate adjustments to the order, shipping, and billing documents.

In some circumstances, you may have to enter the batch specification or the valuation type after picking has been completed, because only at that stage will the necessary data be accurate. For example, some process industries have to expect a variation in the makeup of the finished product, because variability in the input materials and the environmental conditions has an effect on the product.

Linking with the MM-WM Warehouse Management System

If you have installed and configured the MM-WM Warehouse Management system, the initiation of picking can take place through this system.

The system maintains materials master data that indicates the fixed storage bin or circumscribed storage area in which the material can be found during picking.

If the warehouse does not use fixed bin storage, it is treated as a random warehouse. The MM-WM Warehouse Management system makes sure that a transfer order is created for each delivery item. When the goods arrive at the picking area, the transfer order is confirmed and the system will enter the picked quantities directly into the delivery items on the delivery document.

Interpreting Picking Status Indicators

Each item in a delivery carries its own picking status, which is normally assigned from the following standard picking indicators:

- Blank indicates that the item is not relevant for picking.
- A indicates that picking has not been started.
- B indicates that the item has been partially picked with respect to quantity.
- C indicates that the item has been completely picked.

The picking status of a delivery item can be found on the first Item Detail screen, which you can reach as follows:

1. Access the Delivery overview screen.
2. Mark the item of interest.
3. Select Item>Item Details.

If picking has taken place for this delivery item under the control of the Warehouse Management system MM-WM, the processing status of the item in the MM-WM system is also shown.

Picking status is also shown from the Delivery screen by Select Overview>Picking>PW column.

Matching Picked and Delivery Quantities

A delivery cannot leave the shipping point if the picked quantity as confirmed by the warehouse is less that the quantity stated in the delivery document. You have two choices:

- Reduce the quantity in the delivery to make it match the quantity picked and so create a partial delivery.
- Call for the picking to be carried out again in the hope that the entire quantity will be picked.

An item that is classed as relevant for picking has to be associated with a specific storage location in the delivery, and the picking has to take place only from stock at that location. If you are operating the MM-WM system, the storage location identified in the delivery document determines which storage location in the Warehouse Management system is responsible for picking.

Whether an item is to be picked depends on the item category to which it is assigned during customizing. For example, text items such as manuals are not relevant for picking.

It is unusual for the picking location to be known when the order is entered, so this is decided when a delivery is being created at the shipping point. There can be a provision for entering the picking location automatically, or you may have to do it manually.

Displaying the Picking Location

The picking location can depend on the shipping point, the plant, and the storage conditions required by the material. You can find this information as follows:

1. Access the Delivery Item overview screen.
2. Mark the item of interest.
3. Select Item>Item Details>Plant/StLocat. Field.

The Picking overview screen includes a SLoc column.

If picking has not yet begun, you can change the storage location from which it shall take place.

The storage condition for a material is an item detail that can be viewed from the material master record on the Storage screen in the Storage Condition field.

Automatic picking location determination depends on the system consulting a set of rules stored as condition records associated with each delivery type. This information has to be established in customizing.

Using a Picking List

You may have to print out an individual picking list to carry out picking for a particular delivery if the Warehouse Management system (MM-WM) is not used in your company, or if picking is always from a fixed storage bin location.

The picking list has to include the following data:

- Delivery number
- Printing date
- Shipping point
- Delivering plant and storage location
- Picking and loading date
- Number and address of the ship-to party
- Gross weight and volume of the entire delivery
- Storage bin, material number, material short text, and delivery quantity in the base unit of measure for each delivery item

To facilitate the physical operation, the picking list for a delivery will have the delivery items sorted according to which storage bin is specified for them. A new page of the picking list is started each time any of the following parameters changes:

- The plant
- The storage location
- The material availability date

The description of a bin location is stored on the Storage screen in the Bin Location field in the material master record. The location description code specifies the physical location of this product in the warehouse.

Setting Up Collective Picking

If you are not operating with MM-WM, or if you are concerned with items not handled by it, you may able to take advantage of the collective picking facility. The picker selects items for several deliveries from the same bin before moving on to the next bin in the picking list.

There has to be a second stage in which the picked material items are assigned to their individual deliveries.

A collective picking list contains a header for general data and an item area.

The collective picking list header includes the following data that is applied throughout the picking list:

- Collective picking request number
- Grouped delivery number
- Shipping point

The following collective picking list header data can be different depending on the delivery and the material:

- Picking date
- Plant
- Storage location
- Storage number for MM-WM only

A picking list sorted and printed from this data will take a fresh page whenever any of these parameters changes, for example, if a collective picking list includes more than one picking date or plant.

The item area of a collective picking list document can contain both collective and individual items.

For each material item in a collective list, the following information is displayed:

- Bin location
- Material number
- Batch type or valuation type

N O T E   When both collective and individual items are available, the batch type is issued.

- Material description
- The quantity of the material required totaled for all deliveries
- A space in which to enter the total picked quantity for the material

Collective items are sorted hierarchically according to bin, material, batch, or valuation type. These collective items can have individual information items assigned to them to explain how the quantity of the material in each case is to be assigned to the various deliveries.

Creating Collective Picking Lists

A collective picking list has to be created and processed from a single shipping point. The following sequence is suitable:

1. Access the Shipping initial screen.

2. Select Grouped Deliveries>Create Spec.Groups>Collective Picking.

3. Enter the deliveries to be picked together. The system will propose the collective picking group type K.

4. Save the group.

Packing into Shipping Units

A shipping unit is a combination of materials or other shipping units represented by a master record in the SAP R/3 system. A shipping unit is packed and shipped at a certain time. Packing is a part of delivery processing where you can select delivery items for packing and assign them to shipping units.

Because a shipping unit can be combined with other shipping units to form a larger shipping unit, there is no limit to the complexity of a shipping unit. You can have items in boxes that are on pallets that are on a vehicle, for example. You can manage these items at any level of shipping unit.

This data structure facilitates the following operations:

■ Maintaining stocks of packing materials

■ Monitoring returnable packaging stocks at the customer or forwarding agent

■ Ascertaining the contents of a shipping unit such as a container if a problem occurs

■ Ensuring that weight and volume limits are not exceeded

■ Confirming that products and materials are correctly packed

Control of packing is exercised directly in the delivery, as follows:

1. Access the Quantities overview screen of the delivery.

2. Select Edit>Packing.

From the Packing screen you can specify the following operations:

■ Pack delivery items into shipping units.

■ Divide individual items between several shipping units.

■ Arrange automatic packing to distribute a specified quantity among several shipping units.

■ Set up multileveled packing in which some shipping units are packed into larger shipping units, and so on.

N O T E   You are allowed to specify just under one million packing levels of shipping unit when you are setting up multileveled packing. ■

■ Unpack particular items from shipping units, of any complexity, previously packed.

■ Set up system warnings or other reactions to occur when weight or volume limits are exceeded.

N O T E   If you have defined the relevant values, the system will pack only the maximum packable quantity and will continue in another marked shipping unit if space or weight limits will not be exceeded by doing so. ■

■ Delete a shipping unit, having first extracted it from its parent shipping unit if there is one, and then unpacked all its contents.

■ Empty a shipping unit by unpacking all its contents.

■ Maintain a shipping unit and its contents manually by using the Fast Entry function.

■ Change packing quantities before goods issue has been posted.

N O T E   Your system may have other restrictions on when you can and cannot change packing quantities. ■

■ Create delivery items from shipping units so you can manage stocks of packaging materials and invoice for them.

■ Display allowed shipping materials by consulting the material grouping master for the shipping material for the goods you are intending to pack.

■ Check for allowed shipping materials for the materials in the items.

■ Review packing proposals in sales orders and scheduling agreements, if you have customized, for a suitable copying control for packing proposals from the sales order to the delivery.

■ Copy packing data from a subsystem, not necessarily SAP.

Packing for Multiple Deliveries in Transportation Processing

At the stage when you are processing the transportation arrangements, you can still initiate the following packing activities:

■ Pack delivery items that were not packed in the delivery and do not necessarily have to be packed there.

■ Pack shipping units, which are on the highest level in the delivery, into larger shipping units for a shipment.

■ Assign free shipping units to a shipment.

Maintaining Shipping Material Masters

Shipping materials are those materials classified as material type VERP, used for packing or transporting products. When packing an item, a shipping material must always be specified. When you build a shipping unit, the master data for the shipping materials will be automatically copied and the net weight and volume will be converted to tare weight and tare volume.

The net weight and volume that you enter in the material master is particularly important to packing. When you create a shipping unit, the system automatically copies the master data for shipping materials and converts net weight and volume to tare weight and tare volume. For example, the tare weight of a container is the weight of the container when empty. The weight of a delivery does not include the weight of the packaging, but the total load weight does.

Interpreting Shipping Unit Structure

A shipping unit in a delivery is represented by a header and shipping unit items. It is assigned an identification number. The header can also include an external identification number visible on the outside of a container, for instance. The header will specify shipping materials and give the weight, volume, and measurements such as the tare weight, tare volume, maximum allowed weight, and maximum allowed volume.

A shipping unit will originate from a plant or warehouse and have a shipping unit category, all of which will be recorded in the shipping unit header. Any special instructions regarding the means of transport will appear at the shipping unit header level.

The header can include specifications for printing and sending output concerning packing such as a packing list. You can specify the printing of sticky labels to attach to the shipping units.

Inspecting Shipping Unit Items

The items in a shipping unit master record are delivery items or other shipping units. You can view them in the Shipping Unit Contents overview.

NOTE The packing quantity will also be marked with the symbol * for each packing level. ** indicates that the item is a package that is itself packed in a larger unit. ▪

You can view the details by doing the following:

1. Access the Delivery screen.
2. Mark a shipping unit.
3. Select Packing Items or Packing Shipping Units.
4. Select Shp.Unit Contents.

Selecting a Packing Overview

There is an extensive range of overviews available in the Shipping module to assist in packing. You can carry out many tasks from these overviews. The following are examples:

- Weight of Items Overview—Reached via the Delivery Packing Items screen. You can pack delivery items only from this overview.
- Volume of Items Overview—Reached via the Delivery Packing Items screen. You can pack delivery items only from this overview.

Part
II

Ch
5

■ Double-line Items Overview—Reached by Select>Overview>Pack>Doub.-line Items. The relevant information on each shipping unit is displayed in double-line format. You can pack delivery items from this overview.

N O T E   Shipping materials can also be created in the Double-Line Shipping overview using the customer material number for shipping materials. ■

■ Weight of Shipping Unit Overview—reached from the Packing Items screen by Select>Overview>Weight of Shp.unit. You can pack shipping units only from this overview.

■ Volume of Shipping Unit Overview—reached from the Packing Items screen by Select>Overview>Volume of Shp.unit. You can pack shipping units only from this overview.

■ Contents of All Shipping Units Overview—reached from the Packing Items screen by Select>Overview>Shp.unit Contents. You mark the unit of interest. You can process all shipping units from this overview.

Creating a Shipping Unit

If you need to create a shipping unit, the following sequence is suitable:

1. Access the Overview: Quantities screen of the delivery.
2. Select Edit>Packing. This presents the Packing Items screen in which you can select the relevant shipping unit field.
3. Enter the external identification number.
4. Enter the appropriate shipping material in the Shipping Material field.

If you enter just a shipping material, the system will propose an internal shipping unit number in the allowed number range. You can change this manually.

Packing Delivery Items

The packing procedure is a matter of setting up data structures that will be used to issue instructions for the physical packaging operations for a delivery. The data structure is comprised of delivery items that can be packed in a certain way. These packages can themselves be packed into shipping units, which again can be assembled into larger shipping units, and so on.

You can create empty shipping units before you begin to pack, or you can work in the All Shipping Units section of the Packing screen to create shipping units as needed.

The following sequence illustrates the packing procedure:

1. Access the Quantities overview of the delivery.
2. Select Edit>Packing.
3. Access the Items to be Packed section of the screen.
4. Mark the items you want to pack together in shipping units.

5. Access the All Shipping Units section of the screen. Select Edit>Pack item.

6. Mark the shipping units you want to use for these items.

If packing according to your instructions is going to be feasible, you will receive a message that packing has been completed successfully. But if your packing proposals will not be physically possible, you will see a message explaining why not. You may have tried to exceed the volume in the intended shipping units, or the weight of the items may have been too much for this type of shipping unit.

If you select Edit>New Shp.Unit if Full, you can allow the system to decide when a sufficient quantity has been packed in a shipping unit and automatically create another.

You may be working with a partial delivery, in which case you have to specify the partial quantity in the Items to be Packed section of the screen.

If space and volume limits permit, the system will propose packing several delivery items or partial delivery quantities together in the same shipping unit.

Dividing Delivery Items for Packing

You or your customer may decide that a delivery item should be completely packed, but that the total quantity should be equally divided among several shipping units.

The following sequence will achieve this:

1. Access the Quantities overview of the delivery.

2. Select Edit>Packing.

3. Access the All Shipping Units section of the screen and create a suitable shipping unit, or identify one that is already created and free.

4. Access the Items to be Packed section of the screen.

5. Mark the items you wish to split up.

6. Enter a value in the Partial Quantity field.

7. Access the All Shipping Units section of the screen.

8. Mark your chosen shipping unit.

9. Select Edit>New ShUn per PartQty.

The system will go on creating shipping units to hold the specified partial quantity until the total quantity of delivery items is allocated for packing.

Packing Shipping Units in Multiple Levels

Before you can have delivery items packed inside packages inside packages and so on, you must set up the shipping units so they will be properly assigned for packing in the intended structure.

Part

II

Ch

5

You have to get to the Packing Shipping Units screen from either of the following overviews:

- Weight of Shp.unit
- Overview Volume of Shp.unit

You can also get to the Packing Shipping Units screen from the Packing Items screen.

When you have decided which shipping units are themselves packable, adopt the following procedure:

1. Access the Packable Shipping Units section of the screen.
2. Mark the lowest level shipping units you wish to pack.
3. Mark the shipping units that will be receiving these units.
4. Select Edit>Pack Shipping Unit.

The standard packing logic will be applied by using the lowest level shipping unit. Packing will continue until all the units have been packed in higher level shipping units, keeping within the weight and volume restrictions defined for each type of shipping unit. 999999 packing levels can be specified.

Changing Packing Quantities in Shipping Units

Until the relevant goods issue has been posted, you are at liberty to change packing quantities in shipping units, as follows:

1. Access the Packing Items screen.
2. Select Shp.Unit Contents>Overview of Contents>Overview of all Shipping Unit Contents.

The screen will display a list of all shipping units with their contents. Alternatively you can mark the shipping unit of interest and select Shp.Unit Contents>Contents of Shp.Unit.

In either case, you will be able to edit the Partial Quantities field of the shipping unit you want to change.

Unpacking Shipping Units

The objective of unpacking a shipping unit is to assemble a list of its contents so they can be repacked in a different way or in a different arrangement of shipping units.

What you have to do is to access the Contents of all Shipping Units screen and mark the items you wish to unpack. Then you can select Edit>Unpack to have the system display for you a list of the contents once again marked as packable items. This will work at any level of the shipping unit structure, because the actual delivery items are not removed from their immediate packaging material. To do this you would have to select Edit>Empty Shipping Unit.

However, unless you have removed the packaging material—a box, for example—from the shipping unit in which it had been packed, the box itself will remain packed, even if you marked it to be emptied. Again this logic applies at every level of the shipping unit structure.

Deleting Shipping Units

By contrast to just emptying a shipping unit, if you have a shipping unit deleted, it will be emptied and also removed from the higher level shipping unit of which it may have been an item.

Displaying Allowed Shipping Materials

You may need help in choosing shipping materials. What you can do is to ask for a list of the shipping materials that are allowed because they are suitable for a particular delivery item. You must mark the item in the Packing Items screen and select Edit>Allowed Shp.Material.

When you find what you want, you can have it copied directly into the delivery document. As you would expect, this information must have been previously associated with the delivery material you are working with by an entry in the Allowed Shipping Materials section of the material master.

Entering Shipping Units Individually

You can select the Fast Entry for Packing Contents function from the Packing Items screen to manually pack delivery items already existing in shipping units or enter new shipping units.

You can mark the items or refer to them by external identification number if it has been assigned.

Using the SD Transportation Functions

The job of transportation is to move goods to and from your company. The job of the SAP R/3 SD Transportation component is to ensure that these movements are integrated with the rest of the logistics chain to ensure that no value is lost unnecessarily by avoidable delays or unjustified expenses.

Transportation planning has to ensure that shipments are dispatched without delay and arrive on schedule. Transportation costs can form a large proportion of product costs, so they must be efficiently managed.

The basic functions of the SD Transportation component are identified as follows:

- Transportation planning and processing
- Freight calculation
- Freight settlement
- Customer freight calculation
- Customer freight invoicing
- Functions for selection service agents

There are two ways of looking at a movement of goods:

- Materials Management sees purchase orders and inbound shipping notifications as the mechanisms for replenishing stock.

Part

II

Ch

5

■ Sales and Distribution sees sales orders and outbound deliveries as the mechanisms of trading with customers.

Both points of view need to look at the shipment document as the prime source of information for customers, service agents, and your warehouse facilities.

Understanding the Role of the Transportation Planning Point

To provide an efficient control center for transportation, the SAP R/3 SD software has been given the task of maintaining an organizational unit referred to as the *transportation planning point*. This unit is both a group of responsible employees and a set of master records to support their activities.

Your company can maintain more than one transportation planning point, but they will each have to be defined at the stage of Customizing for the Corporate Structure before they can become operational.

You can choose your transportation planning points as you like. Geographical location may make sense. Type of transportation may be better. The essence of the notion is that each shipment will be assigned to a particular transportation planning point for planning and processing. There must be no splitting of responsibilities for a shipment. However, the transportation planning point is not attached to any other organizational unit within the logistics chain.

Using Functions in the Shipment Document

The shipment document has to take part in all of the following tasks:

■ Combine deliveries to form an outbound shipment.

■ Combine shipping notifications to form an inbound shipment.

■ Specify shipment stages in terms of legs, border crossing points, and load transfer points.

■ Assign goods to be transported to shipping units.

■ Assign service agents.

■ Specify planned transportation deadlines.

■ Record actual transportation deadlines.

■ Specify the outputs required for transportation, such as transportation papers or EDI messages.

■ Define transport-relevant texts.

Using the Structure of the Shipment Document

The shipment header carries the shipment type and number, and it identifies the transportation planning point responsible for its creation. The service agent and the deadlines are also held in the header because they apply to the whole shipment.

You can identify a route in the header that will be used for automatic leg determination. The shipping type or the leg indicator will have been predefined for the shipping document type you are using.

If you are planning an inbound shipment, the items will be shipping notifications. If you are planning an outbound shipment, the items will be deliveries.

The shipment can arise from several points of departure and be destined for several ship-to parties. On the way, it may require several modes of transport and have to undergo operations such as customs inspection at border crossing points and trans-shipment from one mode of transport to another. Several service agents will probably be involved at these various stages.

The logic of all this is represented in the SD Transportation module as a set of stage master records.

Interpreting Information in the Shipment Document

A shipment needs a means of transport, and each means of transport is defined as a shipping unit. It may be a box, a truck, a pipeline, or a cargo vessel. You can define what you need to use as a shipping unit. The system needs to know its characteristics, such as the volume and weight of the shipping unit, both loaded and empty.

A shipping unit, such as a truck, needs a crew and will be operating in a country for which it will need legal papers. These will include the transportation papers.

Using Freight Codes in the Transportation Papers

Each of the following types of organization can specify a freight code set that includes the particular freight codes needed to classify the goods to be transported:

- Forwarding agent
- Rail company
- Shipping company

The following are examples of freight codes:

- 4001 Methyl alcohol
- 4002 Glycol
- 4003 Alcohol
- 4004 Formaldehyde

The first phase of identifying the correct freight code is an automatic determination of the freight code directory. A separate directory can be maintained for each combination of the following criteria:

- Country of origin
- Shipping type, such as truck, rail, air

- Forwarding agent or forwarding agent freight group identified in the vendor master
- Route identification, if an external transportation planning system is being used

Having identified an appropriate freight code directory, the actual code is chosen automatically according to the following parameters:

- Freight code set
- Material or the material freight group identified from the material master

Packing Deliveries in Shipment Documents

If you have to pack several deliveries identified in a shipment document, the following sequence is suitable:

1. Select Logistics>Sales/Distribution>Transportation.
2. Select Shipment>Create or Shipment>Change.
3. You reach the Overview: All Deliveries screen.
4. Mark the shipment document of interest.
5. Select Header>Shipping Units>Packing Items screen.

If there are any delivery items that have not yet been fully packed, their shipment deliveries will be displayed with the individual items in the Items to be Packed section of the screen.

If all items have been packed, you will see a display of the shipping items. You can still pack these further, as you would if you were packing in the delivery document.

Using Shipment Stages in the Shipment Document

The SAP R/3 standard instrument that a transportation planning point operates with is the shipment document. The object of interest in a shipment document, apart from the cargo, is the shipment stage, which represents the various operations performed on the shipment. The following are examples of shipment stages:

- Legs that are defined as, for example, preliminary, main, and subsequent legs and have to be defined by starting and finishing points.
- Load transfer points are defined by the operation of unloading a shipment from one means of transport and loading it on to another.
- Border crossing points are defined by the national boundaries the shipment has to cross, which can be significant in terms of the legal requirements for inspection and documentation.

The starting point or end point of a transportation leg can be specified in a number of ways, for example

- A transportation connection point such as a rail depot or a seaport
- A shipping point
- A loading point within a shipping point

■ A plant

■ A storage location within a plant

■ A customer location

■ A vendor location

■ An address you define or copy from a document

To make this system work, you have to ensure that each transportation connection point is classified as a load transfer point or a border crossing point.

Creating Shipment Stages Manually

The following procedure will create a shipment leg in the shipment document:

1. Select Overview>Stages from the initial Shipment screen or from any of the shipment overview screens.

2. Select Stage>New Stage>Leg.

3. In the Departure Point field, enter a departure point that has been predefined as a transportation connection point in Customizing for Shipping.

4. In the Dest.Point field, enter the intended destination point. This destination point must also be predefined as a transportation connection point.

If you do not have predefined transportation connection points, you must adopt the following sequence to identify the information:

1. Select Address when your cursor has marked the required Departure or Destination section.

2. Select Extras and identify the nature of the address you have chosen as a shipping or loading point, plant, or warehouse.

If you use the Address function to define a departure or destination point, it is not possible to overwrite it with a predefined point.

You may want to use a different service agent to the one defined automatically in the shipment header for one or more stages. To do this, enter the agent's name or number in the Service Agent field for the stages that are affected.

The system will automatically propose the shipping type and the leg indicator, having consulted the values set up in the shipment type master. Again, you can alter these.

Before you save the shipment document, you should edit the planned and actual transportation deadlines as necessary.

Creating a Load Transfer Point Manually

A change of mode of transport entails passing a load transfer point, which you must record in the shipment document as follows:

Part

II

Ch

5

1. Select Overview>Stages from the initial Shipment screen or from any of the shipment overview screens.

2. Select Stage>New Stage>Load Transfer Point.

3. Enter a transportation connection point that has been classified as a load transfer point.

4. Unless you are content to use the agent defined in the shipment document header, enter the name or number of the service agent or forwarding agent who is responsible for the load transfer at this load transfer point.

5. Before you save the shipment document, you should edit the planned and actual transportation deadlines as necessary.

Creating a Border Crossing Point Manually

The procedure for creating a border crossing point is almost identical to the load transfer point sequence, except that you can specify a customs agent rather than a forwarding agent.

Deleting Stages in the Shipment Document

Once you have accessed a shipment overview screen, you can delete any stages by doing the following:

1. Select Overview>Stages.

2. Mark the stages you intend to delete.

3. Select Stage>Delete Stages>Save.

This deleting operation can be applied to legs, border crossing points, and load transfer points.

Understanding Automatic Leg Determination

If it has been set up in Customizing for Transportation, a shipment document type can be allowed to call on automatic leg determination.

If so, the preliminary, main, and subsequent legs for a shipment are copied into the shipment document on the basis of these settings in Customizing. The associated transportation data will be copied at the same time so that the shipping point and the ship-to party will appear in the document. Each delivery in a shipment is automatically assigned to the correct transportation legs.

The following attributes define a leg:

- A leg indicator
- A shipping type
- A service agent

An additional leg indicator can be specified in the header of the shipment document to signify whether this shipment is part of transportation chain and whether it has the role of preliminary leg, main leg, or subsequent leg. It also can be identified as an isolated shipment that is not linked to other shipments, a direct leg, or a return leg. These definitions are used to control the scope of automatic leg determination, so that, for example, the route for a preliminary leg is not continued into stages already defined for the main leg.

Calling on Automatic Leg Determination

There are various ways in which a transportation leg can be designed. The following are examples of transportation scenarios that call for different leg determination strategies:

- Milk-run shipments that require the route to link all the destinations specified in the deliveries that comprise the shipment. Thus the itinerary can entail picking up goods in turn from shipping points and delivering them to customers or ship-to parties.

- Collections and deliveries are characteristic of some shipments that can share a common main transportation leg, but have their own preliminary and final legs.

- If you are shipping a large amount and have to split the shipment over several deliveries, you may need a preliminary leg and a subsequent leg for each delivery.

The SAP R/3 SD Transportation module provides for all possible variations and combinations of the different types of collection and delivery strategies. It supports the generation of legal documentation as required for each type of shipment as it passes a border crossing point between all the possible pairs of countries and regions of legal force for which a common business framework is operating. There is a specialized shipment document type for each of these scenarios.

Noting Service Agents

Customs agents and forwarding agents are examples of service agents. They will be identified in the header of a shipment document, although you may need to refer to several of them and associate them with particular stages.

Differentiating Shipment Document Types

There is a range of standard shipment document types you can call upon to take advantage of the predefined parameters that will be automatically entered to facilitate the type of business transaction you wish to control.

The following are examples of standard shipping document types:

- LF Delivery
- LO Delivery without reference
- LR Returns delivery
- NL Replenishment delivery

If you enter a delivery with reference to an order, the system will automatically propose a shipping document type suitable for the underlying order.

You may be working with decentralized shipping processing, in which case the shipping delivery document type LO will be appropriate because decentralized deliveries are not created from an order.

Interpreting Shipping Document Control Elements

The functionality of standard shipping documents, and any that your system administrator has defined specifically for your company, is determined by tables of control elements that can be adjusted to suit the way you do business.

For example, you may have document types that can be differentiated by some or all of the following attributes:

- Is the document number drawn from the internal or from the external number ranges?
- Which partner functions are assumed, and which are allowed to be entered?
- Is it essential to have an order on which to base a delivery?
- If items can be included that are not dependent on an order, what conditions apply to the selection of these items?
- Are there restrictions on redetermining the route?
- If a storage location is not specified, by which rules shall it be determined automatically?
- Which output types are allowed for the business transaction recorded in this document type? On what basis is this set of output types determined?

Recognizing Item Categories in Shipping Documents

The purpose of an item category assigned to a material in a delivery is to allow more precise control over the way the material is processed. If a standard item category is assigned in a standard order item, it will become a standard item in the delivery.

If a delivery is created without reference to an order, the system will use the delivery type and item category group of the material in the item to propose an item category in the delivery. The following are examples of standard item categories:

- DLN Standard item in a delivery without reference to an order
- KBN Consignment fill-up
- KLN Free-of-charge item from a delivery free of charge
- KLX Service free of charge from a delivery free of charge
- TAK Make-to-order production from a standard order
- TAN Standard item from a standard order
- TANN Free-of-charge item from a standard order
- TATX Text item from a standard order

Understanding Work Lists for Transportation Planning

In transportation planning, two main types of work list are available:

- A shipment due list, which records the deliveries and shipping notifications that are due for shipment so you can create the shipment documents and arrange the shipment items in order.

- A transportation planning list, which allows you to complete transportation planning by filling available capacity and making arrangements for transport, loading, and booking service agents.

There are two other types of work list that can improve efficiency:

- Utilization of the Shipments, which is a special work list you can structure to show the percentage rate by which the shipment is utilized in terms of either weight or volume.

- Free Capacity of the Shipment, which is a listing that allows you to locate any shipment that has spare weight or volume enough to take a package you wish to assign.

Building the Shipment Due List

There are various ways to have shipment due lists assembled. There are separate selection screens for inbound and outbound shipments on which you indicate such variables as whether you are going to assign deliveries manually or have them assigned automatically. The Inbound Selection screen offers choices of vendor and destination plant. The Outbound Selection screen offers choices of sold-to party and departure shipping point.

The details and format of these standard views can be altered by having suitable user exits configured.

Using a Work List Screen

A work list screen has one section for the shipment document and another for listing the deliveries still waiting to be assigned to shipment documents. At this stage you can still create new shipment documents and move deliveries or shipping notifications within a shipment or from one shipment to another.

What you cannot do is aggregate deliveries with shipping notifications in the same shipping document because this would attempt to mix inbound and outbound movements.

If you have a problem of insufficient capacity, you can remove shipment items from the shipment due list. If you have spare capacity, you can look for additional shipment items in a more recent shipment due list. However, at this stage you will not be allowed to remove items within a delivery and relocate them in another.

Creating a Shipment Due List

The following is the sequence for building a shipment due list:

1. Select Logistics>Sales/Distribution>Transportation.
2. Select Shipment>Create.
3. Enter a transportation planning point.
4. Enter the code for the type of shipment document you are interested in, possibly with an additional variant identification.

N O T E   A document type can be copied and edited as a variant so that particular default values can be entered automatically when it is selected. ▪

5. Select Edit>Choose>Deliveries.
6. Enter the selection criteria for the list.

The Transportation Planning Stat. field will contain A to signify not yet planned or B for partially planned. The Goods Movement field will show the value A to signify that goods movement has not yet started, and you have time to change a shipment. The system will use these values to select items for your shipment due list.

When you are setting up transportation planning, you should mark the Plan field if you want the selected deliveries due to be assigned automatically to a shipment document. You should then select Program>Execute.

If you select Edit>Selection Edit>Selection Log, you will get a report showing the total number of deliveries and items selected, the selection criteria used, and any problems that occurred.

If you select Edit>Choose Edit>Choose Deliveries, the system will allow you to repeat the selection procedure if you still have spare capacity.

If you select Edit>Save Edit>Save as Variant, the system will allow you to supply a code and a textual description for the current search specification, which can then be subsequently reused to create a shipment due list.

Creating a Transportation Planning Work List

You can adjust the standard criteria to generate a transportation planning work list to your own specifications by doing the following:

1. Select Logistics>Sales/Distribution>Transportation.
2. Select Shipment>List>Transport Planning.
3. Select Edit>New Selection.
4. Deselect and select criteria from the dialog box items offered and select Copy.
5. On the revised screen, enter criteria for selecting the shipment documents you require.
6. Select Program>Execute.

Modifying the Utilization Work List Selection Screen

The very best shipment planning entails attending to the available capacity in relation to the materials being shipped. Thus, you might want to have a different threshold for displaying percentage of capacity utilization for certain materials. Some materials may be best packed by volume, others by weight.

When you have built a work list, you can alternate between the following views of the data:

- Exact details of the percentage of the shipment capacity utilized by weight and volume plus general data such as the transportation planning point, shipment type, and forwarding agent.
- Deadline specifications.

A work list of shipments with available capacity can be generated by doing the following:

1. Select Logistics>Sales/Distribution>Transportation.
2. Select Shipment>List>Utilization.
3. Select Edit>All Selections if you wish to extend your specification with additional selection criteria.

N O T E A search specification that you develop to build a work list of shipments can be saved as a variant for subsequent use.

4. Enter the percentage of spare capacity that should be used to select shipment documents.
5. Select Program Execute.

You can use this work list function to find another shipment with sufficient capacity for an existing package. As an extra search parameter, you have to specify the weight and volume of the package and mark whether or not it can be divided between several shipping materials.

Processing Shipment Documents

You can process a shipment by applying the normal Change function to the shipment document by doing the following:

1. Select Logistics>Sales/Distribution>Transportation.
2. Select Shipment>Change.
3. Enter, or use the Possible Entries button to select from the Find Shipment selection screen, the number of the shipment document you intend to change.

N O T E How the Find Shipment screen is displayed can be controlled online by using the Edit>New Field function to select or deselect display columns.

Part

II

Ch

5

You can maintain data—deadlines, shipping units, output data, and stages—from the shipment document's Deliveries overview screen.

You can also process a shipment from the transportation planning work list.

Storing Deadlines

A transportation activity takes time to organize and time to execute. This data is treated as planning deadlines and will be compared with actual deadlines when the activity has taken place.

When all the planning has been completed, you can set the status of a shipment to Planned. This will prevent anyone from changing the delivery and can be set to initiate automatic leg determination.

Once you have completed the planning activities for a shipment document, you can set the Planned status. As soon as you set this status, you can no longer carry out planning activities for this shipment document (remove deliveries from the document or move deliveries within the document). Leg determination is carried out automatically.

Maintaining Planned and Actual Deadlines in the Shipment Document

From the overview screen of a shipment, proceed as follows:

1. Select Header>General Data>Status and Deadlines.
2. Complete the Planned For and Carried Out On fields as appropriate.

If you set the status, the system will automatically propose the current date. If you enter the date, the system will set the status.

Managing Deliveries in Process

Large volumes of shipping data and the risk of bottlenecks are situations that are best managed from a scrutiny of the work lists for all the shipping points. You will probably want answers to some or all of the following questions:

- Which deliveries are ready for goods issue?
- Which deliveries are being processed?
- Which materials occur most frequently in deliveries?
- To which inquiries, quotations, and sales orders does a particular delivery refer?
- Which deliveries resulted from which sales orders?
- Which order items were included in which deliveries?

You need selective lists of deliveries and document flow lists for particular deliveries. You may perhaps need to sort these results and use the options to define how the selected items are totaled.

If you know them in advance, you can arrange for the relevant selection criteria to be saved as a variant. Otherwise you can adjust the criteria online when you see what the system has found for you.

Displaying Document Flow in Deliveries

The document flow is a list of the preceding and subsequent documents that exist for a particular sales and distribution document. What you have to do is generate the list that includes the document you are interested in and refine search criteria for the displayed items until you can mark the document you want. If you then select Environment>Document Flow, you will reach the Document Flow screen, on which you can mark any document identification and select Document to see it in detail.

You may be interested in the document flow of an individual item in a delivery. What you have to do is to mark the document and opt for Choose. This will show you the document, including the individual items from which you can select one, mark it, and then select Environment>Document Flow to see all the sales documents associated with this particular item.

Locating the Functions for Deliveries in Process

You will expect to find any shipping function you need in the SAP R/3 SD application. It may be helpful to see where they have been located in the various overviews that are available when you are processing or monitoring deliveries in process.

The following functions are located in the Picking overview:

- Select deliveries according to your selection criteria that have been picked or partially picked.
- Pass deliveries on to Warehouse Management (MM-WM) separately.
- Create transfer orders for deliveries relevant for MM-WM.
- Display data relevant for picking for the current work list at delivery and item level.

The following functions are located in the Loading overview:

- Select deliveries according to your selection criteria that are due for loading.
- Display data on loading for the current work list.

The following functions are located in the Transportation overview:

- Select deliveries to be transported according to specific criteria.
- Display data on transportation for the current work list.

Part

II

Ch

5

The following functions are located in the Picking Confirmation overview:

- Select deliveries according to your selection criteria that contain items for which picking data has yet to be confirmed.
- Display data relevant to picking confirmation for the current work list.
- Confirm online.
- Confirm in the background.

The following functions are located in the Goods Issue overview:

- Select deliveries according to your selection criteria for which a goods issue is yet to be posted.
- Post a goods issue.
- Display data on goods issue for the current work list.

The following are common functions available in all areas:

- Create a group of deliveries to enable you to select and edit deliveries using one group number.
- Print shipping forms such as picking lists or delivery notes.
- Display or change deliveries.

From Here

This chapter is about the ways in which the Sales and Distribution application of the SAP R/3 system uses the Shipping component to manage the transportation of goods to and from your company in ways that add value where possible and make the best use of available resources. You might want to check out the following chapters:

- Chapter 6, "Trading Worldwide"
- Chapter 7, "Managing the SD Communications"
- Chapter 12, "Interpreting SD Organizational Structures"

Trading Worldwide

Understanding Foreign Trade Processing

Trade areas, each with a particular set of laws and regulations strictly enforced, are permanent facts of modern business life, although their details may change all too often. Even in domestic trade, within your own trading area, you are required to adhere strictly to the laws and regulations.

The SAP R/3 system supports the data processing requirements of foreign trade throughout the supply chain. The legal requirements of foreign trading areas often affect all the links in the logistics chain:

- Importing raw materials and finished and unfinished goods
- Sale of goods
- Transfer of data to materials management
- Financial accounting

Maintaining Foreign Trade Data

Data fields containing information specific to foreign trade are found in the following master records:

- Customer master
- Vendor record
- Material master
- Purchasing info record
- Route

This data has to be entered and maintained for accuracy and compliance to the relevant regulations. The following groups of functions are available to assist in maintaining foreign trade data:

- Copy data that is specific to foreign trade, as well as to purchasing, sales, and distribution documents
- Communication interface of functions for the retrieval of foreign trade data

The uses to which foreign trade data is put can be classified according to the following tasks:

- Export control
- Declarations to authorities
- Preference processing

This chapter examines each of these.

Defining Foreign Trade Areas

You could define one trade area as the whole world. In practice, your company will probably specify worldwide trading by nominating a set of trade areas, such as the European Union (EU) and NAFTA.

If you are keeping track of deliveries outside your own trade area, perhaps worldwide, you are legally required to differentiate exports from imports, which you probably do for accounting purposes. However, if you are delivering within a trade area, you have to differentiate dispatches from receipts.

Recognizing the Differences Between Economic Zones   An *economic zone* is a useful aggregate of countries that share economic and accounting practices, although not all zones share the same conventions, nor do they all operate with the same set of aspirations. For example, NAFTA is a set of three nation states that intends to eventually abolish the custom regulation procedures that currently operate between them. The EU is a customs union that has already achieved this deregulation to a large extent and is seeking to standardize VAT as well as adopt a common currency.

Identifying Memberships of Economic Zones   Countries that are, at present, formed into the various economic associations are listed in the following sections. Other countries may be allowed to join an association if they meet legal and commercial conditions.

The ASEAN (Association of South East Asian Nations) is comprised of the following nations:

Brunei

Indonesia

Malaysia

Philippines

Singapore

Thailand

Vietnam

The EU is comprised of the following nations:

Austria	Ireland
Belgium	Italy
Denmark	Luxembourg
Finland	Netherlands
France	Portugal
Germany	Spain
Great Britain	Sweden
Greece	

The MERCOSUR (Mercado Comun del Sur) is comprised of the following nations:

Argentina

Brazil

Paraguay

Uruguay

The NAFTA (North American Free Trade Association) is comprised of Canada, Mexico, and the U.S.A.

For SAP-supported business purposes, each country in an economic zone as defined by these lists is assumed to have accepted the business and legal practices defined in the SAP component developed for their zone.

Communicating for Foreign Trade

SAP R/3's standard EDI interface enables information to flow efficiently between the R/3 system and others. One internal interface and two external interfaces are provided for creating foreign trade documents, such as declarations to the authorities.

There are the following possibilities as of release 3.0:

- Create the important documents for foreign trade (such as T2, UZ, and EUR1) from the ABAP/4 Development Workbench, which is internal to the R/3
- Connect external partner systems to the SAP R/3 system
- Send an EDI message to an EDI external subsystem using standard EDI tools

Transferring Export Data During Foreign Trade Processing

There are three methods for passing on export data:

- Automatic output determination
- Send data for the billing document view and the export billing IDoc
- Print out the export report or the single administrative document (AUS2), using one of the following calls to transfer the data:

    Call SAPscript

    Call an external system

    Call an external EDI subsystem

Controlling Output in Foreign Trade

In order to effect automatic output determination and supply data for the billing document view and the export billing IDoc, SAP R/3 (as of release 3.0E) generates the output types AUS1, AUS2, AUS3, and AUSJ.

You can print the following foreign trade documents via SAPscript:

- Single administrative document (standard output AUS2)
- Goods movement certificate EUR1 (standard output AUS3)
- Japanese export report MITI1 (standard output AUSJ)

The output types are identified by automatic output determination, and printing is carried out under copying control. Every export document is assigned an output type from the following list:

- EDI communication (output AUS1)
- Document printing of single administrative document (output type AUS2)
- Document printing of goods movement certificate (output type AUS3)
- Document printing of Japanese export report (output print AUSJ)

Each of these output types is preset in the standard system with a set of parameters to control the communication.

Using an Export Billing IDoc as a Data Interface   The IDoc EXPINV01 is used as a data interface in foreign trade. It has a header and one or more item segments.

Function module IDoc_OUTPUT_INVOIC fills the segments of EXPINV01 with document information taken from the Billing-Print-View component. This reads the header and item data necessary for exporting goods (such as the export license data and the packing data from the dependent deliveries, if required).

Printing is effected by creating an IDoc with the function module IDoc_OUTPUT_INVOIC. The data records from this IDoc are imported to the function module RV_EXPORT_DOCUMENT_PRINT, which sends them to SAPscript.

Printing Out the Export Report/the Single Administrative Document (AUS2)   The single administrative document is used in the EU area for the following external trade functions:

- Declaration of export to a non-EU country
- Declaration of shipping (T1) for the transportation of non-community goods between two locations in the EU customs area
- Declaration of shipping (T2) for the forwarding of goods between the EU and European Free Trade Association (EFTA) countries
- Declaration of the import of goods into the EU customs area

There are occasions when the single administrative document can be used for EU internal trade of European Community goods, as follows:

- If Community goods are to be transported between EU member states via an EFTA country (or via a third country other than an EFTA country), customs legislation may permit the single administrative document to be used
- In trade between the areas of the EU in which the 6th VAT directive applies and in the areas in which this directive is not valid (such as the Canary Islands and the British Channel Islands)
- In the transportation (between EU countries via an EFTA country) of products to which consumption tax for mineral oil, alcoholic beverages, and tobacco goods applies
- As a substitute for the specific INTRASTAT form

Using the Copies of the Single Administrative Document   Copy 1 can be used as follows:

- Document for export declaration
- Document shipping declaration T1 or T2 for the point of departure
- Document for a certificate of goods upgrading/improvement for passive upgrading for the customs office
- Document for the export control declaration
- Multiple document for mineral oil export declaration

Copy 2 can be used as an export declaration for foreign trade statistics.

Copy 3 can be used as follows:

- Copy of the export declaration/export control declaration for the dispatcher/exporter
- Copy of the upgrading/improvement certificate for the upgrader

Copy 4 can be used as follows:

- Copy of shipping declaration T1 or T2 for the destination point
- Shipping document T2L
- Two-part document for shipping goods to Switzerland

Copy 5 can be used as a three-part document for shipping declaration T1 or T2 as a return copy from destination point to departure point.

Copy 6 can be used as follows:

- Document for the various customs declarations for the customs office
- Multiple document as import control declaration
- Multiple document for free movement of goods for special use and other customs procedures at the customs office

Copy 7 can be used as follows:

- Two-part document for various customs declarations for statistical purposes
- Four-part document for shipping declaration T1 or T2 for statistical purposes

Copy 8 can be used as a three-part document for various customs declarations for the declaring party.

Interpreting Data on the Single Administrative Document   The system determines the following uses automatically and appends a second subfield according to the export procedure:

- COM—Goods movement between member states of the EU
- EU—Goods movement between the EU and EFTA
- EX—Goods movement between the EU and third countries

Reviewing the Printable Fields   A wide range of printable fields enables the document to communicate whatever information is required according to its function and the legal requirements of its context. Not all of the numbered fields are assigned (see Table 6.1).

Table 6.1	Printable Fields
Field No.	**Description**
01	Declaration
02	Dispatcher/exporter
03	Forms
05	Items
07	Reference number
08	Receiver
10	First country of destination
11	Trade country
15	Dispatch/export country
15a	Dispatch/export country
16	Country of origin
17	Destination country
17a	Destination country code
18	Indicator and nationality of the means of transport at border crossing
19	Container
20	Terms of delivery
21	Indicator and nationality of the active means of transport at border crossing
22	Currency and total amount entered in invoice
24	Type of transaction
25	Mode of transport to the border
26	Internal mode of transport
29	Office of exit
31	Packages and description of goods
32	Item number
33	Commodity code

continues

Part
II
Ch
6

Table 6.1	Continued
Field No.	**Description**
34a	Country of origin's country code
34b	Region of origin code
35	Size
37	Procedure
38	Tare mass
41	Special unit of measure
44	Export license (number, valid from date, and valid until date)
46	Statistical value
53	Destination customs office and country of destination
54	Location and date

Creating a Goods Movement Certificate Using AUS3 The SAP R/3 output type AUS3 can be evoked by output control to generate a goods movement certificate EUR.1. This certificate constitutes a proof of preference, which is deemed to exist between EU-associated states or between the EU and states that have entered into free trade, preference, or cooperation agreements with the EU. The goods movement certificate is not required for goods movement wholly outside the EU or those states that have preference agreements with it. The customs office responsible will provide a layout set EUR.1 to the exporter.

In addition to the EUR.1, a certificate of origin—created and signed by the exporter—is needed in order to trade with developing countries. There are variations in this:

- To trade with EFTA nations, you can make a declaration of origin on the trading value for transactions up to a value of about 11800 DM (German marks).
- Turkey requires special certificates.
- Layout set EUR.2, which is based on output type AUS3, is suitable for low-value trade with EFTA and some countries in Eastern Europe. You have to specify the ceiling value for each country in the output determination records.
- Exports from Japan with a net value of more than 5 million Japanese yen must be declared to the authorities using the export report Yushutsu Hokokusho MITI1.

Interpreting Technical Data on the Goods Movement Certificate EUR.1

The fields in the goods movement certificate EUR.1 can be entered by your SAP R/3 system (see Table 6.2).

Table 6.2   Fields in Goods Movement Certificate EUR.1

Field No.	Description
EUR-01	Exporter
EUR-02	Preference trade nations
EUR-03	Receiver
EUR-04	State group—short
EUR-05	Destination state
EUR-08	Goods description (current number, character, numbers, and material data, including number and quantity in packages)
EUR-09	Mass
EUR-10	Billing doc. no.
EUR-12	Location and date

The goods items are compressed by substituting their commodity codes.

Selecting the Data Transfer Option for Foreign Trade

Before you can send data by EDI to an external subsystem or to an internal system such as SAPscript, you must define the port, a partner profile, and the initial parameters required by the particular subsystem.

If you are going to use SAPscript, you can enter the program framework and the corresponding forms by calling the Process Output and Forms function when you are customizing for output control in SD. When it runs, the program framework calls the function module IDOC_OUTPUT_INVOIC and passes the data on to SAPscript.

If you are going to use an external subsystem via output medium 6, you have to define the command file and the outbound file. The external subsystem is called by program RSNAST00, which has to be called by the RSNASTED program.

If you are going to use an external EDI subsystem via the transaction technique from the EDI Basis interface, the details of the interface must have been established in the SAP communications server.

Appreciating the SAP Communications Server

The method of sending and receiving data through the SAP communications server is known as the *store-and-forward procedure*. If you are going to send a series of EDI documents, for example, the communications server has to link to the SAP system. It fetches the EDI documents from the SAP system and stores them in the communications server-reserved environment. Next, the communications server's Control component passes the series of EDI documents to one or more communications component. Each component will then consult the communications server's time plan and dispatch the relevant documents on the due date.

A similar sequence is adopted in reverse for incoming documents.

The communications server initiates these data exchanges between an SAP system and the communications server only if scheduling instructions have been entered in the configuration file.

Maintaining the Communications Server

The communications server is controlled by a configuration text file, which you can edit with a text editor. The parameters in this file control the following logic:

- The SAP systems with which the communications server can exchange data
- How you use communications components to operate the communications server
- Which activities are to be conducted by the communications server
- When the prescribed activities shall take place
- The routing and channel that the communications follow

The communications server configuration file also specifies to which SAP system an incoming document is forwarded.

Using the Communications Components

In the context of the communications server, a communications system is a mechanism that carries out the actual data transmission. An adapter card with the appropriate file transfer program is an example.

A *communications component* is the mechanism that connects a communication system with the communications server. Each communication system has a separate communications component assigned for this purpose. The connecting function is started and stopped by the communications server's Control component because the communications component's program is set up to respond in this way.

The communications component named SAP has been designed to meet the SAPcomm standards, which are being adopted by a number of independent communications system vendors. Data exchange is based on the CPI-C protocol.

SAPcomm-API is a communications server interface that allows you to link with other communications systems.

Maintaining the Data Interface for Foreign Trade

The data interface for foreign trade is comprised of a partner profile and a port definition.

Establishing a Partner Profile

Administration Process Technology in Tools Administration provides access to the Partner Profile IDoc into which you have to enter a partner number. That number determines the master record in a system application such as Sales and Distribution. The partner type has to be selected as vendor, customer, or logical system.

The rest of the profile is composed of the initial screen and the Output Control screen, together with the parameters that control the inbound and outbound documents.

Creating a Port Definition

The data interface for foreign trade uses external calls, so a port definition has to be created for them. Administration Process Technology in Tools Administration provides access to the Port Definition IDoc, where you place the file entries for the command file, the outbound file, and the status file before saving the partner profile.

Locating and Interpreting Foreign Trade Data

Foreign trade processing includes the operation of copying the foreign trade data held in master records as default values to the relevant documents. If the data is not directly copied, it will be interpreted to allow automatic determination of further export-relevant data, which is copied into the documents.

The master records that hold foreign trade data are as follows:

- Material masters
- Customer masters
- Vendor masters
- Purchasing info records

There are three types of foreign trade data in the master records:

- General data on foreign trade
- Data on export licenses
- Preference data

Foreign trade data can also be extracted from the sales and distribution documents and from purchasing documents.

Maintaining Foreign Trade Data in the Material Master

Foreign trade data in the material master can be accessed and maintained from the foreign trade or the Plant data screens. In particular, the commodity code has to be accurately assigned. This code is used by customs authorities in certain countries to classify goods in accordance with either the Harmonized System (HS) or the Combined Nomenclature (CN).

The foreign trade data screen includes the following elements:

- Goods' country of origin
- Goods' region of origin
- Export/import group, which associates similar materials for export or import transactions
- Export control
- Preference

Maintaining Foreign Trade Data in the Customer Master

The following foreign trade data elements are available for maintenance in the customer master screens:

- Address
- Country, to clarify which are export transactions
- Region, needed for declarations to the authorities
- Export control data
- VAT registration number

N O T E The customer's VAT registration number must be entered in billing documents that pertain to tax-free deliveries and services from non-EU members. ■

Maintaining Foreign Trade Data in the Vendor Master

The following foreign trade data elements are available for maintenance in the vendor master screens:

- Address
- Country, to clarify which are import transactions
- Region, needed for declarations to the authorities
- Control data
- Export control data
- VAT registration number

N O T E The vendor's VAT registration number is copied into the purchase order from the vendor master record as a default value; this is done when the vendor is identified during creation of the purchase order. For companies within the EU, this number will be referred to when completing taxation procedures. ■

- The Purchasing data screen in the Control data section indicates the mode of transport used to take goods over the border, both exports and imports.
- The Border Customs Office field contains the code that signifies the office of exit normally used for these goods.

The Extras option gives access to tariff preference, which is needed for foreign trade where it is operating.

Accessing Foreign Trade Data in Purchasing Info Records

The General data screen allows you to maintain foreign trade data in the purchasing info record. The following elements are available:

- Certificate category, such as the certificate of origin issued by the vendor
- Certificate number
- Date until which the certificate of origin is valid
- Country of origin
- Region
- Import procedure

Maintaining Statistical Values

The European Union requires that the INTRASTAT contain a statistical value for every item imported or exported. These values are used to compile foreign trade statistics.

The SD application includes procedures for calculating statistical values automatically on the basis of parameters and logical conditions that have been set up to use the material prices, transportation costs, and insurance in accord with the regulations and the sales area involved.

When you are exporting, the statistical value includes the material costs of the goods plus the proportion of the transportation and insurance costs that arises in the exporting EU member state—from when the goods cross the border until the customer receives them.

If you are importing, the proportion of the transportation and insurance costs that arise before the goods reach the border has to be subtracted from the total costs in order to arrive at the statistical value.

Using a Precautionary Checklist in Foreign Trade

Importing and exporting each entails a fairly complex set of data processing tasks that can be different according to the goods or services involved and the trade areas taking part in the transaction. A list of checkpoints has been found useful in preempting the more common errors in completing master data, check objects, and proposal objects. The topics are as follows:

- Number range
- Commodity code
- Procedure
- Business transaction types
- Mode of transport
- Customs offices

Part II

Ch 6

- Control of import data screens
- Countries
- Currencies

Checking the Number Range   Follow this Implementation Guide menu path: SD>Foreign Trade>Define Number Ranges for Import and Export Processing.

Checking the Commodity Code   Follow this Implementation Guide menu path: SD>Foreign Trade>Products for Foreign Trade>Define Commodity Codes by Country>Object: Table T604.

Checking the Procedure   Verify the procedure definition by following this Implementation Guide menu path: SD>Foreign Trade>Products for Foreign Trade>Define Procedures and Default Value>Define Procedure>Object: Table T616.

Verify the SD procedure default value by following this Implementation Guide menu path: SD>Foreign Trade>Products for Foreign Trade>Define Procedures and Default Value>Define Procedure Default Value>Object: Table T616Z.

Verify the MM default value from the purchasing info record by. selecting Logistics>Materials Management>Purchasing>Master Data>Info Record in the initial R/3 screen.

Checking the Business Transaction Types   Verify the definition by following this Implementation Guide menu path: SD>Foreign Trade>Products for Foreign Trade>Define Business Transaction Types and Default Value>Define Business Transaction Types>Object: Table T605.

Verify the SD default value by following this Implementation Guide menu path: SD>Foreign Trade>Products for Foreign Trade>Define Business Transaction Types and Default Value>Define Business Transaction Type Export>Object: Table T605Z.

Verify the MM default value by following this Implementation Guide menu path: SD>Foreign Trade>Products for Foreign Trade>Define Business Transaction Types and Default Value>Define Business Transaction Type Export>Object: Table T161B.

Checking the Mode of Transport   Verify the definition by following this Implementation Guide menu path: SD>Foreign Trade>Transportation Data>Define Mode of Transport and Assign Routes>Define Modes of Transport>Object: Table T618.

Verify the SD default value by following this Implementation Guide menu path: SD>Foreign Trade>Transportation Data>Define Mode of Transport and Assign Routes>Route Definition>Itinerary>Routes.

Verify the MM default value in the vendor master.

Checking the Customs Offices   Verify the definition by following this Implementation Guide menu path: SD>Foreign Trade>Transportation Data>Define Customs Offices and Assign Routes>Define Customs Offices>Object: Table T615.

Verify the SD default value by following this Implementation Guide menu path: SD>Foreign Trade>Transportation Data>Define Customs Offices and Assign Routes>Route Definition>Itinerary>Routes.

Verify the MM default value in the vendor master.

Checking the Control of Import Data Screens   Follow this Implementation Guide menu path: SD>Foreign Trade>Control of Import Data Screens>Object: View V_T001U.

Checking the Countries   Follow this Implementation Guide menu path: Global Settings>Setting Countries>Define Countries.

Checking the Currencies   Follow this Implementation Guide menu path: Global Settings>Currencies>Enter Exchange Rates.

Locating Export Control Data in the SD Documents

Deliveries and billing documents can display foreign trade data in headers and at the item level. The following data sources should be considered:

- Data proposed from the customer master record
- Data proposed from the material master record
- Data derived by considering the route
- Data inferred on the basis of the item category
- Data at header level that has been copied from the underlying order items

Differentiating Foreign Trade Data in SD Document Headers

An SD document header contains the following data elements:

- Partner data as:

   Ship-to party, which is a ship-to party key

   Country key, which is a ship-to party country key
- Customs data as:

   Mode of transport used to take the goods across a border

   Office of exit, which is a key for the customs office where the goods are loaded onto the border-crossing transport

   Inland mode of transport used from the delivering plant
- Data on the means of transport as:

   Indicator for the means of transport with which the goods leave the vendor location

   Country of the means of transport with which the goods leave the vendor location

   Indicator for the means of transport used to cross the border

   Country of means of transport used to cross border

   Container indicator

Part

II

Ch

6

The partner data is copied from the order in the delivery and the billing document.

If the appropriate setting has been made in Customizing, the customs data is determined on the basis of the route. The delivery and billing documents include this customs data by default.

Differentiating Foreign Trade Data in SD Document Items

Each item may contain its own foreign trade data concerning the material, its origin, transaction details, and its value. The document item data adopts the following structure:

- Material data as:

  Material, which is a material key for the delivery item or the billing document item

  Description, which is a description of the material in the delivery item or the billing document item

  Batch, which is only relevant in deliveries of materials that are managed in batches; comprises the batch number of the delivery item

  Commodity code

- Origin data as:

  The goods' country of origin and region of origin

- Transaction data as:

  Export procedure used to report the goods in dispatch/export transactions either in foreign trade statistics or in INTRASTAT

  Transaction type, which is the specification necessary for declarations to the authorities, such as when reporting import or export within the EU in the INTRASTAT

- Value data as:

  Statistical value, which is defined as the untaxed value of the goods, including the transportation and insurance costs that arise in the exporting member state

The commodity code is the only data element you can change because the material data is copied into the delivery and billing documents from the material master records.

You can enter the batch number for each item of any material managed in the delivery batches. This number can be seen in the material data by using Screen Overview>Picking.

The origin of material items is automatically entered into delivery and billing documents from the material master records as default values.

Transaction data is entered into the delivery and billing documents automatically according to the specification set in Customizing. The export or import group or the item category is taken into account.

The statistical value will have been calculated during pricing in the associated sales document. If the billing document has not been released to financial accounts, you can still influence the computation of the statistical value by entries in the order and in the billing document.

Maintaining Foreign Trade Data in Deliveries   You can enter or update an element of foreign trade data in the delivery by performing the following steps:

1. Select Header>Foreign Trade Data, and then enter the export data.

2. Mark a document item you want to edit>, select Item>Foreign Trade Data, and then enter the export data.

Once a delivery has been invoiced, you are not allowed to change the export data in the delivery.

Maintaining Foreign Trade Data in Billing Documents   If you need to enter or update an element of foreign trade data in the billing document, you can do so as follows:

1. Select Header>Foreign Trade Data, and then enter the data.

2. Mark a document item you want to edit>, select Item>Foreign Trade Data, and then enter the data.

Once a delivery has been invoiced, you are not allowed to change the export data in the delivery.

Maintaining Statistical Values in the Billing Document   If you need to update the statistical value calculation for an item in the billing document, you can do so as follows: Mark the billing document item you want to update>, select Item Pricing>Item Conditions Screen, and then enter the percentage rate or the actual value for the statistical value.

Once a billing document has been released to financial accounting, you are not allowed to change the data in the billing document.

Foreign trade data is displayed in the purchase order and in the shipping notification at header and item levels. This data is proposed from the delivery, material, or purchasing master record.

Differentiating Foreign Trade Data in Purchasing Documents

The purchase order and the shipping notification may include foreign trade data in the document header and in the document items.

The document header may include the following:

- Partner data as:

  Vendor, which is the vendor key

  Delivery vendor country key

  Vendor country key

- Customs data as:

  Mode of transport used to take the goods across a border

  Office of exit, which is a key for the border customs office where the goods are loaded onto the means of transport

- Data on the means of transport as:

  Indicator for the means of transport with which the goods leave the vendor location

  Country of means of transport with which the goods leave the vendor location

  Indicator for the means of transport used to cross the border

  Country of means of transport used to cross border

The partner data is taken from the purchase order into the shipping notification. The customs data is taken from the vendor master as a default value and entered in the purchase and dispatch notification document.

Maintaining Foreign Trade Data in Purchase Order   If you need to enter or update an element of foreign trade data in the purchase order, you can do so as follows:

1. Select Header>Import>Import Header Screen, and then enter the data.
2. Mark the purchase order item>, select Item>More Functions>Import>Import Item Screen, and then enter the data.

Maintaining Foreign Trade Data in Shipping Notifications   If you need to enter or update an element of foreign trade data in shipping notifications, you can do so as follows:

1. Select Header>Import>Import Header Screen, and then enter the data.
2. Mark the shipping notifications item>, select Item>More Functions>Import>Import Item Screen, and then enter the data.

Understanding Export Control

There are three reasons a nation might attempt to control its foreign trade:

- To conserve natural resources and raw materials
- To support national security
- To meet international obligations and agreements

A foreign trade transaction can be restricted in any or all of the following aspects:

- The destination country
- The customer
- The particular goods
- The moment at which the export transaction is to be carried out

Even in light of this, it can happen that a particular export is freely allowed without a license. It may be allowed if a license is obtained; it may be prohibited under any circumstance.

The goods in question may be produced in the exporting country, or they may be wholly or partly assembled from constituents that have been imported. In particular, the U.S.A. has a set of strictly followed re-export regulations.

If your system knows that a particular material can be exported only if a license has been obtained, the appropriate type of license is automatically determined. The system checks to see if a license already exists and whether it is still valid. This is the essence of export control processing.

Political situations changing regulations is a facet of worldwide trading. Therefore, the business data processing mechanisms must be able to operate flexibly and keep in touch with the trading environments.

Markets change, and some of the new trading partners will operate under regulations that have not been experienced before. The data on these restrictions must be kept up-to-date.

Identifying Export Control Regulations

Each trading community will be defined, at least in part, by the legal regulations that are in force across the region. The following legal documents are recognized:

- Export Administration Act (EAA)—U.S.A.
- Export Administration Regulations (EAR)—U.S.A.
- Außenwirtschaftsgesetz (AWG, the Foreign Trade Law)—Germany
- Außenwirtschaftsverordnung (AWV, the Foreign Trade Regulation)—Germany
- Kriegswaffenkontrollgesetz (KWKG, the Law for the Regulation of Military Arms)— Germany

The types of export license needed for each legal framework are established when your R/3 is customized. If your company operates under the EAR, for example, you may have to set up the following:

- Exemption license
- Validated license
- Individual validated license
- Sammelausfuhrgenehmigung (collective export license)

If your trading domain is governed by the AWV, you need the following:

- Allgemeine Genehmigung (general license)
- Sammelausfuhrgenehmigung (collective export license)
- Einzelausfuhrgenehmigung (single export license)

Understanding Export Control Country Classification

Your system will have to store relevant information for each destination country, and perhaps for the countries through which your exports have to travel:

- Whether the country enjoys membership of certain international organizations
- Whether the country is, at present, under a general embargo
- In which particular country classification lists the destination country currently appears

This is a flexible system because the Export Control function can look at each legal regulation in turn, decide if a license is needed, and determine the appropriate type of license.

Interpreting Export Control Class Numbers and Grouping

As you would expect with an SAP R/3 function, there is a classification of logical codes. The *export control class* is a numerical classification with a code number; a product or service is assigned a number by the legal control mechanism.

Each legal system may use a particular list of export control class numbers, as illustrated by the following examples:

- Germany refers to the export list number from the Export List.
- The U.S.A. refers to the Export Control Classification Number (ECCN).
- The U.K. refers to the Classification from the International List (IL).

An export control class grouping is not a legal concept, but rather a matter of convenience to the particular trading community. The export control group is a collection of export control classes that can be legally assigned the same processing function. For example, the correct license type for the group can be assigned and the system can be allowed to identify the corresponding export licenses. If you have some similar products or services that need to be handled differently according to export law, you can arrange this by assigning them to different groupings.

Export control is an integral part of SD document flow because the information on the purchase order is compiled from three sources:

- Material master
- Customer master
- Export control reference to the license master

If you are operating with an Active Export Control function in place, every material in the system could be subject to export control. You want to avoid unnecessary processing by signifying that certain materials are exempt from scrutiny for the purpose of export control. You will assign such a material an exemption certificate via an entry in the material master through the Foreign Trade screen or, equivalently, in the SD General Plant data screen. The Exemption Certificate field is significant only if it is set to B, which indicates that an exemption certificate has been issued. The material is subject to export control scrutiny unless the material master bears this value.

The following sequence allows you to maintain the export control data in the material master: Foreign Trade Screen>Extras>Sales Details>Export License.

Maintaining Individual Material Masters for Export Control   Assume you set the indicator for export control in the master records' definition object for a particular legal regulation—the system automatically makes all material masters subject to export control, unless you issue exemption certificates. This can be done as part of the process of defining the export control class and the grouping for all material masters.

Maintaining Export Control Data in the Customer Master   The customer master includes data fields for the following information:

- Export block indicator
- Date of the last check for the export block indicator
- Mainly civil use
- Mainly military use

You might want to temporarily block trade with a particular customer or group of customers. For instance, there are special boycott lists from time to time mandated by U.S. legislation. These restrict the re-export of goods from the U.S., no matter who the exporter. An export block indicator added to each of the customer masters is the appropriate instrument. The following list types are cited as examples of boycott lists that have been used:

- TDO list (table of denial orders)
- SDN list (specially designated nationals)
- DHRP list (diversion high risk profile)

If a customer appears on one or more of these lists, the respective blocking indicators should be set in the customer masters; you record the date when you checked whether a customer had been mentioned in the current boycott lists.

As of November of 1996, EU law (Dual-Use-Regulation) and U.S. law EAR establish that the use of the finished product shall be considered a crucial factor in determining the license type to be issued. Mainly civil versus mainly military use is the current dichotomy. This is used to assign goods and services used primarily for military purposes only to those customers who have been designated to deal primarily with the military.

Editing Export Control Data   The Foreign Trade screen gives you access to the export control data in the customer master. Export control checking examines the headers of orders and deliveries and ascertains the relevance of the boycott list. At the item level, export control will also look for partners that appear on the boycott list. It does not matter which country has been responsible for adding a customer to the boycott list.

If a boycotted customer or ship-to partner is identified, the system issues a warning on the order and an error message on the delivery.

Operating Export Control from the Sales and Distribution Documents

The following functions are available to manipulate export control in the SD documents:

- Export control in the order
- Export control in the delivery
- Export control in the order and in the delivery

Part

II

Ch

6

The similarities and differences between these possibilities are discussed in the following sections.

Interpreting Export Control Data in the Order

The transaction type indicates whether an export is permanent or temporary. This is stored at item level. When export control has considered the legality or permissibility of an order item, the outcome can be recorded in the order.

Each legal regulation that has to be checked can give rise to a different outcome for each order item. Therefore, the following fields have to be updated for each item in the order and for each legal regulation that is relevant:

- Export control class
- Export list number
- Grouping for export control
- License type
- License number

The required delivery date is entered at header level during export control. The responsible person can perform a manual check at header level on the basis of personal knowledge regarding a particular transaction. However, formal export control has to be carried out on each item. This is required because the ship-to party might be different for each item in the order, and one or more of these destinations may not fall within the scope of the license.

The system should have been configured so that no one can generate a delivery for an order item that is blocked because it failed the export control check.

The system status EXLS duplicates the results of the export control check. You can also set up indicators as part of user status that are specific to an individual user or to a particular transaction. The EXLS changes the user status flag from FREE if the export control check initiates a block on the order or an item in it.

The current state of an SD object, such as order, is a logical combination of the active statuses and has the effect of controlling what happens next. The status limits what business transactions are permitted.

Each status can control transactions:

- Permit a transaction
- Permit a transaction with a warning
- Disallow a transaction

The user status can be initialized or replaced only with an assignment number, and this is documented as a changed document. The structure of a user status record is made up as follows:

■ Status profile (8-figure)

■ Status (4-figure)

■ Transactions dependent on object category

The status profile is activated in the SD document types when an export license check is required. For example, the FOREIGN user status profile is active, so that the SALES ORDER ITEM object category can control the following transactions:

■ Create inquiry

■ Create quotation

■ Create billing document

■ Create delivery

■ Post goods issue

Interpreting Export Control Data in the Delivery

You have to be able to carry out export control in the delivery because there could be a long time between the creation of the order and the delivery, during which the boycott situation may have changed.

The date of goods issue recorded in the delivery header is important for export control. A delivery can only contain items for a particular ship-to party, whereas an order may include items for several destinations.

Export control for a delivery is performed automatically during picking in the warehouse management system. If you have created a delivery on the basis of an order, the export control checks are carried out at goods issue—if you have allowed this via your settings in Customizing. Export control is a physical quantity check, so the last possible stage for export control is when the goods issue is posted for the delivery.

Applying Export Control Blocking

A *block* is a stop on further transactions. An export control block is applied to an order or delivery either automatically or manually.

Export law requires that all exports be checked to discern what they are to be used for. A user can block a document from further processing by appropriately setting its status. If automatic blocking at the item level is in operation, the system can be customized to display a log of the export control actions when a document is posted. In either case, the block is recorded on the document.

Processing Blocked Documents

If authorized to do so, an export control operator can remove a block manually by assigning the order or item a previously created active export license; that license cannot exceed its limit as a result.

The EXLS function can also be used to unblock an item that has been blocked due to an embargo. The following sequence is appropriate:

1. Select Logistics>SD>Foreign Trade.
2. License>Export Control Data>Change.
3. Enter the sales document number.

Simulating Export Control

You should simulate export control because the checks carried out in Simulation mode call up accurate and important information; that information includes whether an export transaction is going to be permitted by the law of the exporting country with regard to the following factors:

- Destination country
- Customer
- Products
- Time of dispatch

If an export license is necessary for a product's export, the simulation automatically tries to find a license that satisfies all the transaction's requirements. The export cannot be authorized without such a license.

Simulating the Boycott List Check

The boycott list check looks to see if the customer or a trading partner is on any of the following lists:

- Table of denial orders (TDO)
- Specially designated nationals (SDN)
- A list compiled by the company itself

The following procedure initiates a simulated boycott list check:

1. Select Logistics>SD>Foreign Trade.
2. Select License>Simulate>Boycott List.
3. Enter the partner identification and, if appropriate, the country key. Select Program Execute.

N O T E If you enter a country key when creating a purchase order, the system determines whether the partner is on the boycott list for that country. If you do not specify a country key, the system checks for the partner on the boycott list for all the countries maintained in the customer master for that partner. The system informs you if the partner appears on the list for at least one of these countries.

Simulating Assignment of Export Licenses

If you want to simulate the assignment of export licenses, you should proceed as follows:

1. Select Logistics>SD>Foreign Trade.

2. Select License>Simulate>Export Control.

3. Enter data and then select Program Execute.

The system determines the exporting country if you enter data such as the exporter plant. The partner identification defines the ship-to party. The material number and currency are the dispatch data.

From the screen that shows you the results of export control in the status field for a marked number, you can select an item and obtain detailed information on it.

If your system has been customized to keep a log of the export control procedure, there are red and green traffic lights that indicate whether the result is positive or negative. A double-click on the adjacent field elicits a dialog box containing further information.

Simulating Export Control in Order Processing

If you need to know what the result would be for an individual order item, you can initiate simulation as follows: Select Sales Document>License>Log from the Order Overview screen. The export control's outcome is shown for each item.

Understanding Licenses

There can be extensive data about individual licenses. To optimize performance, this data is stored on an independent database that can be linked as required.

Each export license master holds the following data:

■ The export list numbers signifying the export control classes to be covered by this license

■ The customer numbers to be covered by this license

■ The type of export license

■ The legal regulation that provides the validity for this license

■ The license master record number issued by the system

You can adjust settings made in the Implementation Management Guide (IMG) during customizing to maintain license types with respect to the following parameters:

■ Destination country

■ Business transaction type

■ Document number of the SD order

■ Terms of payment

Part
II

Ch
6

Displaying Export Licenses

Your export control information can be displayed as follows:

- List of all customers on a license
- List of all export control classes on a license
- Selection of all sales documents on a license
- Selection of all documents that are still blocked
- Selection of all existing documents according to certain selection criteria

Perform the following steps to obtain a list of all customers on a license:

1. Select Logistics>SD>Foreign Trade.
2. Select License>Export License>Display or Change.
3. Either enter a license number or press the Possible Entries button to find the license number using the search procedure.
4. Select Contract Data>Select Customers or Export Control class.

Perform the following steps to obtain a list of all sales documents for an export license type:

1. Select Logistics>SD>Foreign Trade.
2. Select License>Monitor>Sales Documents.
3. Enter the required selection criteria and then select Execute.

N O T E   To display a single document when creating a purchase order, place the cursor on the corresponding line and select Displayline>Display Document.

Perform the following steps to obtain a list of all sales documents that have been blocked by export control:

1. Select Logistics>SD>Foreign Trade.
2. Select License>Monitor>Blocked Documents.
3. Enter the required selection criteria and then select Execute.

N O T E   To display a single license when creating a purchase order, place the cursor on the corresponding line and select Changeline>Display License>Change License or Change Export Control Data.

For a list of all available licenses, follow these steps:

1. Select Logistics>SD>Foreign Trade.
2. Select License>Monitor>List Licenses.
3. Enter the required selection criteria and then select Execute.

N O T E To display a single license when creating a purchase order, place the cursor on the corresponding line and select Displayline>Display License. ▧

Updating a License Master

There are two updating functions to be considered:

- ▧ The transactions required for manual maintenance in the individual license master
- ▧ What happens if the license is to be updated from the order itself

When export control is carried out in the order document, the information that needs to be changed on the license master is the outstanding value remaining on a license. An export license can have a maximum value, a maximum quantity, or both. This data defines the upper limit for the validity of the license.

Several orders or deliveries can be processed using one license until the cumulative order value approaches the upper limit, in quantity or value, according to the way the limit is defined on the license. Another license has to be issued if an additional order overshoots the limit.

A license can be defined in terms of export control classes or customer numbers, according to the type of export license that has been configured in Customizing.

A license master record can be created by the following procedure:

1. Select Logistics>SD>Foreign Trade.
2. Select License>Export License>Create.
3. Enter or select the legal regulation, the license type, and the company code.
4. Enter the validity period and the data; save the license.

Understanding Declarations to the Authorities

In order to record and evaluate all goods deliveries inside and outside an economic zone, the relevant authorities demand that foreign trade deliveries be recorded and declared using a standard procedure. The declaration is published on paper or diskette. The vendor declaration performs dual duty as information source and proof of origin. The declaration to the authorities is important for everything directly or indirectly involved in the movement of preference-relevant goods between the EU and other countries.

The following economic zones are serviced this way by the standard version of SAP R/3:

- ▧ EU
- ▧ EFTA
- ▧ NAFTA
- ▧ Japan

Declarations to the authorities are assembled in the following sequence, which may be carried out live or as a test run:

- You enter selection criteria to identify relevant foreign trade documents (such as export billing documents or goods receipts with corresponding incoming invoices or purchase orders).

- Having assembled the data, the system creates the corresponding declarations for the selected documents.

Designing Declarations

The information on the relevant member countries of an economic zone will be identified during billing document selection. It then has to be formulated to accord with each country's requirements. You can also specify whether the declaration should be made using tape or paper.

If you have many declarations to make, you can have the creation take place in the background. Otherwise, you can have the process conducted as a dialog. Selecting billing documents and incoming invoices is best carried out in background processing.

Consulting the Goods Catalog   A *goods catalog* lists a company's goods, which can be imported or exported within the scope of the licensed transaction. They include commodity codes from the nomenclature of goods used to compile foreign trade statistics. In some cases, such as the INTRASTAT declarations, the declaration is only accepted on diskette or on magnetic tape (if goods catalogs are maintained by the authorities responsible in that country).

Selecting Data for Exports and Dispatches   For selection of billing documents relevant for export, you must invoke report RVEXST00 and enter the selection criteria using the following screen sections:

- Selection Criteria, which allows you to control what billing documents are to be examined by selecting or by nominating a range of values.

- Billing Document Types, which allows you to mark the billing documents you require.

- Maintaining INTRASTAT, which accepts the reporting month and other data needed for the declaration.

- If you select Additional Specifications, you can enter or edit additional parameters, such as the material number from the Federal Bureau of Statistics in Germany.

- Specifying Incompletion Log, which differentiates between a test run and a live run by either displaying the selected data or by saving it in a file. You may specify the fields to be reported as an incompletion log in either case.

The incompletion log can include any of the following fields:

- Type of Transaction
- Office of Destination
- Nationality of Means of Transport
- Special Unit of Measure
- Country of Destination
- Region of Destination
- Gross Weight
- Container Transport
- Exporting Federal State
- Tare Mass
- VAT Registration

- Office of Exit
- Statistical Value
- Invoice Value
- Commodity Code
- Country of Origin
- Region of Origin
- Export/Import Procedure
- Mode of Transport
- Name of Means of Transport
- Incoterms
- Harbor Where Goods Are Loaded

If you need to search with other criteria, you can call an additional screen—Maintaining Additional Specifications.

Initiating Data Selection for Dispatches

The procedure for setting up data selection for dispatch is as follows:

1. Select Logistics>SD>Foreign Trade.
2. Select the function and economic zone.
3. Enter the corresponding selection criteria.
4. Enter live or test in the Log Type field.
5. Select Program Execute.

Specifying Data for Arrivals

Data selection for arrivals utilizes report RMIMST00. The system selects all relevant goods receipts in the reporting month and locates the corresponding invoice receipt documents.

If you set the Delivery Vendor indicator, the vendor specified in the purchase order, not the vendor in the goods receipt document, is used in the INTRASTAT declaration.

If you set the Shipping Notification indicator, you can control whether the data relevant for import is to be taken from the shipping notification instead of the purchase order. The shipping notification may well contain the more up-to-date information. The German INTRASTAT declaration, for example, has to be sent to the relevant authorities within five working days after the end of the reporting month. If no invoice exists at that time for a goods receipt following the reporting month, then declaration of this goods receipt is postponed until the following month. If there is still no invoice a month later, the purchase order is used to determine the value of the goods and the goods movement is reported.

Part
II

Ch
6

Perform the following steps to select data for arrivals:

1. Select Logistics>SD>Foreign Trade.
2. Select the function for the economic area.
3. Enter the corresponding selection criteria.
4. Enter type of log field as "test run" or "live run."
5. Select Program Execute.

If you have chosen Issue List on the Selection Criteria screen, the data appears on the screen and can be printed as required. If you chose to have the data issued in the form of a file, a file is created with the name you assigned to it.

Troubleshooting Declarations

If your declarations are unsatisfactory, you should first check the data in the customizing tables:

- Own VAT registration number
- Key for place of manufacture
- Special unit of measure
- Default business transaction-type table
- Import/export procedure
- Completeness check
- Currency conversion; make sure that the currencies are maintained for conversion in both directions
- Route definition (only relevant for dispatch)
- Transportation connection point definition (only relevant for dispatch)

The master data should be the second level of checking:

- The material masters should contain all data relevant for export and dispatch.
- The customer masters should each contain the customer EC VAT registration number in the Control screen for the customer master record.
- The vendor masters should each contain the vendor EC VAT registration number in the Control screen for the vendor master record.
- Mode of transport.
- Customs office.

The document data should be the third level of checking:

- Foreign trade data must be maintained for all documents needed for the INTRASTAT declarations.

N O T E   Documents with no foreign trade header or item data cannot be selected for INTRASTAT.

■ Pricing data has to include the invoice value or purchase value, and the statistical value must be maintained.

N O T E If statistical values are to be calculated, the condition type GRWR must be maintained in the pricing procedure and the corresponding condition records must be created for condition type GRWR. ■

■ Delivery/Billing (SD) requires that the foreign trade data include dispatch data in the header and in the items.

■ Purchase Order (MM) requires that the import data include goods receipt data in the header and in the items.

Understanding the **INTRASTAT**

The single European market was established on January 1, 1993. Despite the fact that the economies of the European Union's member states have become increasingly interdependent and some internal tariffs have been removed, they still need to assess their international competitiveness. They also require a perspective on the dependency of their individual products and sectors on import and export. Prices and developments in foreign trade are as important as ever and the EU member states must keep statistical records of trade within EU borders. It was for this purpose that the INTRASTAT was created.

From January 1, 1993, companies with a turnover of more than 200,000 DM in the current or previous year have been required to make regular intra-EU trade statistics declarations. All deliveries made and received within the EU during the reporting period of a calendar month must be reported in the INTRASTAT declaration. The declaration has to be sent to the authorities within five days of the end of the reporting month.

Table 6.3 shows the identification of the report used for each country for paper and diskette issue.

Table 6.3   Declarations for the EU

Country	Report on Paper	Report on Diskette
Belgium	RVEXPAIB	RVEXDAIB
Germany	RVEXPAID	RVEXDAID
Finland	RVEXDAIL	
France	RVEXPAIF	
Great Britain	RVEXPAIU	
Greece	RVEXPAIG	
Italy	RVEXPAII	

continues

Table 6.3   Continued

Country	Report on Paper	Report on Diskette
Ireland	RVEXPAIR	RVEXDAIR
Luxembourg	RVEXPAIL	RVEXDAIL
Netherlands	RVEXPAIH	RVEXDAIH
Portugal	RVEXPAIP	
Spain	RVEXPAIE	RVEXDAIE
Austria	RVEXPAIA	

Establishing Customer-Specific Settings

When you want to arrange exactly how the declarations are to be produced, you must call report RVEXST00 and individually specify which types of billing documents and which item categories shall be used; this is required because this report selects the export billing document. In addition, you may have to modify program RVEXKUEI at the coding level to accommodate your particular requirements.

Managing Return Deliveries

Returns from customer to vendor as well as incomplete deliveries are handled in the INTRASTAT declaration as sales. The INTRASTAT declaration has to report the value of the returned goods as an intra-EU delivery from the customer to the vendor.

Return deliveries in SD export processing are not reported in the INTRASTAT declaration. You have to generate a manual correction report for the authorities responsible.

Reporting the Value of Goods

There are two amounts that have to be reported in the INTRASTAT declaration:

- Invoice value, which is the amount stated in the invoice in the relevant currency
- Statistical value, which is the value of the goods before tax, including transportation and insurance costs that arise in the exporting member state when the export is made

Identifying Goods Movements Exempt from INTASTAT

The INTRASTAT does not require that every goods movement be declared. The following goods movements are not relevant:

- Tax-free goods movement between bonded warehouses
- Goods movement between free trade areas
- Free shipments to non-EU states of non-resaleable samples

Declaring the EXTRASTAT

The *EXTRASTAT* is a declaration of business transactions with non-EU members. If you call report RVEXEX00, it selects the data from the billing documents and records the information in a work list. You have to select EU declarations to issue an EXTRASTAT declaration.

Declaring the KORBA

This declaration is used for certain sensitive goods only for Germany. If you call report RVEXK000, it selects the data from the billing documents and records the information in a work list. You have to select EU declarations to issue a KORBA declaration.

Using Declarations to the EFTA

Declarations to the authorities for EFTA is used for declarations for Switzerland. If you call report RVEXCH00, it selects the data from the billing documents and records the information in a work list. You have to select EU declarations to issue an EFTA Switzerland declaration.

Using Declarations to the NAFTA

NAFTA is comprised of the U.S.A., Canada, and Mexico. There are three types of declarations needed for dispatches and export:

- Automated Export Reporting Procedure (AERP)
- Shipper's Export Declaration (SED)
- Harbor Maintenance Fee (HMF)

NAFTA declarations to the authorities are created by either report RVEXSE00 or RVEXSE01, which selects data from the billing documents and writes it on a work list.

Exporters and forwarding agents need to follow different procedures even though a standard data layout record (AERP) was set up on January 1, 1995.

Two screens allow you to specify which exports should be selected and how the items with the same commodity code are to be accumulated within a billing document. The following factors may influence the method of accumulating:

- Statistical value
- Net mass
- Special mass unit
- Gross weight
- Whether an export license requiring declaration is assigned to the export item

Part
II

Ch
6

N O T E If an item requires a license, it is not accumulated. ▥

When the work list is produced, it is accompanied by the necessary Shipper's Export Declaration (SED) specifications and a general overview.

Applying Technical Criteria

In the third screen section, you can specify whether the output should be issued in list or file form; you also specify the criteria for including or excluding items from a NAFTA declaration.

The criteria for including export item transactions in a NAFTA declaration are as follows:

▥ Export item value is greater than 2500 USD

N O T E An export license requiring declaration is assigned to the declaration automatically during order creation, without regard to the ship-to country or the value of the export. ▥

▥ In-transit exports that are to leave the U.S.A. by ship

Items can be excluded from a NAFTA declaration on the basis of the following criteria:

▥ Export item value is less than 2500 USD
▥ The ship-to country for the export is Canada
▥ Dispatch is by post, and the item value is less than 500 USD
▥ The item is an in-transit export, which is not leaving the U.S.A. by ship

If the legal requirements change, you have to alter the code of the declaration to authorities software.

Understanding the Shipper's Export Declaration (SED)

You have to make a Shipper's Export Declaration to the United States Department of Commerce every month. It must include all exports leaving the U.S.A. that are not going to another NAFTA member state, although exports to Mexico have to be declared.

If you call report RVEXPEIS, it selects the data from the work list and creates a paper version of the Shipper's Export Declaration.

Understanding the Automated Export Reporting Program (AERP)

The U.S.A. Census Bureau installed the AERP in 1970 in order to collect statistics about foreign trade. This program enables exporters and forwarding agents to use electronic media to declare their export activities each month directly to the Bureau of the Census. The Shipper's Export Declaration in paper format is no longer required.

You have three options for communicating the AERP:

- Direct computer transmission
- Magnetic tape
- Diskette

From R/3 release 3.0 the SAP system has supported the magnetic tape and diskette procedures.

Report RVEXDEIS selects data from the work list and writes the declaration in a file, from which a magnetic tape or a diskette may be generated.

Understanding the HMF Declaration

The Harbor Maintenance Trust Fund was established by the Water Resources Development Act of 1986. It levies 40 percent of the cost of maintaining harbors in the U.S.A. by charging each time a ship is loaded or unloaded, be it cargo or passengers. A fee of 0.125 percent of the value of the goods transported is levied and paid to the Department of Treasury.

The regular SED reports the value of all dispatches from the U.S.A. that leave a U.S.A. port by ship. From this information, the HMF declaration must be created four times a year and sent, with the fee, to the authorities.

Understanding Declarations to Authorities in Japan

There are two reports used in Japan:

- The MITI export report
- The customs declaration for import

Understanding the Japanese MITI Export Report

Yushutsu Hokokusho is the name of the export report form required by the Japanese Ministry of Finance for statistical and currency control purposes. Exports with an export billing value greater than 5 million Japanese yen must be declared to the Ministry of Trade and Industry (MITI) using the export report.

An original and two duplicates have to be completed and submitted to the customs authorities after the customs inspection has been carried out. The second duplicate is checked, stamped, and returned to the exporter. The customs authorities pass the original to MITI and the duplicate to the Ministry of Finance.

The MITI export report includes the following data:

- Name and address of the shipper
- Ship-to party
- Commodity code
- Freight category number

Part
II

Ch
6

- Official bank confirmation on foreign currency
- An items quantity
- FOB value and total invoice amount
- Currency
- Means of payment
- Date of payment
- Number of the valid export license issued by MITI (if applicable)

Customs Declaration for Import to Japan

Yunyukamotsu no shiharai ni kansuru hokokusho, customs form no. T2010, is needed for customs declarations of imports to Japan. The following fields are included:

- The date
- Address of the importer
- The quantity, value, and customs tariff number for the imported goods
- The type of payment and the payment deadline

Understanding the Aims of Preference Determination

Preference determination is part of a sequence of processes that is referred to as *preference processing*.

Preference determination has to first establish whether preference is to be authorized for a product that is represented by a bill of material. The results of this calculation can cause the preference indicator in the material master to be changed. The preference ID and the date of preference determination are automatically recorded in the material master.

If the ID B, Qualifies for Preference, is recorded, that material master can be updated automatically.

Second, condition records containing the determined preference price are created for each material and preference zone. The preference pricing procedure PREF000 is used in the standard system for preference determination.

The standard condition record type is called PREF and used in SD pricing. In the sales order, the system will compare the sales price of each material with the preference price stored in the condition record. If an order item qualifies for preference, this fact is displayed in the Item Detail screen, both in the order and in the billing document.

Proving the Origin of Goods Produced In-House

Preference determination includes the process of establishing the proof of origin for goods that are produced in-house. In particular, you have to determine the make-up of these goods in terms of constituents or components that are themselves classifiable as originating or non-originating goods with respect to a particular preference zone.

You have to determine the total value of all component parts in the structure according to the following places of origin:

- European Community
- EFTA
- Third country
- Associated countries

If you have produced a component that is also a part in a single-level bill of material, you must also consider the valuation price of this part when the value of the exploded structure is taken into account.

The system will take a bill of material for a product produced in-house and evaluate all the components used in order to identify each according to its origin.

One of the tasks of preference processing is to calculate the price at which a product for export is authorized for preference. This price may depend on the details of preference agreements that already exist between the individual preference zones. The preference rules defined for these areas affect the critical export price.

Preference determination can be performed individually or collectively.

Using Individual Determination   Each component is valued by multiplying the quantity by the standard price or the cost price per price unit.

A bill of material may include items such as texts that are not subject to preference determination. Such items are ignored by preference processing because they are not classified as material bill of materials type M.

If there are not too many components in the corresponding BoM, individual determination for new materials can be carried out online using the following sequence:

1. Select Logistics>SD>Foreign Trade.
2. Select Preference Determination>Individual.
3. Maintain the selection data for the material and BoM.

The following entries are mandatory:

- Material number of the BoM
- Plant of the BoM
- Usage or application

Part

II

Ch

6

- Tariff alternation
- Price unit

The following entries are optional:

- BoM alternative
- BoM validity date
- Simulation
- Additional back-up percentage

If you are working with assemblies for which preference determination has not been carried out, you have the option of exploding an alternative assembly that may have a very similar structure.

Performing Collective Determination   If you have made suitable agreements with the appropriate authorities, you can carry out collective determination in the background at certain intervals. The following procedure is available:

1. Select Logistics>SD>Foreign Trade.
2. Select Preference Determination>Collective>Preference Determination for BoM Explosion in the Background.
3. Maintain the selection data for the materials and the BoM.

N O T E   You should specify as many restrictions as possible when setting up selection data for materials, in order to minimize database access time.

You may decide to run a simulation. If so, collective determination can also be simulated. When you have checked and processed the simulation log, the real preference determination run can take place, and the preference data can be updated.

Using the Results of Preference Determination   The outcome of a preference determination run is recorded in a spool file, where it can be inspected by the customs authorities or by the external auditor. In addition to this legal record, the relevant material masters are updated on the basis of the preference determination results.

The other outcome of a preference determination run is the creation of condition records for each preference zone, plant, and material number. These condition records can be used during an SD pricing procedure to determine whether a particular item is authorized for preference.

Meeting the Prerequisites for Preference Determination

If you want to decide whether a salable part or an in-house produced assembly can be subject to preference processing, you have to make sure that the following criteria are available and accurate:

- A material bill of material must exist.
- A commodity code must be maintained in the material master.

■ Preference rules must be defined for the commodity code.

■ The sales and purchasing views of the material must be maintained.

■ A commodity code must be defined in the material master for all components at the lowest explosion level of the bill of material.

■ A vendor declaration ID must be defined in the foreign trade view of the material master for all externally procured components.

You must maintain each preference ID manually in the material master's foreign trade view for all in-house produced assemblies that cannot be exploded unless preference determination has been performed previously for these components.

In order to carry out preference determination, the vendor declaration indicators from the individual purchasing info records must have been summarized in the material master.

Using a Bill of Material Explosion in Preference Determination

A bill of material explosion allows the program to perform preference determination for all components.

Although the bill of material is exploded into its multiple levels, externally procured parts are not exploded further, even though they may have been assigned a bill of material. This can happen, for example, when an assembly can be both procured externally and produced in-house.

If a special procurement key is assigned to these components in the material master record, the procurement type will be determined using this key and the explosion controlled accordingly. If this key is not assigned to the components, they are treated as if externally procured and will not be further exploded, even if a bill of material exists.

If one of the components is an assembly with a multiple BoM, the corresponding bill of material is selected and exploded on the basis of required quantity for the components.

All the material items are displayed after a BoM explosion. If any errors are detected, the processing will stop with the production of an error note.

The stages of preference processing are as follows:

■ Request/dun vendor declaration

■ Summarizing the vendor declarations in the material master

■ Preference determination

■ Using the preference results in the sales and distribution documents

■ Printing the EUR 1 document (goods movement certificate)

These phases are discussed in the following sections.

Part

II

Ch

6

Understanding the Vendor Declaration

The vendor is obliged to issue a vendor declaration for certain goods movements between the EU and other countries.

The critical decision to be made is whether goods can be treated as originating in the exporting country and are therefore relevant for preference processing when they are exported to a particular destination country. The key information is contained in the vendor declaration that is produced at regular intervals.

The information is usually reduced to a brief key known as *the summarization of the vendor declaration indicator.*

The *vendor declaration* is the proof of origin of a product. It is used by customs offices as the basis for the issue of preference certificates. A vendor declaration is valid only if the issuing company is based in an EU member state.

The issuer has to declare the origin of a product as part of the vendor declaration. There are two categories used in ascertaining origin:

- The goods must be manufactured fully in the EU or in a partner state.
- The goods must have been processed or enhanced to a significant degree within the EU or partner state.

If a product has not been manufactured or significantly worked on within the EU, it requires a preference certificate.

Defining EU Partner States

Table 6.4 lists the states that are recognized as EU partner states for the purpose of deciding whether preference certificates are necessary. The ID codes refer to the vendor declaration formats used.

Table 6.4   EU Partner States

ID	Partner State
CH	Switzerland
CZ	Czech Republic
LI	Liechtenstein
SK	Slovak Republic
CY	Cyprus
BG	Bulgaria
IL	Israel
RO	Romania

ID	Partner State
MT	Malta
DZ	Algeria
CE	Ceuta, Melilla
MA	Morocco
FO	Faeroe Islands
TN	Tunisia
P	Poland
XY	States in African, Caribbean, and Pacific regions
SL	Slovenia
XB	Overseas areas and countries
H	Hungary

Requesting or Dunning a Vendor Declaration

The vendor declaration serves as both information source text and proof of origin. If a valid declaration fails to be provided, it has to be requested or dunned after a specified number of tolerance days.

Interpreting the Vendor Declaration Data Structures

If a valid vendor declaration exists for a vendor material, an entry will appear for relevant preference zones in the database table LFEI, which is linked to the purchasing info record. Table 6.5 illustrates the format.

Table 6.5   Vendor Declaration Information

Plant	Zone	VDI	Dec.Date	DC	*Dunning Date*
0001	MOEL	A	31.12.98	0	
0001	CARI	B	31.12.98	0	
0001	EFTA	C	31.12.98	0	
0001	MEDI	D	31.12.98	0	

The following interpretations of the columns are appropriate:

- Plant to which the specifications refer
- Preference zone for which the vendor declaration indicator is valid
- VDI, vendor declaration indicator

Part
II

Ch
6

■ Declaration validity date

■ Dunning code

■ Dunning date determined by the system on the basis of the dunning code

The permissible VDI values are as follows:

■ A—not checked—no specifications from the vendor

■ B—checked—marked as originating goods by the vendor

■ C—checked, originating—long term declaration exists and no dunning will take place because this vendor declaration is valid until canceled by the vendor

N O T E You are advised to set B as the default for the vendor declaration indicator when requesting or dunning a vendor declaration because preference determination checks the validity
date of the vendor declaration only when B is set. The legal maximum validity is one year. Long term
refers to the option to renew after one year. ■

■ D—checked—vendor cannot confirm as originating goods

The vendor declaration date is recorded as the date on which the vendor declaration expires. If this date is overdue, the vendor is sent a reminder or dunning letter, depending on the dunning code. The validity expiry date for the vendor declaration, the dunning code, and the dunning date are be same for each material and plant in all preference zones.

The dunning code indicates the current level of dunning and is increased each time the vendor fails to respond within the time allowed. A typical dunning scheme is as follows:

■ 0 or blank—First reminder letter to the vendor. This is sent when the vendor declaration has ceased to be valid for longer than the number set for "tolerance days 1." The system sets the matchcode to 1 and the dunning date to the current date.

■ 1—First dunning letter to the vendor. This is sent when the vendor declaration has ceased to be valid for longer than the number set for "tolerance days 1" and when the number set for "tolerance days 2" has been exceeded. The system then sets the matchcode to 2 and the dunning date is set to the current date.

■ 2—Second dunning letter to the vendor. This is sent when the vendor declaration has ceased to be valid for longer than the number set for "tolerance days 1" and when the number set for "tolerance days 3" has been exceeded. The system then sets the matchcode to 3 and the dunning date is set to the current date.

The following procedure is appropriate when requesting or dunning the vendor declaration:

1. Select Logistics>SD>Foreign Trade.

2. Select Preference>Vendor Declaration>Request/Dun.

Understanding the Data Blocks of the Vendor Declaration

The screen for requesting or dunning the vendor declaration is divided into the following organizational units:

- Purchasing organization. This is where you enter the purchasing organization of the vendor for whom you are carrying out the dunning run.
- Plant. The dunning data and the tariff preference data can be specific to each plant. You can limit a dunning run to a particular plant in the purchasing organization.
- Purchasing group. You can make an entry here to ensure that the dunning run is carried out only for info records within a particular purchasing group.
- Material. You can control the run by selecting material numbers or number ranges.
- Vendor. This entry can select vendor numbers or vendor number ranges.
- Material group. This parameter can be used to select info records for materials from particular material groups.

Controlling the Processing Mode or Level   The processing mode or level is controlled by the following selectors:

- Simulated Run. If this field is activated, the request letter is printed but the dunning data from table LFEI are not updated. This is the default case.
- Processing Level: Vendor? This indicator can be activated to ensure that the vendor declaration records are processed entirely at the vendor level without being separated by specific materials. The key field MATNR in structure LFEI is therefore blank. The advantage of this processing mode is that the vendor declaration data only needs to be entered once per vendor by using the Create/Change Vendor Master function.
- Equalize Info Records? This indicator can only be used when Simulated Run is deactivated and Level: Vendor? is activated. If the system is in update mode, the activation of this field causes the system to display and update both cross-material and material-specific vendor declaration records. In this case, the preference data of the superior LFEI record is copied fully to all the material-specific records.

N O T E   If you choose to equalize the info records when entering the vendor declaration data, the contents of all already existing material-specific LFEI records will also be updated or equalized to conform with the values you have entered.

Controlling the Content of the Dunning Letter   The content, style, or prepared format for the requesting or dunning communication can be controlled by the following options:

- Request Letter. If this field is activated, the system only creates the first request letter to the vendor along with the dunning code and validity expiry date. No dunning letters are printed.
- Dun—First Level. Dunning is only carried out to the first level.
- Dun—Second Level. Dunning is only carried out to the second level.
- If you make all three fields active, the system will print all dunning levels.
- Request Text, Dunning Text, and Outline Text. You can use these fields to indicate, via their text numbers from standard text processing, what shall be printed instead of the standard default "dunning text," "additional dunning text," and outline text from T001W.

- Print Parameters for Batch or Without Online Listing.
- Print Without Online Display? This indicator allows the system to print the corresponding letter without displaying it on the screen.
- Print Error Log. This indicator is used during background processing or online processing without online display. It causes the system to print out an error log displaying the material-vendor combinations for which some of the essential vendor declaration data is missing or invalid.
- Other Print Parameters in This Block. This is used to control printing during a background run or when the Print Without Online Display? indicator is activated.

Reviewing the Results of the Vendor Declaration Run   The results of the run are presented as a list that gives you an overview of which requests or dunning letters must be issued to the vendors according to your specification. The system will generate a letter with a dunning text and an outline text for each vendor and each dunning level, and which covers all the material-vendor combinations implied by your parameters.

Every preference zone entry in a plant-related info record will be chosen if it meets the following criteria:

- The preference zone entry is contained in a valid info record that has not been marked for deletion.
- The preference zone entry points to plant-related info record with a validity date that has exceeded the tolerance period set.
- The preference zone entry points to a plant-related info record with incomplete vendor declaration data.

An error log is created for these situations.

The following items are not selected for the dunning run:

- Material-vendor-preference zone combinations for which there are no plant-specific info records for the plant(s) selected
- Material-vendor-preference zone combinations that have a long-term vendor declaration (vendor declaration indicator is set at C)

If the processing is being carried out at vendor level, at least one plant-specific info record must exist for a selected plant. Only the vendor declaration indicator and the validity date in the non–material-dependent LFEI record are relevant at the vendor-level processing.

Using Function Buttons   The following function buttons empower the actions as indicated:

- Error Log>Branch to the Display of LFEI Records Still to Be Maintained>Print the List Separately>Branch from Here to the Master Data Display.
- Info Record>Mark with Your Cursor the Item Line of the Letter in Question>Branch to the Vendor Declaration Data of an Individual Info Record. The data on all preference zone customs areas for the plant-material-vendor combination is displayed.

N O T E Branching to the info record during processing at material level is impossible. ■

■ Vendor>Mark with Your Cursor the Item Line of the Letter in Question>Branch to the Vendor Master at the LFEI Data Records.

Using the Preference Results in the Sales and Distribution Documents

The results of preference determination can be evaluated in the material master as well as during order processing and billing processing. You might want to do this because the preference status of a sales product is not actually determined until the sales transaction is effected.

The Ex-Works price is compared with the preference condition record at condition type PREF during the business transaction. If the Ex-Works price is higher than the limit set by the condition record at type PREF, the preference indicator is set in the document against the item. You are allowed to print an EUR 1 document, which is the goods movement certificate.

Printing the EUR 1 Document (Goods Movement Certificate)

The EU uses the goods movement certificate primarily as proof of preference validity that the countries involved and the goods in question are covered by one of the following types of preference arrangement:

■ Free trade agreement

■ Preference agreement

■ Cooperation agreement

These agreements may also extend to cover partner states associated with the EU.

The relevant customs office provides the exporter with layout set EUR.1. The forms are to be used as follows:

■ Form A certificate of origin for goods movements involving developing countries.

■ For goods valued up to ca. 11800 DM, moving between EFTA member states, a declaration of origin in the commercial documents is sufficient.

■ A special certificate A.TR.1 is required for Turkey, which is an EU-associated state.

Layout set EUR.2 can be used for low-value goods movements involving EFTA and some East European states as a declaration of origin issued and signed by the exporter.

Reviewing the Preference Determination Sequence

The process of determining preference is normally carried out in accord with the following sequence:

■ The plant is determined.

■ The material master data for the main part is determined.

■ The preference ID in the material master is interpreted to control the checking.

Part
II

Ch
6

Preference ID interpretations are as follows:

- A—The check is carried out.
- B—The check is carried out using the EU commodity code. If this code is not available in the material master, this is noted in the log.
- C—No check is carried out because preference is generally authorized. A message appears in the log.
- D—The check is not carried out because preference is generally not authorized. A message appears in the log.
- E—The check is carried out, but the material master is not updated. A message appears in the log.
- F—The check is carried out and the price for this main part is recorded, but the material master cannot be changed here. This indicator is needed for products of mixed origin, such as an in-house produced part assembled with an externally procured part. A message appears in the log.

The indicators E and F are special cases only assigned to insignificant parts of a material assembly.

All indicators except B must be entered manually. B is entered automatically in the material master after preference determination.

If the material master record indicates the need, the following customizing tables are consulted to determine the material share for each preference zone:

- Commodity Code and Preference Rule by Preference Zone. This table defines the standard rule that contains the procedures for preference determination. The valid rules are processed for each preference zone. If no rules are found, a message is recorded in the error log.
- Preference Rule/Percentages. This table includes the preference procedure, the HS (Harmonized System) number, and the corresponding percentage for each preference rule and sequential number.

The preference price for the main part in an assembly is defined as the highest determined price in the preference zone most recently processed in the sequence. Where an alternative rule has been defined, the preference determination is performed on the basis of this rule as well. The adopted preference price is the lower of the two determined prices.

There is a separate preference price determined for each preference zone.

If the goods include externally procured components, all the plant data in the material master record is consulted to determine the ID and validity date of the vendor declaration. There is also a check, which determines if any alternative items have been defined for the BoM. If there are any, they are checked, evaluated, and selected for each preference zone.

As part of preference determination, the following values of the material share by preference zone are calculated:

- Originating value
- Non-originating value with classification change
- Non-originating value without classification change
- Collective value

Changing the Classification Between Originating and Non-Originating

One of an assembly's important characteristics is the proportion of the value that has been added in the country seeking to export it. This proportion is one of the key factors that determines whether an assembly of in-house and externally procured goods is subject to export preference processing.

The components have to be classified between originating and non-originating. When sufficient value has been added to a non-originating component, it can undergo a change of classification.

For each component in the bill of material, the vendor declaration is checked to see if a change of classification is warranted. The results of the check are recorded as follows:

- A—Not checked. Non-originating goods.
- B—Checked and valid.
- Validity date>Current date or Validity date>Current date.
- Originating goods or non-originating goods.
- D—Checked and invalid. Non-originating goods.

The first four digits of the main part's commodity code are compared with the first four digits of the components' commodity code.

N O T E The number of digits designated as significant when consulting the commodity code of components can be defined using parameters during customizing for pricing.

Part

II

Ch

6

Setting the Percentage for Classification Change

A significant proportion of goods that originated outside an exporting country may be brought up in value by the work done on them, or they may be warehoused until a more favorable market appears. In such circumstances you could argue that a composite assembly of which they are a part should be reclassified as goods originating in the exporting country. The argument turns on what percentage of added value should be considered critical. The reference material is always the main part. It is the main part that is reclassified.

Considering Preference for BoM with Alternative Items

After the BoM has been exploded, the components are examined for alternative items that can be used as substitutes. The system will check for each new preference zone with which alternative items might be traded. Different preference zones might have different preference rules. Therefore, it might be possible to choose different alternative items according to the preference zone.

The system automatically suggests the item that has the worst effect on the preference price of the main part, starting at the lowest BoM level.

Using an Assembly with Exploded BoM

The rule is that if an alternative item is an assembly and cannot be exploded because of a selection parameter, each alternative item is to be treated as a main part.

This entails a separate preference determination for the material of the alternative item. However, it has to be the commodity code of the main part that determines the procedures and rules to be applied.

If your BoM includes components produced in-house, they can qualify for preference. They must meet the following criteria:

- The components have been included on the basis of the selection data in the most recent preference determination without changing the material database.
- A valid preference ID and a preference price could be determined for these components.

Using an Assembly Without Exploded BoM

If an alternative assembly item cannot be further exploded on the basis of the selection parameter, the system will assume that preference determination data is already available for it.

In particular, components that have been produced in your company will normally qualify for preference. The data for this will be available if preference determination has already been performed for them. They will then have a valid preference ID in the material master record and corresponding preference price condition records.

Components procured externally will qualify for preference determination if they have a valid vendor declaration.

Examining the Results of a Determination Run

The following logs are created during preference determination:

- Preference log
- Error log
- Process log

If you conduct preference determination as a background job, the logs will be created automatically. If you are operating online, you will be invited to authorize updating the material master after preference determination.

Another option is to call for a simulation. This will perform preference determination in the background and generate the logs, but the data will not be saved.

Reading the Preference Log

A compilation of the preference log takes place for each successfully processed material. The first part of the log contains information on the main part or master assembly:

- Material number
- Material description
- BoM data
- Commodity code
- Date and ID from the last preference determination
- Date and ID from the latest preference determination

The second part of the preference log refers to the preference zone:

- Preference rule used
- Material value of the components
- Preference price determined

The values in the third part of the preference log are reported for each preference zone:

- Components used including the material number, material description, commodity code, quantity, and value
- Vendor declaration ID for externally procured components

Reading the Error Log

The system differentiates three types of errors:

- Error messages and notes regarding the main part
- Error messages and notes regarding the components
- Error messages and notes regarding the table entries

The first part of the error log identifies the main part. The second part of the error log displays the error messages and the notes for each error that has been detected.

Reading the Process Log

The process log lists which materials were selected for preference determination and whether preference determination was successfully carried out.

Maintaining Preference Data in the Material Master

Your Import department will normally maintain the preference data for import and export in the Foreign Trade screen as part of maintaining the material masters. If you select the Tariff Preference Function button, you will have access to the preference authorization; it's an indicator that records in the material master the least favorable preference situation for the material concerned. The codes are interpreted as follows:

- A—Preference has not been checked.
- B—Preference has been calculated and the preference price must be taken into account when pricing the order.
- C—It has been decided that this salable part may benefit from preference. The price has no influence.
- D—Preference is generally not authorized, but this indicator may be set manually.
- E—Preference benefits generally apply to this salable part. This indicator may be set manually.
- F—Preference benefits generally apply to this salable part, and the material is of mixed origins.

Preference determination requires precise definitions regarding the vendor declaration. The Least Favorable vendor declaration situation is coded in the material master as follows:

- A—No check has been made regarding the vendor declaration.
- B—The individual vendor declaration has been checked and can be used.
- C—The vendor declaration has been checked and a long-term declaration exists that is valid until canceled by the vendor.
- D—The vendor declaration has been checked and cannot be used.

The date of vendor declaration is stored in the ID record and signifies the last date on which the vendor declaration is valid.

Maintaining Preference Data in the Purchasing Information Record

The details regarding the vendor declaration status are the same in the purchasing information record as in the material master. However, the purchasing information record stores the following additional data:

- Dunning indicator
- Requisition date of the dunning notice

The preference data in the purchasing info record may be accessed by the following sequence: Select Extras>Tariff Preference.

Locating Preference Data in the Vendor Master

The vendor master and the purchasing information record both store the same preference data. The purchase information record is read first during calculation. The vendor master is read if the record does not exist.

The preference data in the vendor master record may be accessed by the following sequence: Select Extras>Purchasing Data>Tariff Preference.

Summarizing Vendor Declaration Indicators

Before you can determine preference, you have to summarize the vendor declaration indicators from the individual purchasing info records in the material master.

The database table LFEI is the data structure holding the vendor declaration indicator for a vendor material; this is where the indicators are stored per preference zone. The structure is linked to the purchasing info record.

The summarizing of all the vendor declaration indicators takes place for each plant and for every preference zone. The summarized vendor declaration indicator is stored in database table MAPE. This database is linked to the material master. The structure is as follows:

- Preference zone
- Preference
- Preference date
- Vendor declaration
- Vendor declaration date

The summarized indicator for the vendor declaration per preference zone can take the following values:

- A—Not checked, or no information from vendor
- B—Checked, marked as originating goods by all vendors
- C—Checked, long-term vendor declaration exists that is valid until canceled by the vendor
- D—Checked, not originating goods

The vendor declaration date is defined as the most recent expiry date of all the vendor declarations for the relevant preference zone. This data can be controlled in the material master, either in the Purchasing screen or in the Sales and Distribution screen.

The following sequence is appropriate for summarizing vendor declaration indicators: Select Logistics>SD>Foreign Trade>Preference>Vendor Declaration>Summarize.

The advantage of using this function is that it enables you to select all existing info records for a particular material. What you need to know is the last purchasing activity for the vendor. The date of the last purchasing activity is compared with the current date. If the purchasing date is earlier than the date allowing for purchasing tolerance days, the info record is not taken into account during summarization.

Now the purchasing info record is always maintained on a plant-by-plant basis. Therefore, the tolerance check can only be carried out successfully for info records that have maintained an association with a particular plant, where the information is updated. You cannot run this check using purchasing info records that are maintained at purchasing organization level.

The vendor declaration indicators are read from structure LFEI for each material, plant, and preference zone and are summarized according to the following rules in the material master:

- Blank equals A
- D before A, B, and C
- A before B and C
- C equals B

The system always adopts the most negative value for each material-plant-preference zone combination.

The following default values are used during preference determination if no valid info records are selected:

- Externally procured material is set to D (checked, not okay)
- Mixed material is set to A (not checked)

The options available for summarizing the vendor declaration in the material master are as follows:

- Plant, which allows you to limit the summarization run to a single plant because tariff preference data is always related to particular plants.
- Purchasing Group, which allows you to confine a summarization run to info records associated with a particular purchasing group.
- Purchasing Organization, which allows you to confine a summarization run to info records associated with a particular purchasing group.
- Materials may be chosen by their individual material numbers or by specifying a range of material numbers.
- Material Group limits selection of info records to materials from certain material groups.
- Preference Zone limits selection for summarization to the specified preference zone.

The default in the standard system for the parameter named Simulation Run does not update the indicators. If this control is removed, the summarized indicators are updated directly into the material master structure MAPE.

From Here

This chapter is about foreign trade, preference processing, and how to locate and interpret the data needed for these business processes.

You might like to move on to one of the following:

- Chapter 7, "Managing the SD Communications"
- Chapter 8, "Using Modern Sales Systems"

Part

II

Ch

6

Managing the SD Communications

In this chapter

Understanding Document Flow in Sales and Distribution

Everything is balanced about the delivery. Before there can be a delivery there has to be a sales order, preceded perhaps by a quote solicited by an inquiry. Billing, with possible credit or debit memos, comes after the delivery. The sales order may have to be supplemented by a returns document and a subsequent or free-of-charge delivery.

The relationships between the various SAP R/3 documents that control these processes is referred to as the *document flow*. This suggests that the documents are in many ways interdependent. What flows between the documents is the information and responsibility for action entailed by a business transaction.

Your company may indeed identify the division of responsibilities by having different departments "own" the various documents. SAP R/3 tends to use departmental titles such as Sales, Shipping, and Billing to identify the business significance of the various modules that comprise the Sales and Distribution application.

Making Use of Sales and Distribution Documents

The SAP business transaction document is a versatile instrument, created automatically and always subject to the rule that changes must be documented and timestamped. These are some of the day-to-day uses to which the SAP document is put in the SD-Sales and Distribution System:

- Pricing
- Availability checks
- Transfer of requirements
- Sales or distribution document printing medium and formatting
- Management of short standard texts or long texts and drawings
- Delivery management and document printing
- Billing management and document printing
- Provision of data to the SD-IS Sales and Distribution Information System

The documents created by the SD-Sales and Distribution System follow the standard SAP R/3 convention of composing a header plus one or more items.

The system differentiates between sales support activities carried on without any specific reference to individual customers and the activities that entail dealing with sales and distribution to individual customers. Computer-assisted sales support is discussed in Chapter 8, "Using Modern Sales Systems."

Configuring for SD Business Transactions

Every business transaction is documented automatically by the SAP R/3 system. The SD-Sales and Distribution module provides for a separate document type to be created for every stage of the sales and distribution chains. Changes to a document, such as revisions of prices or quantities, are stored in the change history associated with each document. Standard business programs are available for executing and displaying the results of all the usual sales and distribution functions, to which you can add your own variants during customizing.

The following documents will be handled routinely by the SD module to generate printed and other output and to conduct electronic document interchange (EDI) with other users:

- Sales documents
- Shipping documents
- Billing documents

The sales documents usually include the following:

- Sales queries, such as inquiries and quotations
- Sales orders
- Outline agreements, such as contracts and scheduling agreements
- Documents such as free-of-charge deliveries and credit memo requests, created when dealing with customer complaints

Although the following functions may be managed in other application modules, they will be important in the SD operations. Perhaps their documentation could be classed as sales documents in this context:

- Delivery scheduling
- Availability checking
- Pricing
- Credit management

Because the SAP R/3 SD system is so able to flex to your particular business process needs, it seems that almost any action can be taken from any point in the SD processes. For example, you can process deliveries and billing documents directly from a sales document. If you post a cash sale or a rush order, you can have your system configured to automatically trigger the creation of corresponding delivery and billing documents.

Reviewing the Background Functions of Sales Order Processing

Any of the following tasks can be brought into the foreground, but they can also take place in the background so that you see only the results or a report. The SD module's base mode offers proposals for all data fields in a document if there is a reasonable method of anticipating what you want to see in the particular field. This mode operates throughout the following basic functions:

- Monitoring the sales transactions
- Checking for availability
- Transferring requirements to materials planning (MRP)
- Scheduling the delivery

Part

II

Ch

7

- Calculating pricing and taxes
- Checking credit limits
- Creating printed or electronically transmitted documents such as delivery notes and confirmations

Appreciating Document Flow in Sales Processing

The typical flow of activities in a Sales department is reflected in the flow and development of the corresponding SD-Sales and Distribution documents. An example follows:

1. A sales representative makes a series of calls to a potential customer, and information is collected in sales activity documents.

2. If the potential customer makes an inquiry, a quotation can be created and assigned a limited validity period. An inquiry document can be created for the same purpose, which can subsequently lead to a quotation.

3. If the potential customer accepts the quotation, a sales order has to be delivered by a specified date.

4. In order to do this, the system must check that the material will be available, and this must be confirmed.

5. Scheduling the necessary transport for the required date has to be arranged.

6. There may have to be a picking control document to collate the order parts.

7. When the goods are about to leave the plant, there has to be a series of stock and value adjustments in the MM-Materials Management and FI-Financial Accounting departmental systems. If the relevant delivery document has not been received when goods are issued, a goods issue document has to be created to initiate the same processes.

8. The billing document may be sent, emailed, faxed, or transferred via EDI to the customer, and the event is recorded with a transfer of data to the FI-Financial Accounting department.

You can find out what is in any previous document at any stage in the document flow, right back to the first contact between your company and the customer. If the flow you are scrutinizing has been completed, you can inspect the delivery document and the invoice. Whatever your query, the automatically generated process documentation will be readily available.

Consulting Processing Status   Progress along this document flow and the transaction processing that it represents are documented automatically and can be controlled by a system of status indicators, which signal the stage reached in the transaction. You can call for information using the status indicator, which causes the system to respond with answers to the following kinds of questions:

- Has the customer accepted all the quotation items, and have they been copied to a sales order?
- Is the sales order complete?
- Which items have not yet been delivered?
- Has this transaction been fully invoiced?

You can issue commands to block the progress of a transaction if, for instance, you see a problem with the quality of the stock that might be assigned to this order.

Locating a Document   You can always access a document by entering its document number. The standard SAP R/3 system of using matchcodes is applied in SD-Sales and Distribution to initiate a search. That search narrows the list from which you have to select the document you require. Matchcodes can be customized to meet any requirements. The following matchcodes are standard:

- Sales activities selected by nominating one or more of the short texts that may have been copied to the document
- Sales documents by customer purchase order number
- Credit and debit memos that have been released for further processing
- Deliveries from a specific shipping point according to a range of goods issue dates
- Billing documents that have not yet passed to the FI-Financial Accounting system

Document flow is both a fact of life and a reporting function in SAP R/3. If you mark any item in an overview screen, you can probably select the document flow function to generate the document identifications of all the events that came before the item you marked—and all the subsequent events that depend on it. You may not be authorized to see some items in the linked documents, but often you can mark a document identification and ask to view the document itself.

Although you may have arranged your screen so that you do not see all the data fields, each entity in the SAP R/3 system has data elements sufficient to determine who owns it. For instance, sales transactions occur within an organizational structure of sales and distribution, which is usually defined by three linked entities:

- One sales organization
- One distribution channel
- One division

Each transaction document will be identified by entries in these three data fields. If your sales organization is more complex, you may have additional organizational structure entities that serve to identify the origin and responsibility for the sales documents. You may well specify the following:

- One sales office
- One sales group
- One sales representative

The logic of citing only one of each when forming a sales document's "ownership" is that it defines each document as a unique entity and also allows any user to select and list the documents at any level. You can scrutinize the sales documents of just one specialist sales group, for instance. You can also carry out analysis and comparisons between organizational entities using this system.

Each sales document comprises two types of entity:

- The document header that carries data applicable throughout the document unless contradicted by particular items
- One or more document items that represent the details of the business transaction for which the document was created

Interpreting Sales Document Data

A sales document item may be composed of a material code and a quantity. If that quantity is not to be shipped as a single delivery, the item will have to include more than one schedule line, each containing the schedule line quantity as intended, the date, and the confirmed quantity of one of the deliveries.

You can inspect sales document data by calling up various screens. An overview screen will show the types of data available and allow you to indicate your interests before calling on details screens; the screens are where the data is displayed and may be amenable to alteration, depending on your authorization and the status of the transaction the document represents.

The most useful overview screens will probably be as follows:

- Customer-Material Information, which reports each material item's company number and the code used by the customer for this material.
- Shipping, which reports for each item and item schedule line, the loading date, the shipping point, and the tolerances for under- or over-delivery, and any customized shipping data you need for your particular business.
- Billing, which reports for each item the net value, the terms of payment, and the standard Incoterms applicable.
- Reason for Rejection, which identifies the standard code that indicates the reason for each item rejected by the customer.

If you require more detail than is provided by an overview screen, the following detail screens are available when you have marked the items of interest:

- Pricing, which shows the prices, discounts, and surcharges used for pricing at the header and item level.
- Account Assignment, which shows how costs are transferred from a sales document to the Financial Accounting system and to any controlling accounts you are running, such as profit center accounting.
- Purchase Order Data, which shows header information such as the customer's purchase order number, the purchase order date, and information about the person who placed the order. This screen also displays for each item the item number and the customer material number.
- Status, which reports the progress of the business transaction and the completeness of the data at the item level. The status of the document as a whole is displayed at the header level and depends on a logical summary of the items' status values.

It will be apparent that some of the data in a sales document is copied from master records, some has previously appeared in records that are part of the document flow, and some values have been computed by the system.

Calling Individual Functions from an Overview

Depending on which overview you are consulting, various options are available:

- From the picking overview you can obtain information and select deliveries that have been picked or only partially picked according to selection criteria you specify. You can also deal separately with deliveries and transfer orders that involve Warehouse Management (MM-WM).

- From the loading overview you can select deliveries due for loading according to specific criteria and determine the loading information for the current work list.

- From the transportation planning overview you can selectively identify deliveries to be transported and obtain information on transportation for the current work list.

- From the picking confirmation overview you can selectively isolate deliveries that contain items for which picking data still has to be confirmed. You can obtain information relevant to picking confirmation for the current work list and confirm online or in the background.

- From the goods issue overview you can selectively identify deliveries for which goods issue is yet to be posted, as well as post goods issue and obtain information on goods issue for the current work list.

The following functions are available in all the overviews:

- Create a group of deliveries to enable you to select and edit deliveries using one group number

- Print shipping documents such as picking lists or delivery notes

- Display deliveries

- Change deliveries

Displaying the Picking Overview

The picking overview does not display deliveries that have already been completely picked. You might want to narrow the choice by specifying picking dates:

1. Select Logistics>Sales/Distribution>Shipping.
2. Select Delivery>Delivery in Process>Picking.
3. Enter your selection criteria in the Shipping Data section.
4. Identify the relevant shipping documents in the Choice of Output section.

N O T E The system will accept a range of values or a list when you enter data for most purposes.

Part
II

Ch
7

5. Enter an indicator to specify the picking type of interest, unless you want to see both deliveries due for fixed bin picking and deliveries picked by the MM-WM system.

6. Select Edit>List>Work List for the Day.

7. Select the picking data you require.

8. For an overview of deliveries due for picking, select Goto>Deliveries List.

9. For an overview of deliveries due for picking that includes the corresponding delivery items, select Goto>Delivery Items List.

Displaying the Loading Overview

The loading overview displays only those deliveries for which no goods issue has yet been posted. You can narrow the choice by nominating a specific loading date or loading point. The deliveries due for loading are reported in the following sequence:

1. Select Logistics>Sales/Distribution>Shipping.

2. Select Delivery>Delivery in Process>Loading.

3. Enter your selection criteria in the Shipping Data section.

4. Identify the relevant shipping documents in the Choice of Output section.

5. Select Edit>Deliveries List.

Displaying the Transportation Planning Overview

The transportation planning overview shows only deliveries for which no goods issue has been posted. You can specify a picking date. The following sequence displays the selected deliveries:

1. Select Logistics>Sales/Distribution>Shipping.

2. Select Delivery>Delivery in Process>Transportation.

3. Enter your selection criteria in the Shipping Data section.

4. Identify the relevant shipping documents in the Choice of Output section.

5. Select Edit>Deliveries List.

Displaying the Picking Confirmation Overview

The picking confirmation overview shows only deliveries that contain items for which the picking data has not been confirmed. The following sequence is suitable:

1. Select Logistics>Sales/Distribution>Shipping.

2. Select Delivery>Delivery in Process>Picking Confirmation.

3. Enter your selection criteria in the Shipping Data section.

4. Identify the relevant shipping documents in the Choice of Output section.

5. Select Edit>Deliveries List.

Displaying the Goods Issue Overview

Only deliveries that have been fully picked are included in the goods issue overview. The following sequence is suitable:

1. Select Logistics>Sales/Distribution>Shipping.
2. Select Delivery>Delivery in Process>Goods Issue.
3. Enter your selection criteria in the Shipping Data section.
4. Identify the relevant shipping documents in the Choice of Output section.
5. Select Edit>Deliveries List.

Customizing the Control of Sales Documents

The Customizing for Sales operation allows your system administrator to establish how sales documents are processed. That's done by setting up classified condition records, which are consulted at the following levels:

- By sales document type
- By item category

NOTE Standard item, free of charge item, and text item are the item categories defined for the standard order.

- By schedule line category

The following situations can be predefined by condition records:

- Shall a credit check take place for a particular type of sales document?
- Shall a failed credit check automatically block a document, or may it be passed for review and be the subject of a request for a credit memo?
- Shall an item's category affect how deliveries and billing are conducted? For example, a material item in a quotation will not be delivered or billed, although certain text items may be delivered but not billed in a quotation.
- Shall a schedule line category be taken as a signal for a particular type of action from the MRP Materials Requirements Planning section and perhaps affect how an availability check is carried out?

Configuring Control Elements for Item Categories

Control elements are held in tables associated with item category definitions. They refine the actions taken automatically by the system for individual items, so as to handle the following types of sales situations:

- Is this item to be processed as a material, or is it a pure value item or text item?
- Is the item included in pricing?

- Is the item relevant for delivery?
- Is billing to be carried out for this item?
- Is a billing block to be set automatically for the item (for credit or debit memo requests, for example)?
- Are schedules lines permitted for this item?

In shipping documents, a similar system of item category control elements is applied to preconfigure the functional logic. Look at the following examples:

- Is the system to check whether the minimum quantity for an item has been reached?
- Is the system to check whether over-delivery is permitted for the item?
- Is an availability check to be carried out?
- Is the item relevant for picking?
- Is a storage location to be specified?

The item categories determine the control in the billing document; the item categories are copied via copy control into the billing document. All item controls are done at the item category.

If a sales item has associated schedule lines, their category will be determined by consulting the rules that apply to the corresponding item and the MRP type assigned to that material type.

Assigning Numbers to Sales and Distribution Documents

Although a sales transaction is associated with a particular sales organization, and this is recorded on the documents created, each document is identified by a separate document number. The number is unique within an SAP R/3 client and does not depend on company code, sales organization, or fiscal year.

If you want to assign a number, you must choose one that has not been used before and is within the range of numbers and letters the SA allocated for the type of document you are creating. This is referred to as *external number assignment*. Alternatively, you can let the system assign the document number internally.

Consulting the Sales Information System

The Sales Information System allows you to filter out and consolidate SD data in whatever manner helps you discern market developments and economic trends. The SIS will also accept planning data against which you can later make comparisons.

The Sales Information System is a component of the Logistic Information System (LIS). The Purchasing Information System and the Shop Floor Information System are also part of the LIS.

A shared set of data selection and analysis tools is available in the LIS and can be applied to extract data relevant to sales and distribution.

Understanding the Cross-Application Document Management System

The CA-DMS Document Management System is an integral part of SAP R/3 and therefore is designated CA, as Cross Application. It is presented in the central part of the Logistics menu. DMS works under the authorization control system so that you can read—but not alter—some documents.

The objects controlled by DMS are technical documents and associated design drawings, photographs, and control files for such processes as computer-assisted manufacturing.

The aims of the DMS design are summarized as follows:

- Avoid data redundancy
- Maintain consistency of data
- Minimize the workload involved in entering and updating data

Each type of "document" is subject to status control and may undergo a unique sequence of milestone stages during its creation. The users responsible are automatically informed of the document's current processing status. SAP standard Engineering Change Management (ECM) procedures are applied to the documents in the DMS.

It is of particular importance to be able to consult archived technical documents. Those documents track a product's processing life cycle because legal liabilities may be at issue and it may not be enough to sample the product to prove its integrity.

ISO 9000 to 9006 is a range of standards that define the criteria for quality management certification. These include the requirement for a high-performance document management system.

The R/3 DMS provides additional functionality to that required for QM certification by allowing you to automate parts of the production and life cycle of technical documents in the following aspects:

- Document creation
- Document storage
- Document access
- Recorded document update

Any DMS document can be accessed immediately from any terminal in an R/3 or mixed-system network. A DMS document can be linked to various implementation entities, such as material masters, change masters, production resource, and tools.

Defining a DMS Document

The DMS object is composed of two parts: A data storage medium contains information and a document info record is maintained to store its history, its processing status, storage location, and general administrative information.

A document's reader may be a user or, if the content is a program or other type of machine control database, another system.

Understanding the Functions of a Document Info Record

The document info record's various functions may be called from the DMS. For example, when DMS creates a document, a unique number is assigned (in the document info record) that can be used to attach the document to another SAP object or to a workstation application. The document info record also keeps track of the version management records; they may have to be synchronized with associated material master records and might be required by CAD systems using the SAP-CAD interface.

When equipment is audited, the associated documents may be accessed using the SAP ArchiveLink. A customer may need to consult a document by reference to its classification, which is stored in the document info record.

Documents in a hierarchy can be accessed in DMS during Engineering Change Management, for example, where they form part of the integrated workflow. SAP Workflow has a Find Document function that accesses the DMS.

Application files—the programs—can be accessed through DMS, with the help of company-specific settings established in Customizing.

The DMS will be home to BoM details that are used to develop production orders and complex sales items from the bill of materials.

The Document Management System's IMG allows you to set up various configuration options so that you can have the DMS specifically suited to your company. For this purpose, the DMS is accessed from the IMG as a cross-application component. You can make adjustments to the following:

- Field and screen selection
- Authorization checks
- Object links
- Number assignment options for documents
- Workstation applications
- User-defined revision levels
- Options for storing original application files

You have to identify to the IMG what types of documents you intend to manage in the DMS and how you want it to handle each of them. For example, you may well insist that every technical drawing of one type of product be linked automatically to the material master that is used when selling it. A complex product with variants may be manufactured using routings and production resources and tools. The routings and PRTs can be stored as a document hierarchy in the DMS and linked with the inspection data as it becomes available.

The production of a document may itself be a project managed by the PS-Project System, but a project may use the DMS to control the associated documents.

If you are calling the DMS within R/3, the following sequence is appropriate:

1. Select Logistics>Central Functions>Document Management.
2. Choose Document, Find, or Environment.

The Document option offers the following choices:

- Create a new document
- Change an existing document
- Display a document
- Create a new version of an existing document

The Find function allows you to define a search specification to retrieve documents, which you can then process.

The Environment option allows a choice of submenus with which to work with bills of material, classification functions, and Engineering Change Management.

A document may be usefully linked to many other SAP R/3 objects and recalled as needed by referring to the edition or variant as required, thus saving the space that would otherwise be needed to keep copies of the documents. There would also be a problem of locating all the copies if updating has to occur. Such links are held in a number of database tables from which they can be rapidly utilized.

Controlling Document Processing by Authorization Objects

Document processing under the DMS is organized in parallel with the structure of your company and its software. Master data for all application areas is usually created at one central location, and extra data specific to a particular application area is added using the Change function.

When one application area requires access to the master data, the authorization system come into play to ensure that each user community gets access to its own selection from the single copy of master data.

Interpreting Authorization Objects and Fields for the DMS

Four authorization object types are defined for the document management system. If a user is assigned one of these objects, there are only certain possibilities open to him or her, as defined in the master record for the particular object. The object types are as follows:

- The C_DRAW_TCD Document Activities object controls the combinations of the activities and document types and fields with which you are allowed to work when maintaining document info records.

- The C_DRAW_STA Document Status object contains values that control which document types you are allowed to work with and which status indicators you can assign to them.

- The C_DRAW_BGR Authorization Group object carries the range limitations to control the numbers of the documents you are permitted to maintain.

- The C_DRAW_DOK Document Access object will specify which fields of original data in a certain document type are available to you for editing.

Using Lists in Sales and Distribution

Lists are very useful for two types of tasks:

- Selecting documents that require attention to make a work list, such as deliveries outstanding

- Extracting and sorting records so as to arrange data in a meaningful way for simple evaluation and analysis

The next section illustrates some of the uses for standard listing functions.

Listing Incomplete Documents

A document may be incomplete because it is used as a pattern or model to which specific information is added before it is posted. Your system may also be configured to allow certain documents to be accepted even though not all fields have been entered. In general, the system is set up to offer the most intelligent suggestion at each stage.

However, a document may be incomplete because the necessary information was unavailable at the time it was created. A document may also be unsatisfactory because it contains a detectable error and failed to be accepted on posting. Incomplete or incorrect documents can be inspected as follows:

1. Select Logistics>Sales/Distribution>Sales.

2. Select Environment>Document Analysis>Incomplete Documents.

NOTE If you require the document analysis function to display documents that are incomplete, you are invited to specify the degree of incompleteness. Typically, you have to do this by selecting selection criteria for the fields of interest. For example, if you want to see documents that require further delivery processing, select the Delivery field. If there are many, for example, you may want to narrow the selection by specifying a range of dates.

3. Enter the incompleteness degree.

4. Enter the selection criteria.

5. Select Program>Execute.

You can mark a document of interest and select Details to see the incomplete data. If there is more than one, mark them all and select Edit>Documents.

The most used of ten search specifications are provided as menu items:

- Order>Incomplete Orders
- Inquiry>Incomplete Inquiries
- Quotation>Incomplete Quotations
- Outline Agreement>Scheduling Agreement>Incomplete Scheduling Agreements
- Outline Agreement>Contract>Incomplete Contracts

Listing Blocked Documents

The sequence for listing blocked orders is as follows:

1. Select Logistics>Sales/Distribution>Sales.
2. Select Environment>Document Analysis>Blocked Sales Orders.
3. Identify the organizational data for the blocked orders that you require and edit the list characteristics if necessary.
4. Select Program>Execute.

The outcome is a list of order values blocked for each month. You can get a list of individual blocked orders sorted by customer or material once you have marked a month line item.

Displaying All Blocked Billing Documents

If you need to display all billing documents that are blocked for forwarding to Accounting, use the following sequence:

1. Select Logistics>Sales/Distribution>Billing.
2. Select Billing Document>Blocked Billing Docs.
3. Enter selection criteria.
4. Select Program>Execute.

Listing Documents Due for Processing

Apply the following procedure to display all backorders in documents due for processing:

1. Select Logistics>Sales/Distribution>Sales.
2. Select Environment>Document Analysis>Backorders.
3. Identify the organizational data for the blocked orders that you require and edit the list characteristics if necessary.

The outcome is a list of the monthly values of backorders. You can view the sorted individual backorders for a month by marking the monthly value line item and selecting either Display Customers or Display Material.

Part

II

Ch

7

Listing Unconfirmed Documents

Sometimes a sales order's order quantity cannot be confirmed for the date required. You can use a matchcode to search for sales orders.

1. Select Logistics>Sales/Distribution>Sales.

2. Select Order>Change.

3. Place your cursor on the Sales Order field and select Possible Entries. You're shown a list of the possible entries, which you can use as matchcodes.

4. Select Unconfirmed Orders>Choose.

5. Enter data that will restrict the list of orders.

6. Press Enter.

   You get a list of all orders in which the order quantity of one or more items could not be confirmed. Mark one of interest.

7. Select Choose.

The order will now appear in the initial screen for changing orders, where you can work on it.

Displaying Documents According to Object Status

One way of selecting sales documents for display is to call for all documents that have a particular status in the Accounting system. Released is a system status.

Another type of status is referred to as a *user status* and depends on a status profile being set up in Customizing that controls which values of the status indicator are allowed for each type of sales document.

The following sequence will select and list sales documents on the basis of their object status:

1. Select Logistics>Sales/Distribution>Sales.

2. Select Environment>Document Analysis>Docs by Status.

3. Enter an object status that is valid in your system.

4. Enter further selection criteria, such as organizational data and sales document data.

5. Select System Status or User Status.

6. Select to search for the status at header or item level.

N O T E Document analysis by status defaults to processing for system status at document header level. ■

7. Select Program>Execute.

You can mark any documents you want to work on.

Making and Using Work Lists

Any summary of objects that meet certain criteria can be treated as a work list if the objects in it require further processing. You do not have to do any work on a work list if you are using it for information!

Making Work Lists for Credit Management

A *credit hold* is a blocked sales order or delivery. If you are in credit control you will want to search for such items, perhaps selectively by using matchcodes to specify parameters such as the following:

- Credit control area
- Credit representative group
- Next shipping date
- Credit account
- Risk category
- Customer credit group

When you have built an overview list, the following data will be displayed:

- Next shipping date
- Credit account by customer number or name
- Document number
- Credit value as the document value
- Currency
- Credit limit used as a percentage
- Terms of payment
- Risk category
- Total status of credit check
- Credit status with blocking reasons
- Date on which the document was created
- Credit representative who entered data
- Document value class

You can use any of these fields to control the sort order and you can arrange to have displayed only those fields you need to work on. In particular, the credit control function will have to arrive at decisions on blocked documents according to the following options:

- The credit limit can be granted and the document will be released.
- The credit limit cannot be granted and the document will be canceled.
- The credit representative will forward the blocked document to another representative.
- The blocked document will be rechecked.

The credit representative can again determine the way priority is assigned for blocked documents. For example, it may be preferable for several documents with a low document value to be given priority and released until their credit limit is completely used up, rather than release a single high-value document that has already exceeded its credit limit.

An overview work list of blocked documents for credit limit processing is made like this:

1. Select Accounting>Financial Accounting>Accounts Receivable.
2. Select Environment>Credit Management.
3. Select Exceptions>Blocked Sales Docs.
4. Enter a selection specification to isolate documents (for example, by credit control area, credit representative group, and other criteria, such as risk category).
5. Select Program>Execute.

The following functions are available at this stage:

- Release documents for further processing
- Decline to extend credit
- Re-run the credit check
- Edit documents
- Branch to credit-related texts in the customer master or the document
- Display the document history and document flow
- Forward the document for review by another credit representative group

As you work down the list, the system will update the status indicator where appropriate. You may need to make a temporary excursion to view other information, such as credit control area data and reports that summarize customer-related credit histories.

Processing Work Lists for Customer-Expected Price

If you are using a customer-expected price to alert everyone of any potential sources of dispute, you can specifically list all orders that are blocked due to a difference in customer-expected price and the determined net price. The following sequence is suitable:

1. Select Logistics>Sales/Distribution>Sales.
2. Select Sales Order>Release>CustExpPrice.
3. Enter your selection criteria and select Program>Execute.

Making a Selection List for Backorder Processing

The backorder processing functions enable you to focus on specific materials and the relevant sales documents. You then process them from the list. The following sequence builds the list:

1. Select Logistics>Sales/Distribution>Sales.
2. Select Environment>Backorders>Backorder Processing>Sales/Distribution Documents.

3. Enter selection criteria such as the plant, sold-to party, and purchase order number in the Backorder Processing screen.

4. Select Program>Execute.

You get a list for each material, and there are relevant fields displayed for each sales document that refers to this material:

- First delivery date
- Order quantity
- Confirmed quantity
- Open quantity

If you mark the documents of interest, you can go through the Environment option to display the document status, the document flow, and the changes that have been made to this document.

Creating Delivery Due Lists

The list of deliveries due is a popular choice, which you can arrive at via the following sequence:

1. Select Logistics>Sales/Distribution>Shipping.

2. Select Delivery>Process Dlv.Due List.

3. Specify the shipping point at which the deliveries are to be created.

If you would otherwise get too many order items, you can narrow the search by one of the following specifications:

- Define a time period to cover the due date of the order items. An order item will then appear only if it has a material availability date or transportation scheduling date within this period.
- Nominate a route or a forwarding agent.

If you want to refine the list by specifying organizational data for the delivery due list, you should select Defaults>Organizational Data. You are invited to nominate a sales organization, a distribution channel, or a division.

It is possible to refine the search even further:

1. Select Defaults>Further Sel.Screen.

2. Specify a range of order numbers.

   or

   Specify a particular sold-to party or ship-to party

   or

   Specify a particular material.

Part
II

Ch
7

If you are responsible for shipping, you may find it helpful to limit the retrieval of delivery due documents according to the capacity of a shipping point. You can express this limit as a maximum work capacity in days and the maximum gross weight or volume.

Monitoring Deliveries in Process

Another useful list is the Deliveries in Process suite of overviews, which focuses on the shipping work stages as follows:

- Picking
- Loading
- Transport planning
- Goods issue

This is the way to manage large amounts of data and keep a lookout for incipient bottlenecks.

Using Billing Due Lists

One of the advantages of working from lists is that you can have the system assemble them on the basis of the work that needs to be carried; they can be arranged, if necessary, in order of priority according to the document's value or age.

For example, you can define some selection criteria and call up the billing due list. You may be able to have several deliveries for the same customer combined in one invoice, thus saving your company processing workload. This is how you do it:

1. Select Logistics>Sales/Distribution>Billing.
2. Select Billing Document>Billing Due List.
3. Define the criteria for your list, such as a particular billing type, the ID number of a sold-to party, and a destination country.
4. Enter the billing date in the To field.

N O T E The current date is the default value used for the To field while assembling a billing due list. ■

5. In the Documents to Be Selected section, record your choice between order-related or delivery-related billing; this appropriately groups the displays.
6. If you are confident, have the invoices created immediately for the documents that fulfill the specified selection criteria. If you are not confident, select Edit>Display Billing to display the check billing due list and unmark any if necessary.

Chapter 4, "Billing," discusses the billing processes in more detail.

Consulting Pricing Reports

If you have to answer any of the following questions, you can have the system look in the pricing data:

■ Which customer-specific price agreements were made within a certain period?

■ Which condition records exist for freight charges?

■ Which condition records exist for customers in a particular region or country?

A suite of pricing reports will have been predefined in SD Customizing and adjusted in accord with the methods used in your company. You can use these reports in many different ways by manipulating the selection criteria; only the system administrator can reformat the reports themselves.

What you can do is have a look at pricing condition records that you select according to the criteria of interest. Do so by selecting Environment>Condition Information.

Using Lists to Monitor External Procurement

If a customer wants to change an order after your company has generated a purchase order, you could find yourself with a deviation between the order data and the data in purchase requisitions and purchase orders. There could also be a deviation when you are managing third-party order processing. If you want to have a look at these deviations, here is how to do it:

1. Select Logistics>Sales/Distribution>Sales>Sales Order.

2. Select Comparison with Pur.>New Selection.

3. Enter a sales order number in the selection screen. That displays the purchase requisition or purchase order for that sales order.

4. Enter organizational data or a set of values in order to retrieve a selected set of purchase orders with deviating data.

5. Select Program>Execute.

There may be various explanatory notes relating to any reported deviations. You may also append notes.

To work on any individual document, mark the line and select Goto>Purchase Requisition.

Here's how to display the last list compiled previously:

1. Select Logistics>Sales/Distribution>Sales.

2. Select Sales Order>Comparison with Pur.>Display.

3. Enter organizational data on the selection screen.

4. Select Program>Execute.

Utilizing Communications in SD

The main communications of interest in the SD domain are as follows:

- To customers as sales order confirmations and delivery notes
- To sales management and electronic mail on the placing of a significant sales order
- To customers and prospects via direct mailings and selective communications, as part of a sales support campaign
- To affiliated companies and partners

There are various ways of controlling the timing and the output media (as well as the target recipients) of these communications.

The SD system makes reasonable output proposals during the processing of sales and distribution documents. These are like default values that you can confirm or alter before release. Alternatively, you may be sure of the requirement and have the output, at least for some customers, issued automatically. If you define the output in a document header, it will usually apply as the default for all the items unless a different output is indicated for any individual items.

The functions for output control are basically to service the creation of a new document or a change in an existing document. The mechanism places data defining the issue of an output in a file where it is queued until the output controller interprets this data and generates the actual output for dispatch using the output media that have been established in Customizing for Sales and Distribution. Some assignments of output to individual media will be prohibited.

The following factors have to be considered when specifying output assignment:

- Output must be assigned to the account group to which a customer belongs if it is to appear as an output proposal for that customer.
- The output must also be assigned to the various partner functions, and to the individual sales and distribution documents.
- Sales and distribution document types will probably be printed on forms that control the layout and content. The output has to be assigned to each of these forms.

Before you can use a new type of output, you have to create a master record for it and then assign it to the entities that will use it.

Defining Background Jobs

Background jobs are first defined in Customizing for Sales and Distribution. When you want to have output issued as the result of a selection run, you select which output types are to be created and when, their language, and the quantity of output to be sent. This information is stored in the customer master record and automatically copied into the sales and distribution documents. You can edit the output for particular transactions before the output background job is released. The actual output is scheduled according to your specification once you have released the background job.

Controlling Output Dispatch Times

The following options illustrate the flexibility with which you can influence the sending of output:

- Send immediately after a document is created (such as a sales order confirmation when the sales order is posted)
- Send at a specified time
- Send only when requested by a user
- Send periodically, such as invoices printed hourly or daily

Printing has to be directed to a named printer and then the print parameters will be proposed in the documents. These parameters are normally dependent on sales organization or shipping point and are defined for each output specification.

The receiving partner must be identified in the customer master record for there to be an automatic output proposal; this relates to sending output by telex, fax, or teletex.

If your system uses EDI, there will be general and application-specific standards to control it.

Operating a Typical Print Procedure

To illustrate the scheme of print control operations, the following example prints an individual picking list:

1. Select Logistics>Sales/Distribution>Shipping.
2. Select Output>Picking.
3. In the Output from Picking screen, enter output type `output medium 1`.
4. Enter the specification for selection of the data.

N O T E If you want to print from the picking lists that you know have been issued previously, you can activate the button for repeat processing.

5. Select Program>Execute.
6. Mark the picking lists you intend to print in the display of all picking lists to be printed that match your selection criteria.
7. If you need to make any alterations, select Goto>Parameter to access a dialog box for output print parameters.
8. Select Goto>Print Preview to look at a picking list before printing it.

You will see a print preview for the selected delivery note when you execute the print program.

The selected picking lists will be printed out when you select Edit>Process.

Issuing SD Output as Internal Mail Messages

You can, in the document header, make arrangements for an internal electronic mail message to be proposed when anyone creates a sales, shipping, or billing document. For example, this message can go to a supervisor who can immediately access the document and check it. Perhaps it would be prudent to allow some staff to work unsupervised within an order value limit.

Another possibility is to allow the creator of the document to decide when a message should be sent and to whom. Again, the message itself would be associated with the document header. Of course, all this logic has to be set up in Customizing for Sales.

Here is how to get an internal mail message into the header of the sales order you are working on:

Access the Output screen and make the following entries:

- Output Type to be MAIL.
- Output Medium to be Output medium 7.
- Partner Function to be MP.
- Partner to be the recipient's username.
- Language to be the language in which the mail should be delivered.
- Enter timing data for the mail message to be sent.
- Enter or confirm the communication data for the mail message.
- Mark either the Functional field (for mail that is not confidential) or the Private field.
- In the Transaction field, signify the transaction the recipient is allowed to use to process the sales order. For example, VA02 is "change sales order" and VA03 is "display sales order."

If you need to create additional text to amplify any standard text you may be sending, select Edit>Editor to acquire the SAPscript editor.

Receiving an Internal Mail Message

If you are the target for a mail message, the following procedure is appropriate for processing it:

1. Select Office>Inbox.
2. In your individual Inbox: <user name> screen, you should mark the incoming mail of interest and then select Document>Display.

If you select Edit>Process after you have read any messages, the system automatically transfers you to the transaction specified in the mail message, where you can deal with the document.

Arranging Output Determination Analysis in Sales and Distribution Documents

If you find that output is not quite what you expected, you may want to see how it was determined. How did the system search for a suitable output formulation? Did the system consult a condition record or the customer master record? Were any intended outputs not actually available? What were the access key combinations used to determine how the output should occur?

You have to select Analysis>Output Determination when you are in the Output screen of the document in question. If you mark any particular output, you can select Goto>Details to reveal more information about it. You can go deeper to probe the fields that were used to access the condition records that controlled the output.

Proposing SD Output by Filtering from the Customer Master Record

For each document type, and for each partner function, a customer master record can assign the correct output in an output proposal when you create a sales and distribution document. The technique is called *filtering* because the system eliminates unwanted outputs according to the business transaction in hand.

For example, if the customer you are working with is the ship-to party, the system will automatically propose a delivery note rather than (for example) an order confirmation, which would be out of place in this context.

Of course, you may have customers that can take on different partner functions from time to time. They may be the sold-to party, the ship-to party, or the bill-to party. For these customers, the system is prepared to propose the following outputs according to the circumstances:

- Inquiry confirmation
- Quotation confirmation
- Sales order confirmation
- Delivery note
- Invoice
- Contract confirmation
- Scheduling agreement confirmation

All of these are specified in the customer master record.

The output proposal made automatically by the system also includes how and when output is to be sent, the quantity, and the language to be used. You can always ask to see the possible entries in the Output screen and choose a different one from the proposal.

Part

II

Ch

7

Proposing SD Output Using the Condition Technique

The *condition technique* is a more flexible alternative to filtering as a mechanism for generating appropriate output proposals. The condition technique is also extensively used in pricing. The benefit is that you can set up conditions to control output proposals so that they suit the customer, the product, the sales organization, the country, or whatever R/3 data elements you choose as criteria for selecting a particular output proposal.

To illustrate the condition technique's use in controlling output proposals, the procedure for creating condition records of an order confirmation is given next:

1. Select Logistics>Sales/Distribution>Master Data.

2. Select Output>Sales Document>Create.

3. Enter the text description for the order confirmation in the Output field.

4. Select Edit>Key Combination.

5. In the dialog box, select a key combination for which you intend to create condition records.

6. Press Enter to access the Fast Entry Output screen.

7. Enter the appropriate key for each condition record being created. This depends on the key combination you selected.

At this stage you have to provide entries for each condition record in the following fields:

- Function
- Partner
- Type
- Timing
- Language

You should check and maintain, if necessary, the communication data before you save the condition records. That includes things like the output media printer and internal mail.

Using EDI Messages in SD Processing

In order to use EDI, you need partners who also use it. Inbound EDI messages are converted by an external non-SAP translator into the SAP format and stored as intermediate documents (IDoc). They are then available to whatever SAP applications you have installed and configured. Outbound EDI messages follow this route in the other direction.

The various partner translators communicate to each other by making an RFC and accessing the NFS.

Understanding the IDoc Structure for EDI

The SAP R/3 standard IDoc is composed of three sections:

■ The control record uniquely identifies what follows as an intermediate document.

■ The data record is composed of several segments that contain business data such as material and quantity specifications.

■ The status records inform you of the current status and history of the EDI message.

For example, a message may have been transferred to the appropriate application, and a document posted. This example generates two status records, one for each processing step completed. Each status record can be interpreted to discern the outcome of this processing step.

Interpreting Inbound EDI Messages

Because an EDI message gets translated to and from a suitable IDoc, the IDoc structure can be predefined to suit the message's purpose message. The standard EDI inbound message types that are assigned to the SAP IDocs as indicated follow:

■ Request for quotes becomes inquiry using IDoc structure ORD-ID01, which equates to the SD incoming sales orders with configurable materials (as of release 3.0D) and uses the transaction set -REQOTE-.

■ Purchase orders and sales orders become IDoc structures ORDERS01 and ORDERS02, respectively, and use transaction set -ORDERS-.

■ Purchase order change requests and sales order change requests become IDoc structure ORDERS01 and use transaction set -ORDCHG-.

■ Planning schedule with release capability becomes forecast delivery schedule using IDoc structure DELFOR01 and uses transaction set -DELFOR-.

■ Shipping schedule (call-off) becomes JIT delivery schedule using IDoc structure DELFOR01 and uses the transaction set -DELFOR-.

■ Credit memo becomes IDoc structure GSVER01 and uses transaction set -GSVERF-.

■ EDL delivery note becomes IDoc structure DESADV01 and uses transaction set -EDLNOT-.

Depending on the SAP R/3 release and the customization settings, warnings generated during processing can be evaluated by the system and used to alert the person responsible.

Interpreting Outbound EDI Messages

Standard procedures for creating outbound EDI message types are defined as IDoc structures:

■ Quote is generated from a quotation using IDoc structure ORD_ID01 and using transaction set -QUOTES-.

■ Purchase order acknowledgment is generated from an order confirmation using IDoc structure ORDERS01 and using transaction set -ORDRSP-.

- Dispatch advice is generated from a shipping notification using IDoc structure DESADV01) and using the transaction set -DESADV-.

- Invoice is generated from IDoc structure INVOIC01 and using transaction set -INVOIC-.

- Invoice list (as of release 3.0C) is generated from IDoc structure INVOIC01 and using transaction set -INVOIC-.

Assigning SD Output for Optical Archiving

One of the functions of output control is to initiate optical archiving of outgoing documents such as letters and questionnaires. The prerequisites include an assignment to the SD document, an appropriate archiving mode, and a suitable archiving document type at the stage of Customizing for Output Control. For example, SDOACTIV is the standard archiving document type defined in SAP ArchiveLink for sales activities.

Incoming SD documents—inquiries, purchase orders, contracts, and complaints—can be assigned for optical archiving from where they may be readily retrieved for planning, processing, and analyzing of business transactions.

SAP ArchiveLink is an interface designed to support the following activities for incoming SD documents:

- Early archiving of incoming paper documents, before an electronic SD document is created and the SAP Business Workflow notifies the person responsible.

- Late archiving, which entails the incoming paper document being processed before an electronic copy is archived.

- Late archiving involving bar codes, which are attached to the paper document in the mail room or at the time of processing and which link the SD document number with the archived copy.

- Simultaneous archiving, which avoids calling SAP Business Workflow or sending mail by creating an SD document at the same time the paper document is scanned for optical archiving.

Table 7.1 illustrates the standard incoming SD document types with their corresponding incoming document type identification, as well as the object type used to archive them.

Table 7.1 SD Incoming Document Types for Optical Archiving

SD Document Type	Incoming Document Type	Object Type
Sales activity information	SDIACTINFO	VBKA
Customer response to sales activity	SDIACTRESP	VBKA
Inquiry (sales activity)	SDIACTINQ	VBKA
Inquiry	SDIINQUIRY	VBAK
Inquiry change	SDIINQUICH	VBAK
Sales order	SDIORDER	VBAK
Sales order change	SDIORDCHAN	VBAK
Complaint	SDICOMPLAI	VBAK
Contract	SDICONTRAC	VBAK
Contract change	SDICONTRCH	VBAK
Delivery schedule	SDIDELPLAN	VBAK
Delivery schedule change	SDIDELPLCH	VBAK
Delivery note	SDIPOD	VBAK

Incoming document types have to be assigned to SD document types in Customizing for Sales and Distribution before optical archiving can be enacted. You can then establish which SD documents shall be optically archived and where bar codes are to be used.

From Here

This chapter is about using some of the common-sense techniques for managing and obviating conventional paperwork. These techniques are recognized as beneficial and therefore worth supporting with SAP R/3 SD functions.

You might like to move on to one of the following:

- Chapter 8, "Using Modern Sales Systems"
- Chapter 9, "Using Internet Applications"
- Chapter 10, "Operating the WebRFC Gateway Interface"
- Chapter 11, "Programming the Internet Transaction Server"
- Chapter 12, "Interpreting SD Organizational Structures"

Part
II

Ch
7

Getting Results with the New Technologies

Using Modern Sales Systems

Aligning the SD System with Customer Requirements

There are several techniques and operational skills that make use of standard SAP R/3 functionality and focus work and smooth the flow. Consignment stock and returnable packaging are examples of special commodities. The theme of keeping in touch with customers is extended by looking at the ways in which the SD application can be set up to build a database for the sales support team and used to locate potential customers.

The SAP R/3 SD application is fully "aware" of the importance of keeping closely in touch with your competitors and their products; it provides valuable techniques for documenting and retrieving this information in ways that can best contribute to sharp pricing and market-leading provision of added value to your goods and services.

You would expect to manage sales activities carefully, and the SD-CAS module does just that. The module is named Computer Assisted Selling, but you might prefer to think of it as Computer Assisted Salespersons. It can call for help from direct mailing functionality and the cornucopia of Internet catalogs, which are always available.

Smoothing the Flow of SD Business

A *backorder* is an order item for which you cannot promise to meet the required delivery date. You will want to do what you can to meet the order as soon as possible. However, you may want to give preference to certain customers if there is a shortage. Smoothing in this area of business may be more of an art than a technique.

What you can do is survey what material availability issues are waiting to turn themselves into problems and customer complaints.

Progressing Backorders

The backorder or backlog processing functions are designed to first show you the sales documents for specific materials and automatically review the materials available to meet them on the due dates. You can then elect to handle the situation in various ways.

For the materials of which there's a shortage, you may be able to assign ATP stock to the order item quantities that are outstanding. You may prefer to withdraw already confirmed quantities and reassign them to different items, even to other customers.

If a material is normally managed in bulk for a customer as a summarized total of his requirements, manual backorder processing is not applicable. Customers with individual requirements can have their backorders processed with a selection list or by material.

Assembling a List of Backorders   You can make a list of backorders with this sequence:

1. Select Logistics>SD>Sales.
2. Select Environment>Backorders>Backorder Processing>SD Documents.

3. Specify your required selection criteria, such as the delivering plant, the sold-to party, or the purchase order number.

4. Select Program>Execute.

For each material identified by your search, the system will display the relevant sales document information, such as the following:

- The first delivery date
- Ordered quantity
- Confirmed quantity
- Open quantity

It is possible to go into an individual sales document and have the document status, the document flow, and changes to the document also be available.

Mark the documents of interest and choose as follows:

- Environment>Document
- Environment>Document Status
- Environment>Document Flow
- Environment>Document Changes

This sequence has to be repeated for each material.

When you see a material and a corresponding sales order you intend to work on, mark it and select Edit>Backorders. You will see the following information quantified in the storage units of the material:

- Previously committed quantity.
- Cumulative ATP quantity, which is the stock available to promise for further use in backorders or new orders; each quantity is displayed by requirements date or inward goods movement date and MRP element.

N O T E   When a date of requirement is generated by a sales order, it will be the same as the material availability date.

- Position your cursor on the MRP element that you intend to process and select Edit>Change Committed Qty.

You will be limited to highlighted MRP elements, which are those selected by your search and for which quantities of the material have already been committed. If additional quantities have been committed for deliveries, they will not appear in this display or order information in backlog.

Nevertheless, the system will recognize that any quantities committed for deliveries are no longer available to promise and so should not be included in the ATP total.

When you see the Change Committed Quantities screen, you will be able to see details of the selected MRP element in the lower section of the screen, under Sales Requirements.

Interpreting the Sales Requirements in Backorders   The following data is displayed for each sales order item:

- Order number
- Item number
- Material availability date
- Open quantity, which is the quantity still to be delivered
- Committed quantity, which is the quantity confirmed during backorder processing
- Total committed quantity, which is the total quantity confirmed for the sales order item or the committed quantity total of all schedule lines
- ATP quantity, which is the quantity available for outward goods movement

Your scope for taking action on backorders is defined by the Sales Requirements screen:

- Distribution of the ATP quantity
- Redistribution of confirmed order quantities

You can reach the sales document by selecting Display>Additional Functions, where you have the following options:

- Variable Views
- Scope of Check
- Exception Messages
- MRP Elements

The main facilities are described in the following sections.

Distributing the ATP Quantities

If you have ATP quantities that you intend to distribute, take the following route:

1. Access Backorder Processing>Change Committed Quantity.
2. Enter a quantity in the Committed field in the Sales Requirements section. This quantity can fulfill some or all of the requirements for the backordered item.
3. Press Enter to display what will be the updated requirements situation, taking into account any action you have just taken.
4. Select Copy to confirm the data.
5. Save your changes by selecting Backorder Processing>Save.

If you marked more than one material, you will be taken back to work on the next.

Redistributing Confirmed Order Quantities

If you decide to take back some or all of an order quantity that has already been confirmed, you will be able to add it to the ATP total or reassign the quantity to a backordered item that has higher priority.

Redistribution is achieved the following way:

1. Access the Backorder Processing: Change Committed Quantity screen.
2. Reduce the quantity in the Committed field by the quantity you need elsewhere.
3. Press Enter to display the updated requirements situation.
4. Select Copy to confirm the data.
5. Distribute the freed quantity.

Managing Consignment Stock

A stock of consignment goods is stored with the customer but still owned by the supplier. The customer does not have to pay for it unless and until it is removed from consignment stock. If any of this stock is not required, it can be returned to the supplier.

If you are the supplier, however, you must include the value of this consignment stock in your accounting system, just as if it were being held in your own plant. You need to keep track of how much consignment stock of each material is held by each of your customers and how much is held by you in your own plant.

Your inventory management accounts will define consignment stock as an example of Special Stock and assign it to individual customers.

There are four actions you can take with consignment stock:

- Create a consignment fill-up on document type KB
- Create a consignment issue on document type KA
- Create a consignment pickup on document type KE
- Create a consignment return on document type KR

You have to use the right sales order type for each processing action, as indicated by the type codes.

Managing Consignment Stock Through a Special Stock Partner   One of the business partner types is a special stock partner. It is recognized as a third party, distinct from the supplier and the customer.

Consignment goods intended for a special stock partner are processed as follows:

1. Create a customer master record for the special stock partner and assign account group 0001 or DEBI.
2. Identify the special stock partner in the customer master record on the Partner screen via the partner function SB. This will become the default partner function in document headers and items for this customer.

Creating a Consignment Fill-Up   Various activities occur when you ship consignment stock to a customer via a consignment fill-up order type KB, as follows:

- If special stock does not yet exist in your inventory for the customer or for their special stock partner, the system creates it when the goods issue is posted.
- The fill-up quantity is removed from regular inventory in your plant and is added to the special stock for the customer. This does not affect the valuated stock for your plant.

The consignment stock remains your company's property and so there is no pricing activity.

The consignment stock fill-up procedure is as follows:

1. Create a sales order using order type KB.
2. Identify the customer, the consignment goods, and the delivering plant.
3. Enter all other relevant data and save the sales order.
4. Create a delivery for the sales order, and after picking has been successfully carried out, post goods issue.

The goods movement type involved is a stock transfer, which causes consignment special stock to be created for the customer concerned when the goods issue is posted. If special stock of this kind already exists in the delivering plant for this customer, the goods are posted to this special stock.

Creating a Consignment Issue   When your customer wants to sell or use some of your consignment stock held in his plant, you have to use a consignment issue order type KE. Various activities will ensue when this order is posted:

- The relevant quantity is subtracted from the customer's special stock and from your own total valuated stock.
- Pricing must now follow because the goods now belong to the customer. An invoice will surely follow.

Creating a Consignment Pickup   The customer may have had enough of your consignment stock and want to return some. You must document the transaction in the system by a consignment pickup order type KA.

When goods issue is posted for the pickup, the system will subtract the relevant quantity from the customer's special stock and return it to your regular stock at your plant, where the goods are returned. There is no effect on the value of your stock because you already owned the pickup quantity.

A pickup can be arranged like this:

1. Create a sales order using sales order type KA.
2. Identify the customer, the consignment goods, and the plant to which the goods are to be returned.
3. Complete the relevant data and save the sales order.
4. Create a returns delivery for the sales order and accept the system proposal of delivery type LR.

5. Post a goods issue to initiate a transfer posting of customer special stock to your plant stock.

Creating a Consignment Return   A customer may want to return some material to consignment stock after it has been issued and he or she has had claim on it. You need to make a consignment return order type KR.

When goods issue is posted, the relevant quantity will be added to the customer's special stock at his plant, where the goods are returned.

Ownership has changed in this case, so billing is relevant in the form of a credit memo for the returned goods. This can be automatically blocked until you approve the request for a credit memo.

Displaying Consignment Stock   You may want to take a look at the consignment stock you own in one or more customers' plants. You can do so with this method:

1. Select Logistics>Materials Management>Inventory Management.
2. Select Environment>Stock>Stock Overview.
3. Enter your selection criteria.
4. Enter the special stock indicator W.
5. Mark all the fields in the Select Display Levels section.
6. Select Program>Execute.
7. Position the cursor on the Consignment Stock at Customer line.
8. Select Edit>Choose.

You will see the current consignment stock with customers for the material selected.

Managing Returnable Packaging

Returnable packaging is material on free loan and is stored at a customer location. It remains your company's property unless the customer does not return it to you by a specified time, in which can you can charge him for it.

If your company does not actually want the returnable packaging back, you can sell it to the third party without ever having it delivered to your plant.

Returnable packaging is rather like consignment stock. You still own it and must include it in your valuated stock inventory, but you have to keep track of what is where so that you can locate its value in a customer's location.

There are three main transactions you can use in support of inventory management:

- Create a returnable packaging shipment using a normal order item or a free-of-charge delivery.
- Create a returnable packaging pickup using order type LA.
- Create a returnable packaging issue using order type LN.

Returnable packaging is managed in the inventory as special stock that is assigned to individual customers. The material master record for a returnable packaging material is classified with item category LEIH.

If you are using a third party in conjunction with returnable packaging, this company must be defined as a special stock partner.

If a carrier is identified in your vendor master records and you want to have it work with returnable packaging, it must also be recorded on a customer master record so that it can be assigned returnable packaging stock.

Understanding Intercompany Business Processing

Intercompany business processing refers to business transactions that take place between two companies at the company code level belonging to one organization. For example, a company orders goods from a plant that is assigned to another company code in the same corporate enterprise.

By definition, a *company code* is a legal entity that completes its own financial documents. Therefore, intercompany business transactions represent value movements between accounting entities.

Intercompany sales could proceed as follows:

1. The sales organization of the ordering company code creates a sales order and orders goods from a plant assigned to another company code.

2. The plant in the delivering company code delivers the goods to the customer for whom the sales organization placed the order.

3. The delivering company code bills the ordering company code with an intercompany billing document via an agreed intercompany price.

4. The ordering company code bills the customer and pays some of the proceeds to the delivering company code.

An intercompany stock transfer might take the following form:

- A purchasing organization assigned to the ordering company code creates a purchase order to get goods from a plant assigned to another company code.

- The plant in the delivering company code delivers the goods to the plant for which the purchasing organization ordered the goods.

When your customer is another company code in the same organization, you have to have a special customer master record for him or her. It will establish the billing procedure and, if appropriate, the currency conversion arrangements. Intercompany condition types are provided to arrange for the internal pricing structure.

Understanding Sales Support

The aims of a business' sales support function may be listed, although not in order of any particular priority, to:

- Promote business development.
- Improve customer service.
- Provide a mechanism through which all in-house and external sales personnel can contribute any useful information to a central facility, from which they can also draw freely in order to further their own sales activities.
- Support sales promotion by individuals.
- Improve communication throughout the sales force.
- Provide methods for evaluating competitors and their products.

A computer-based sales support function would also be expected to automate as many of the Sales department's routine tasks as possible. Master data and the documented evidence of business transaction processing are sales support's prime sources of direct information. The SD-IS Sales and Distribution Information System is a further source of analyses based on sales summaries and the statistics of sales orders. The sales support activities also provide input to the SD-IS Sales and Distribution Information System.

Defining the Role of Sales Support

Many, if not most, sales by your company may be to existing customers. The first target population has to be your existing folio of customers. However, you need new business and new customers.

A realist might say that computer processing does not sell, but that computer-assisted sales representatives are more effective than those who rely on memory or on ancient card indexes. Be that as it may, the SAP R/3 SD application has two elements to its sales support facilities: data about sales and data about salespeople (your own and those of your customers and prospects).

N O T E A sales activity is represented as an SD document and is primarily a record of previous contact with a customer.

Just in case you think there must be very little information that could be stored in sales support, consider the following list of SD master records and those that are consulted from other applications:

- Customers
- Sales prospects
- Competitors
- Your products

- Your sales materials
- Your competitors' products
- Your competitors' sales materials
- Sales activity masters, with records of the contacts made and their outcomes
- Analyses of optical archives that store the incoming and outgoing documents, such as customer letters and complaints
- Optically archived responses to direct mailing, and marketing flyers identified with particular sales activities

As you would expect, the Sales Information System is directly linked to the Sales Support component and offers an extensive reporting service. You can call for help in planning sales and marketing strategies on the basis of previous marketing history. You can later analyze the outcomes of your sales activities, such as incoming orders by sales office and sales group.

If your operator has learned how to exploit the SD list functions, there can be a list of all open sales activities on the screen as soon as the caller's or target prospect's identity has been determined.

If you are responsible for a sales activity, you can elicit a history of the activity and the sales or inquiries resulting from that activity.

Building Master Data for Sales Support

Nothing is for nothing. You must have master data in your sales support environment before you can use it.

For example, you may want to set up systematic recording of information on the following types of person or company:

- Sales partners and customers
- Sales prospects
- Competitors
- Contact people
- Internal sales personnel

You will, of course, maintain immaculate master data on your products.

Recording Information on Sales Prospects

The management of customers and sales prospects constitutes a major part of the SD-CAS sales support software component. The customer master record holds most of the information in the standard SAP format of *attributes*, which are clusters of thematically related data fields.

A customer master has records for general details, as well as the following:

- Company organizational structure, annual sales revenue, number of employees, industry sector, status as a valued customer of your organization, and market areas of goods and services

- Contact persons by name and position
- Contact person details such as first name, form of salutation, birth date, marital status, buying habits, sales strategy to use, visiting hours, home address, business address, interests, and pastimes

If you are looking for a particular contact person, you can search for the company by name or number; alternatively, you can search for the person's details, which enables you to keep track of that person if he or she moves from one of your customers to another. You may have a very large database of potential customers on whom you are keeping a watching brief and a diligent data-collecting effort.

There are no restrictions on the definition and number of attributes maintained in your master records for customers, sales prospects, and contact persons.

A *prospect* is handled by the SD-Sales and Distribution module as a customer without a record of past purchases. The detailed record fields and processing functions are the same, except that you will not (yet) need to activate billing or output control, although you may want to try a mailing.

If a sales prospect becomes a customer, you can upgrade the master record from prospect to customer simply by changing the account group.

Recording Information on Internal Sales Personnel

A sales visit, a telephone call, a sales letter—these are all sales activities that can be identified on a master record and hence associated with whatever the outcomes are. In particular, the system can relate these records to the records in HR-Human Resources, which identify a particular person in your company.

Linking Optical Archiving with Sales Support

ArchiveLink is the connection between sales support and the optical archive through which information can flow from the contacts to the population of customers and prospects.

If you are in sales support, and if you can find a way of analyzing the optical archives, then you may be able to tap a rich source of information on how your sales activities and product development should proceed if these expenditures are to lead to better results.

The optical archive will also contain your company's responses to contacts from the business community and the general public. You may be able to trace links between information releases and sales.

Even if you are not aspiring to subtle analysis, the optical archive is a valuable resource of stored technical, sales, and marketing literature that can be efficiently accessed because of the retrieval facilities available in the R/3 system.

The details of optical archiving are touched on in Chapter 8, "Using Modern Sales Systems."

Defining Sales Partners

Because they represent your company in the market, each sales and sales support person is given a master record in the SD-Sales and Distribution System.

Sales personnel are defined as people who are documented in the HR-Human Resources System as your company's direct employees, and who also are recognized by the SD-Sales and Distribution module because of the roles they may play in sales and distribution activities.

Sales partners are recognized and documented in the SD-Sales and Distribution System as consultancy partners or sales agents, but they are not direct employees of your company and do not necessarily have personnel records in your HR-Human Resources System.

Accepting Automatic Proposal of Partner Functions

If the same employees are always responsible for sales to a particular customer, you can record their personnel numbers and functions in the customer master record's Partner Functions screen. For example, ER denotes a person who is the employee responsible (any department), PE denotes a sales employee.

If you subsequently create a sales activity for this customer, the system will suggest that you use the same partners, or the appropriate partners in terms of their sales area responsibilities.

Recording Information on Sales Partners and Customers

Existing customer master records can be accessed from sales support, and you may be authorized to create new masters. You may be dealing with companies that have the status of sales partners because you have an agreement with them to cooperatively market your products, their products, or both. You will want to maintain master records for these sales partners.

Thus, you have a system of master records—each assured to be unique by the internal numbering system—that can document the following entities and their activities:

- Customers
- Sales prospects
- Competitors
- Sales contacts
- Sales personnel
- Sales partners

Interpreting the Sales Summary

The *sales summary* is a condensation of the most important information your company can collate about your customers with sales records, and about your prospective customers with a null sales record.

The sales summary displays order data and payment terms from the customer master and transaction data, such as sales figures and sales activities.

The sales summary is zoned into information blocks, which can be combined into views that contain related data on a particular customer. Each user can be assigned a suitable view of the sales summary according to his or her areas of responsibility. These assignments are made in Customizing for Reporting. The default is the standard view.

If you are in a sales activity, you can select Information>Sales Summary and be shown the summary for the customer you are currently working with.

If you are in the Initial Sales Support screen, you should select Business Partners>List>Sales Summary. You can then define the organizational data and customer names of interest.

If you have the address list for a direct mailing, you can mark a customer in the list and select Information>Sales Summary.

With all this information, you should be well prepared to make a sales visit or phone call.

Utilizing Automatic Messaging

If you have previously set up suitable personnel master records and sales personnel data, you can link them so that an incoming sales activity document that requires attention can be automatically sent to the person responsible.

Creating and Maintaining Sales Personnel Data

Any person you identify in SAP R/3 must be represented by a personnel master record, which is most conveniently managed in the HR-Human Resources application. Once he or she has a personnel master record, you can identify that person by a unique personnel number.

To set up automatic messaging and other functions that nominate a person from a sales document, you must maintain sales personnel data from the Sales Support screen. This record will include the follow information:

- Employee's personnel number
- Plant to which the employee is assigned
- Address in the company
- Organizational location
- Sales data

To prepare for automatic messaging, the personnel number has to be linked to the system username of the sales employee by the infotype 105 and the communication type 0001.

Identifying Employees Responsible and Sales Employees

In order to nominate the person responsible, assign to that person the Responsible Partner function in the master records of any sales activities for which he or she is responsible.

If you want to nominate an employee who is knowledgeable about a sales activity but is not the person responsible, you can assign the Sales Employee Partner function in the sales activity's master record.

Using Sales Personnel Information

Once you have set up sales personnel information that is linked with the HR personnel files, there are various possibilities for using this information. The following examples illustrate this facility:

- A person in the sales office staff can call for a list of all the follow-up telephone calls for which he or she is responsible for a particular workday.
- A salesperson can call for a retrospective report on the sales calls he or she made over a specified period.

These kinds of lists can obviously be used as work lists.

Maintaining User Master Records

One of a user master record's functions is to elicit a particular reaction from the sales support functions when that user calls upon them. The following examples illustrate this facility:

- Propose, as defaults, the details of the user's sales area, which is defined by the user's sales organization, distribution channel, and division.
- Propose the user's sales office and sales group.

The system administrator can maintain the details of a user:

1. Select System>User Profile>User Parameters.
2. Edit the parameters that have changed.
3. Save the user profile data.

Recording Information on Contact People

A *contact person* may be an individual buyer or a person you know of in a customer or prospect company. In SAP R/3, a prospect is recorded on a customer master, although there will be no sales history. The Sales Support component provides storage for building additional information records that can be linked to the customer master as necessary. These records allow a salesperson to enter information in whatever attributes have proved useful. The system offers some suggested types of data attributes to record information such as the following:

- Contact people in the customer company
- Sales prospects
- Sales partners
- Visiting hours
- Buying habits of particular contacts
- Topics of interest to the contact person

This database of sales information can be used in sales staff training and in preparing for a sales call. You may be able to consult the database when choosing target companies or persons for a promotional campaign. There may also be hints as to the type of promotional gift that might be appreciated.

You can create and maintain contact information directly in a customer, sales partner, or sales prospect master record. You can also access the Business Partner menu in the Sales Support System.

The advantage of working within Sales Support is that you can search for an existing contact person record, even if you have only a fragment of relevant information, such as the last name of the contact person or part of the telephone number.

Salespeople may change companies or work for several companies at the same time. Therefore, as of SAP R/3 release 3.0, you can link one contact person master record with several other customers or prospects by assigning them the partner function AP. This allows you to make contact with a person who is perhaps no longer in the company with which the initial contact was made.

Documenting Competitors and Their Products

New markets and new market segments are often detected by closely observing what your competitors are doing and not doing. You can store this kind of data systematically in the SD-Sales and Distribution System.

You can use the system of master records to store data on your competitor companies, using the same structure you use for customers, but with some important additions:

- Industry classifications
- Annual sales
- Employees
- Other information about the competitor, stored in a structured format that allows you to conduct searches and compile statistical summaries

You need a database that includes all the details that are important for your own products, but if you want to make a comparison, you also need your competitors' products to be entered, using a compatible set of master attributes. A special kind of material master record type is defined for this purpose. Like your own, competitive products can be assigned to product hierarchies upon which a comparison can be based.

You can also assemble structured texts to locate critical information in ways that are susceptible to classification and search techniques. You might store your competitors' marketing profiles and details of key people this way.

Working in the Sales Support Environment

The sales support environment is designed to accept useful information in the form of material master data for your own and your competitors' products. You may well hold as much data about competitive products as you do about your own.

For example, you can create and maintain as product proposals those predefined aggregates of materials that constitute useful models. It's from those that you copy reference data into quotations and sales orders.

Accessing Other Sources of Information

Your electronic mail inbox can be accessed from the Sales Support component, as can the records from which you can compile lists of such items as sales, shipping, and billing documents. You might focus on a list compiled online for the parent company of a contact person who is talking to you on the telephone or via email.

The SIS-Sales Information System can be accessed from the Sales Support component if you need to evaluate customers on any criterion. Thus, you might view actual orders and planned orders by individual salespersons, by sales office, by customer, by product, and so on.

As you would expect, it's not difficult to access pricing data from the Sales Support component. You can also create and maintain prices, discounts, and surcharges there if you have the authorization.

Exploiting Sales Activities and Promotions

The outcomes of previous sales activities have to be stored in order to become an input to the design of the next sales campaign. The SD-Sales and Distribution System stores all interactions with the potential customer population in the sales activities data structures. The following are examples of activities by SD-CAS Sales Support that are documented by recording the outcomes of sales activities in such records:

- Sales calls in person
- Telemarketing calls
- Brochure mailing
- Calls received from potential customers
- Presentations
- Conferences
- Promotions

The standard SD-Sales and Distribution System recognizes three activity types:

- Sales call
- Sales letter
- Telephone call

You may define other sales activity types to add to this list during customizing.

The basic information on the SAP document (generated as a result of a sales activity) includes the following data elements:

- Customer number
- Contact person at the customer company
- Your sales organization or sales group conducting the sales activity
- Date and time of the sales activity

- Type of sales activity carried out
- The reason for the activity, which can be entered using standard keys
- The outcome of the activity, which can be entered using standard keys and can have additional standard short text or free-form text; for example, "sales order" and "invitation to give a presentation" are standard activity outcomes that the system will offer as options

Authorization may be required to change or display a sales activity document.

When an authorized salesperson is processing a sales activity, the data from the SD-IS Sales and Distribution Information System can be accessed to show, for example, sales trends for this market segment or for this customer.

You can amplify the information carried by a sales activity master record by defining a set of standard texts that specify how a set of keys is to be interpreted. For example, you can set up codes for preparation notes, reports, and reactions to sales promotions. If you attach one of these codes to a free-text note or a standard short text phrase, you can store the data in a way that will make it easy to access, classify, and use in the future.

Your sales activities will often have specific follow-up actions that can be predefined and permanently associated with the sales activity. They can be scheduled by elapsed time or given a firm date for completion. When you are planning your sales support work, you can call for a display of the planned sales activities and follow-up actions that are outstanding. The system also gives you complete histories of previous sales activities.

Using the Sales Activities

The standard version of the SAP R/3 system recognizes sales calls, telephone calls, and sales letters as sales activity types.

The types of sales activity available and the data maintained for each are things the system administrator controls during Customizing for Sales.

However, you can maintain up to 10 freely definable attributes, which can be applied to sales activities that take place in your company. For example, you might want to have an attribute that can specify whether a sales activity is associated with a consulting project. You might also want to have a signal to show that the sales activity has been triggered by a problem, for which you could possibly append an explanatory text.

Entering Sales Activities

Your administrator will have configured each sales activity so as to collect certain data and make some proposals. The following sequence portrays one such activity, a telephone call, being handled by the Sales Support System:

1. Select Logistics>SD>Sales Support.
2. Select Sales Activities>Telephone Calls>Create.
3. Enter your sales area definitions if they have not been proposed by default.

4. Enter a value in the Customer field; it will identify the customer.

5. Select one or none of the contact people that will be suggested automatically.

6. Enter data as necessary.

At this stage you can record information in any of the following standard fields (to which Customizing may have added others to suit your business):

- Comment, which is a short description of the activity. This will be used as a matchcode for locating the sales activity master records.

- Date and time of the activity.

- Activity reason, outcome, analysis, and status. Default values for these fields may have been defined in Customizing. They can be used to build lists of follow-up actions and for reporting.

- Follow-up activity and when it should be made. For example, another telephone call is normally proposed automatically as the follow-up of a telephone call.

- Enter text as required under any of the standard headings such as Report and Telephone Notes.

N O T E   Your logon language will be determined by your user profile, and this will be used both when you make entries and when the system responds. If you want to enter text in a language other than your logon language, select All Languages on the text screen and prefix the text with the language code that identifies the one you intend to use.

- If your telephone call is fruitful, you can move directly to create sales documents if your distribution channel and sales division have already been identified to the system.

- If you intend to take one of the predefined follow-up actions, select Goto>Follow-Up Sales Proc.

When you save your sales activity document, the incompletion log may have been set to offer you a dialog box in order to remind you that the document is incomplete. You can save it as an incomplete document or access the incompletion log where you can edit the data.

Processing Special Sales Orders

Promotions and sales deals are agreements. They are usually treated as special sales orders. A promotion marketing plan may include several different sales deals covering several product lines.

A sales deal for a product line may be defined to offer a variety of promotional arrangements, such as customer-specific discounts or material-based discounts.

Each deal will be processed by the system in accord with specific condition records linked to the sales deal. These may be existing condition records or newly created condition records, which could have been made by copying and editing existing records.

If there is a link between a sales deal and a promotion, the condition record will also carry the promotion number, so that you can analyze the contributions of the sales deal to a specific promotion.

Defining Agreement Types

A promotion or a sales deal has to refer to an agreement previously defined. This will be established to set limits to the following data elements:

- Internal and external number ranges allowed
- Condition types and condition tables that can be used in the agreement type
- Which overview screen the user sees when creating master data
- Which validity period is proposed as default
- Additional control data for the condition types that can be used for the agreement

If the types of promotions and sales deals you intend to use have been previously defined, you can enter the master data in the system. Each agreement will need general data, and sales deals will also have to specify individual condition records.

Managing Direct Mailing

The standard SAP R/3 direct mailing function requires you to provide the following data elements:

- Address list for direct mailing
- Content and layout for the correspondence
- Enclosures for each addressee

This information will be stored in a direct mailing master record so that you can use it again or take it as a reference model when creating a new mailing.

You can use selection variants or search specifications to cull addresses from customers, sales prospects, and contact persons. Editing and all variants of customized texts can be used to make each mailing specific to each company in your group and, if necessary, specific to each of the units in your customer's company.

If you buy address lists, the system will automatically check that potential customers' new addresses are in accord with the information you already have.

The person responsible for each mailing can be identified in the mailing master record.

The direct mailing is defined as a sales activity and will be precise as to its contents, such as the following:

- A sales letter
- An invitation to a trade fair

- A product sample
- A brochure or product documentation

A direct mailing master record can also specify a follow-up activity and the date on which it is to be carried out.

The mailing list is usually assembled from the following types of elements:

- Existing customers
- Sales prospects
- Contact people

You can specify whether the addresses used shall be private or business. You may well assign the mailing as a background job.

The mechanics of the mailing itself depend on your having the following elements available and correct:

- Correspondence.
- Enclosures.
- Master data records for the direct mail recipients.
- A customer master record maintained with your own organization as the sold-to party. This will be used to accumulate the costs of any enclosures for assignment to the Marketing department account.
- Master data for the sales personnel responsible for the direct mailing.
- Master data for any enclosures you want to send with the correspondence.
- Condition records for the output type MAAK for carrying out the direct mailing. These condition records control printing the direct mailing, creating the internal order for any samples, and initiating any follow-up activities.

Creating Correspondence

The SAPscript word-processing environment operates with standard texts into which variable text can be inserted using the INCLUDES function. You can create a standard text from Sales Support via the following sequence:

1. Select Logistics>SD>Sales Support.
2. Select Sales Promotions>Standard Texts.
3. Enter the name of your correspondence in the Text Name field.
4. Assign SDMD as the Text ID used for standard texts in Sales Support.
5. Enter the language of the text if it not to be the same as your logon language.
6. Press Enter to create the standard text.

You will probably want to have variable text, such as the address of the recipient and perhaps a signature section, in your standard letter. An INCLUDE is a placeholder for a parameter, such as an address that will be inserted when the text is being assembled for printing or other output. When you are in the word processing screen, you must follow this sequence:

1. Put the cursor on the line where you want the INCLUDE to appear.

2. Select Include>Text>Standard.

3. In the Include Text dialog box, enter the name of the INCLUDE in the Text Name field.

N O T E   SD-CAS-BEISPIEL-ADDRESS and SD-CAS-BEISPIEL-GRUSSFORMEL are standard
INCLUDE names. ■

4. Enter SDKI in the Text ID field to signify that you are referring to INCLUDES for use in Sales Support.

N O T E   When you are using the word-processing system to prepare a text for a specific customer,
the system automatically selects the recipient's language as defined in their master
records. ■

5. Press Enter to have the INCLUDE appear in your standard text.

Creating a Direct Mailing

If all the preparations have been made, you can create a direct mailing:

1. Select Logistics>SD>Sales Support.

2. Select Sales Promotions>Direct Mailing>Create.

3. Enter a short description of the mailing in the Comment field. This comment can be used to search for the mailing later.

4. Enter a report name in the Selection Report field or search for possible entries from which to select. RVADRSEL is a standard report that can be used to create and maintain a mailing list. You will be offered any report classified CASS.

5. Display the possible entries. The system automatically lists all reports that belong to the report class CASS.

6. Identify a selection variant (if you have one that will select the data you require).

7. Select Edit>Find Correspondence.

8. Maintain a follow-up activity and follow-up activity date.

9. Enter your selection criteria and press Enter.

N O T E   If you entered a short description or title of the direct mailing when you were setting it up,
this title will appear in the direct mailing's Short Title field. ■

10. Save the direct mailing before you attempt to create or maintain your list of addresses.

Creating a Mailing Address List   Long list generation is a task you will want to assign to background processing. Use the following procedure:

1. Select Logistics>SD>Sales Support.
2. Select Sales Promotions>Direct Mailing>Change.
3. Enter the ID number of your direct mailing and press Enter to display it.
4. To create the list of mailing addresses, select Edit>Address List.

If you previously entered a selection variant, the system will create the address list for you to accept or edit. If you did not enter a selection variant, you will have the chance to enter your search criteria. You will be offered the choice of Create Immediately or Create Background, in which case you must indicate the date and time you want the background job to run.

The next stage is to either save the direct mailing or go directly to the Attaching an Enclosure procedure.

One or more users can edit an address list in *intervals*, which are blocks that start with 100 addresses, and you can assemble an address list merely for evaluation purposes.

Attaching an Enclosure to a Direct Mailing   Having created a direct mailing, you can include an enclosure:

1. Select Goto>Sample Enclosure.

N O T E   The system treats a sample enclosure as a product proposal representing a sample order of what you intend to send to each addressee. The sales order to an internal sold-to party is completed by adding the quantity when the mailing is sent to the printer. ▤

2. Enter the identifications of the product samples, brochures, documentation, or promotional gifts that you intend to send to each direct mailing recipient.
3. Save the direct mailing.

Maintaining a Product Catalog on the Internet

Your company will probably have a product catalog in paper form. You may also offer it as a CD-ROM in order to make it cheaper to distribute and easier for the prospective customer to search. The CD-ROM also allows the inclusion of multimedia presentations. However, there are several extra advantages to maintaining a product catalog on the Internet. The following factors may be significant for your company:

- Global availability with minimum distribution costs.
- Errors can be corrected as they are detected.
- An Internet product catalog can be continually updated with up-to-the-minute information without incurring additional production expenses.
- An Internet catalog can be justified for short production cycles (reduced layout costs).

- No paper or other materials need be consumed or processed in production or distribution.
- An Internet catalog can be provided with direct email ordering or inquiry mechanisms available continuously, worldwide.
- Peak ordering times can be smoother and less order entry staff are needed.
- Response times can be reduced.

Reviewing the Product Catalog

The Product Catalog LO-MD-AM is an SAP application component that can be implemented as a passive catalog or as a product catalog with integrated sales order entry over the Internet. This component uses data from the Advertising Media Planning module in the SAP R/3 system.

The purpose of the advertising media planning functionality in R/3 is to save, call, and manage data that has been created in connection with advertising media such as catalogs, brochures, CD-ROMs, online catalogs, and multimedia point-of-sale terminals.

The Internet product catalog allows the viewer to browse freely and assign items to be ordered to a *shopping basket*, which is finally checked by the viewer before it is sent to the supplier as an inquiry, a request for a quote, or as a sales order, depending on the configuration and the wishes of the viewer.

Browsing is facilitated by search options and the following standard structure levels:

- Overview of the shop; shown as layout areas at the advertising medium layout's top level
- Detail screen for a shop
- Product lists
- Detail screen for the product

Text, pictures, and sound extracts can be associated with objects at the shop level and with items in the product lists.

The standard search functions provide the following services:

- List of products falling within a specific price interval
- Detail screen of the product when you enter its name
- Product lists sorted by product name or price

Operating a Product Catalog with Sales Order Entry

If you want a customer to have a quote created for the items in the shopping basket, your customer must be logged on with an SAP customer number and the initial password. The customer can then change the initial password.

Suppose you are offering a product catalog with sales order entry. The authorizations belonging to the object class Sales and Distribution have to be maintained for the R/3 users, with which the IAC logs on to the R/3 system via the ITS.

The product catalog can be configured to use the following methods of identifying your products:

- Material number (product)
- Material short text (short text)
- Heading from Advertising Media Processing (title)
- Heading from Advertising Media Processing (title)

From Here

This chapter is about techniques for smoothing the flow of business, which is done by having many automatic functions that are designed to anticipate the data you might otherwise have to enter by hand. In particular, the labor-intensive activities of Sales Support have been looked at from this point of view.

You might like to move on to one of the following:

- Chapter 9, "Using Internet Applications"
- Chapter 12, "Interpreting SD Organizational Structures"

Using Internet Applications

Introducing the SAP R/3 Internet Application Components

This chapter is about R/3 Internet Application Components (IACs) that have been programmed by SAP so as to integrate smoothly with the rest of your R/3 system. The Internet is developing rapidly and there are several different avenues of development. The IACs available now are being supplemented by additional software components as new developments in communication and presentation technology are released for general use.

This chapter discusses three IACs that are in widespread use in the sales and distribution business area:

- Sales Order Creation
- Sales Order Status
- Available to Promise

These IACs can be used by your staff and by your business partners. They work equally well on the Internet or on a company intranet.

Understanding the Benefits of an IAC

The purpose of an IAC is to connect SAP R/3 to a World Wide Web browser, which becomes the user interface to the SAP R/3 system. IACs are handled by a standard software program called the Internet Transaction Server (ITS) .

A Web browser is a user interface that can interpret and respond to dialogs written in Hypertext Markup Language (HTML) . This is a standard language for creating document pages that can be processed on the World Wide Web. The language's syntax is based on a set of tags or markers, usually arranged in matching pairs. These tags are recognized as commands to display the intervening text in a particular format. Tags have been defined to carry out almost all the operations that are necessary for a user to receive messages from a host computer system and to respond to the host as appropriate. As new media are brought into the scope of HTML, extra tags have to be defined. For example, there are HTML tags to change the format and color of the text included within the matched tags. If your computer does not have a color display, you will still be able to read the text in your display's default color.

N O T E   HTTP refers to the Hypertext Transfer Protocol, which defines how files are passed across systems if they are written in HTML. ▓

HTTP allows Web communication with very little restriction on the type of hardware devices that can take part. However, the HTML protocol is limited in its scope and can be inefficient in operation.

HTML functions are provided within SAP Internet Technology, which is distributed as the CA-ALW module. The SAP R/3 ITS is a program designed to improve the effectiveness of the connections between R/3 and the Internet. The software is available as of R/3 release 3.1G and runs under Windows NT 4.0 (server version).

Although the HTML protocol is conceptually simple and easy to generate on any word processing system, it demands strict adherence to the language's conventions. For example, the tag that begins a message has to match with exactly one tag that signals the end of the message. A complicated display, such as an input form, can be difficult to proofread and troubleshoot. Internet Application components for important business applications have been developed by SAP to provide a stock of standard HTML files; those files can be used either directly or as templates that you can edit to suit your particular requirements.

Part

III

Ch

9

Exploring the Standard IACs

The following sections illustrate some of these standard Internet Application Components. The IACs are grouped according to the type of business scenario in which they are most likely to be needed.

N O T E   HTML syntax has become a useful tool for creating Help documentation because it allows the reader to jump from a highlighted item in a document to another page in the same document, to another page in another document, or to a page on another computer if a suitable network connection has been established. *Internet* is the term used to include all kinds of systems that can be accessed via an HTML link, including other files in your own computer. *Intranet* is used when the network referred to is limited to a specified set of users, such as your company and its business partners. The WWW is, by definition, excluded from an intranet's scope. ▨

The number of users on the Internet is doubling each year. One of the services that these users call upon is the World Wide Web, which was developed as a mechanism for exchanging texts and performing controlled searches to locate textual strings within them. A company will typically offer a catalog in which potential customers may search for information of interest. There will be a few HTML links to promote efficient navigation through the catalog and a `Mailto` link through which a customer may place orders or email queries.

SAP R/3 IACs are designed to increase the variety of interaction modes available to Internet contacts. At the present time, the customers who have used the Internet recognized the following advantages:

- Low communication costs to many possible suppliers
- Easy procedures using a Web browser that may well be the standard desktop presentation for the user's operating system
- Continuous availability worldwide
- Outgoing and incoming messages can be dealt with when convenient, in contrast to phone calls, which are difficult to stack

Recognizing the Potential of Internet Business

As a provider of goods and services, you will probably recognize the following additional advantages of Internet business:

- Many business stages can be conducted at low cost over the Internet.
- Business processes may be overlapped and integrated, as when the buyer sends product data directly to the warehouse, which is readily interrogated to determine availability of stock.
- The customer can directly enter order and delivery data in order to accelerate the purchasing processes and reduce costs.

One benefit that all Web browser users have recognized is their rapid acquisition of skill. This is due to their manipulating the same browser for all their transactions. This will probably be the same system they use for personal Internet access. There may be a substantial reduction in staff training costs that seriously extends a company's use of a browser for business transactions and general communication.

Exploring the Mechanisms of an Internet Application Component

SAP R/3 uses two different methods for communicating with the ITS:

- IACs based on Web transactions
- IACs based on the WebRFC Gateway Interface

The differences in design and operation are discussed separately in the following sections.

Understanding IACs Based on Web Transactions

SAP R/3 IACs based on Web transactions use the DIAG interface to exchange screens and their fields' contents. You will find that they provide most of the services of the SAPGUI user interface via HTML pages and forms.

SAP R/3 standard transactions are conducted by programs written in the ABAP/4 business processing language. The ITS will not accept ABAP/4 commands directly because it has to comply with the specifications of the Business Application Interface (BAPI) . This requires that screen design and user authorization procedures be consistent across all SAP R/3 BAPIs.

The ITS uses a service name, which you can assign, to stand for each IAC that you need for your business. When you are using an IAC, the ITS will hold copies of the technical information that might be required. For example, the ITS will hold information so that the service name you assign for the IAC will be associated with all the necessary transactions that may be called for on the SAP R/3 applications, which have been installed and configured in your implementation. The ITS will manage these configuration files, along with language resources and templates that you might need to build Web pages in HTML.

Understanding IACs Based on the WebRFC Gateway Interface

SAP R/3 can call upon associated systems to perform tasks using the RFC technique. In particular, R/3 can be linked to the ITS by the RFC methodology. Any IAC that is based on WebRFC will be able to use this link to exchange data between the ITS and an R/3 system. When requested by a Web user, the ITS calls a special function module in the R/3 system. From this module—the WebRFC Gateway Interface—any program can be called and any report can be initiated. The output will then be translated into HTML format and passed to the ITS for transmission to the Internet. There will normally be various opportunities for the user to intervene and make necessary manual adjustments.

Recognizing How the IAC Build Systems Scenarios

You will seldom want to operate just a single business function on its own in the course of your business activities. Your work will take place in a specific context, as part of a routine workflow sequence. SAP has recognized these familiar sequences and prepared scenarios of IACs. These IACs conduct Web transactions between customers and your business and between one business partner and another. The following lists suggest how these scenarios of IACs are grouped and identified.

Identifying a Logistics Scenario   It will come as no surprise to discover that SAP R/3 has IACs to cover the logistics functions. In particular, there are specific IACs tuned to operate the following functions over the Internet:

- Product catalog
- Sales and distribution
- Sales order creation
- Sales order status
- Available to promise

These logistics services are provided by the R/3 system, which is linked to users through the IACs and is hence available to most Internet browser types.

Identifying a Financial Accounting Scenario   There are only two IACs available at present—Customer Account Information and Asset Information—for the Financial Accounting services.

Identifying a Controlling Scenario   The IACs developed in the controlling area concentrate on the remote management of activities and internal price lists:

- Internal Activity Allocation
- Internal Price List

Identifying a Project System Scenario   Although the project system has but one IAC, it is able to support remote management of projects by providing access to project data: Project Data Confirmation. The project system IAC collects project data and reports on it with equal facility.

Identifying a Human Resources Management Scenario   The following IACs are supported by the HR-Human Resources application:

- Employment Opportunities
- Application Status
- Who Is Who
- Calendar of Events
- Booked Events (R/3 Users)
- Booked Events (Web Users)

The HR IACs provide a comprehensive personnel system available over the Internet.

Identifying a Materials Management Scenario   The standard MM IAC is confined to control of consignment stocks and is intended for the use of business partners who have a close and continuous relationship based on the management of consignment stocks. Consignment Stocks Status is the MM IAC.

Identifying a Quality Management Scenario   The IACs associated with the QM module are concentrated on the control of certificates and notifications:

- Quality Certificates
- Quality Notifications

Identifying a Plant Maintenance and Service Management Scenario   Plant maintenance and the provision of services are both served by the following IACs:

- Service Notifications
- Measurement and Counter Readings

Identifying a Production Planning and Control Scenario   The KANBAN system of production management is fully supported by the KANBAN IAC.

Identifying an Intranet Scenario   A group of IACs has been developed to serve the shared requirements of an intranet of connected business partners:

- Materials Management
- Requirement Requests
- Requirement Request Status
- Collective Release of Purchase Requisitions
- Collective Release of Purchase Orders

Identifying a Basis Scenario   The SAP R/3 Basis system is the foundation of all R/3 activity and is particularly served by the Integrated Inbox IAC. This inbox is designed to facilitate an efficient use of communications, no matter where they originate or what channels of communication they employ.

Building and Maintaining an Internet Application Component

Even though an extensive range of IACs is already available as standard, your particular company may need or prefer to develop a unique connection between its business data processing and the sources and users of this data.

You may well need to repeat the development cycle to develop a successful IAC. You will probably need to make changes to the SAP R/3 Web Transaction function if you have developed Web objects for your new R/3 IAC.

A Web transaction is usually defined from an executable R/3 transaction by adjusting a copy and making it compatible with the ITS. The Web Studio support tool is designed to facilitate this process.

> **N O T E** Web Studio runs outside the R/3 system under Windows NT 4.0 and is included in the standard version of the Internet Transaction Server. ▓

For each Web transaction, a service description must exist in the file system of the computer on which the ITS is running. The *service description* is a file that contains all of the information that the ITS needs to call the R/3 transaction. These files can be created with Web Studio and later edited by a standard text editor.

No separate language resources need be created if an Internet transaction uses only the language-specific graphics, filenames, or texts that are supplied directly from the R/3 system. However, you have to identify the language resource files if you want to refer to graphics or texts that are specific to your particular implementation. An HTML template should contain placeholders that can be associated at runtime with the logon language's resources. These language resources are consulted by the ITS to locate suitable entries for the placeholders.

Each R/3 transaction screen needs a corresponding HTML template that uses HTML business instructions to identify the fields in the screen. These templates can be created from a screen description using Web Studio, which will automatically generate the corresponding placeholders and control instructions. The HTML pages will usually require manual editing after changes have been made. Some screen techniques, such as the use of frames, cannot be applied automatically by Web Studio.

Web Studio has the following functionality:

- Generate HTML templates that include an R/3 function's remote call
- Generate service descriptions
- Edit all external text-based objects
- Communicate with the R/3 correction and transport system
- Communicate with the CheckIn/CheckOut functionality for the Web objects

Web Studio supports activities executed outside the R/3 system. For example, Web Studio places in the directory structure all files required by the ITS and makes sure that all objects are stored in the R/3 system. Any file required by an IAC based on Web transactions can be edited in Web Studio. Service descriptions can be generated by Web Studio under the control of dialog boxes and do not require manual editing.

The ITS Debugger is an ITS operating mode for testing an IAC. In addition, you can call for status information by specifying special parameters in the URL that calls the IAC.

Understanding How the ITS Works

You cannot access the R/3 system directly from a Web browser or via an HTML server because the two systems use different protocols and data formats. The ITS acts as an interface. When an SAP user sends a request to the HTML server, the server prompts the ITS program to set up a connection to an R/3 system.

The SAP system's screen can then be used to send information to the ITS and to the R/3 system with which it has connected. The R/3 system does not have to know that the user is using a terminal through the ITS. It converts the screen data supplied by the SAP system into an HTML document. The HTML document is passed, via the HTML server, to the Web browser where it is displayed. In the opposite direction, field contents in HTML forms can be converted to screen data. The user's browser acts as a standard SAPGUI.

In practice, the ITS is an extremely complex application. Various components will be resident while others are loaded only when required. The ITS will manage the various Web users, their different Internet transactions, and the system resources they need.

Understanding R/3 Development Objects for the Internet

Data exchange to and from the Internet is carried out using SAP R/3 transactions and function modules. Various software development objects are needed to create and transmit service messages. They will normally be configured during customizing. For example, the material availability service provided over the Internet is defined as follows:

- Development class—MDW1
- Transaction—CKAV
- Function group for the screens—W61V
- Function modules—BAPI_MATERIAL_AVAILABILITY

The ITS controls data output by inserting data in the appropriate fields of nominated output forms, which are presented to the Internet or to your company's intranet in the HTML format. It's done in HTML so that they can be read by the various browsers that serve the users.

The output forms are held in the TEMPLATES directory's CKAV subdirectory. The following forms are used:

SAPMAVCK_500.HTML	CKAV_D.HTRC
SAPMAVCK_600.HTML	CKAV_E.HTRC
SAPMAVCK_1100.HTML	CKAV_J.HTRC
SAPMAVCK_1200.HTML	
SAPMAVCK_1300.HTML	

Dealing with Security

The ITS is linked in two directions: to the HTTP server and to the R/3 system.

Communication between the HTTP server and the ITS is based on the ISAPI (MS IIS 2.0) and NSAPI (Netscape Enterprise Server 2.0).

Web transactions between the ITS and the R/3 system are based on the SAPGUI protocol, or in the case of the WebRFC Gateway Interface, on the Remote Function Call (RFC) .

Part

III

Ch

9

Special certification services, such as Kerberos or SecuDe, are under development to provide extra security for the links between the ITS and your R/3 system.

Applying the Authorization Concept

Each IAC is supplied with a unique *service user*. This user is not apparent when you establish a connection to the R/3 system through the ITS—it deals only with the ITS. However, any connection between the ITS and the R/3 system is initiated through the R/3 system's standard logon procedure. Thus, each R/3 service user has to have a password that is stored in encrypted form in a service file on the ITS. The encryption method uses the DES-accepted industrial standard. The passwords are permanently encrypted when the ITS is installed and cannot be changed unless the ITS is reinstalled.

The service files are restricted to the Windows NT administrator by using Windows NT security mechanisms. Firewalls should be installed to protect the ITS from unauthorized network access. Communication should only be allowed on the HTTP server's TCP/IP port. Network access to the HTTP server should be restricted to authorized personnel.

SAP recommends that the HTTP-S protocol be used between the browser and the HTTP server. This protocol is based on Secure Socket Layer 3.0, which is an enhancement of the HTTP protocol.

Exploring Internet Scenarios for Sales and Distribution

SAP has preconfigured a set of IACs to support the main business scenarios that are being managed over the Internet in addition to the normal operating systems. The next few sections indicate how these fit into a business background and illustrate how they are operated in the sales and distribution context.

Using the SD-SLS-SO Sales Order Creation IAC

This consumer-to-business IAC is responsible for receiving orders from customers through the Internet and forwarding them as sales orders into an R/3 system. The most attractive situation is where there is a catalog available or where the customers know exactly what they want and are primarily interested in a price comparison and a quick delivery offer.

The following customer benefits are recognized:

- Customers can submit orders around the clock.
- Your customers can enter their orders directly using your screen layout on your Web server (without using the telephone or fax).
- Your response can be quick, with up-to-date price data and delivery times.
- Your customers can trace the progress of their orders at any time.

The advantages to the supplier business are based on the speed of the transactions:

- You can design the screen layout to help your customers enter data quickly and easily.
- You receive the sales order very soon after it is entered, and you can therefore deliver that much sooner.
- You can prepare for the peak times for sales orders entries and can therefore improve performance.

The SD-SLS-SO Sales Order Creation IAC normally operates in the following sequence:

- You offer your customers a product catalog. They assign their selection to a *shopping basket*.
- If they ask for a quote for the article in the shopping basket, they will be given a customer-specific price and delivery date.
- If they accept the quote, a sales order is automatically created in your R/3 system, where it can be processed without delay.
- The customer gets the order number that can be used to inquire about the status of the order.
- Your company now has a choice of either placing the Internet order on a work list waiting to be checked or immediately generating a work list from the orders outstanding.

You have to arrange for authorizations and security before a customer can enter a sales order over the Internet. You have to assign each customer an SAP customer number and an initial password. The customer should then replace the initial password with his or her own. The system will ask for the SAP number and password when the customer first assigns an article from the catalog to the shopping basket.

Authorizations are assigned according to the SD object class and maintained in the internal global user master record. These authorizations must not be restricted.

When a sales order is entered on the Internet, your R/3 system attempts to generate a sales order. You have to ensure either that the necessary data is available as default or maintained entries in the global user master record, as follows:

- AAT (Order Type)—Default TA
- VKO (Sales Organization)—Default 0001

- VTW (Distribution Channel)—Default 01
- SPA (Division)—Default 01

Using the SD-SLS-GF Sales Order Status IAC

If one of your customers wants to find out what has happened to her purchase orders, she can access your Sales Order Status IAC from the Internet. She can determine whether shipping is in progress for each purchase order and whether the goods are already on their way.

The Sales Order Status IAC operates in this way:

- You give your customers the option to view the status of their purchase orders, which exist in your SAP system.
- The customer will have used an SAP customer number and password when logging on. The existing sales orders for this customer number can be selected and displayed.

Filtering can take place:

- Order data from
- Order data to
- Order number
- Purchase order number
- Material number

Your system will then transmit to the customer a list of one or more sales orders, which contain the following information:

- Quantity of a material that has already been assigned to deliveries because the Shipping department has started picking the goods and preparing for transportation
- Quantity of a material that is already on the way to a customer

N O T E If you are accessing a SAP R/3 system through an IAC, additional information (on a shipment, for example) may be available over the Internet by clicking a hyperlink in the browser display, which connects you to the transportation agent. ▧

Using the SD-BF-AC Available to Promise IAC

The Available to Promise IAC's purpose is to allow an authorized person to check the availability of the necessary resources before making critical decisions or commitments. If your company is focused primarily on your customers, you need unrestricted access to reliable information on the availability of resources at all times. Your salespeople need to be able to quote reliable delivery dates.

The standard R/3 system availability check provides a service to many logistics operations at all organizational levels. You can call for information at plant level, storage location level, and at batch level.

The Available to Promise IAC screen shows the results of the material availability check as an overview.

Customer-oriented companies in the high-tech and consumer goods branches of industry are likely to be interested in this IAC, particularly in production planning and in sales and distribution. Their customers may be invited to use the Available to Promise IAC for the following reasons:

- Available to Promise is available to users all over the world and around the clock.
- The application is simple and easy to use because you can identify the product lines in the display in order to specify the products you are interested in.
- The Internet availability check need not entail communicating with the Sales department if a customer master record has been created for the material of interest.
- Vendors can use the IAC to find out which products are available and how much is available. They can therefore anticipate deliveries.

Selecting Material   You receive a graphic overview of the range of products after logging on. As a salesperson, MRP controller, or customer, you can check to see whether sufficient quantities of a product are available on the required date directly through the Internet.

You can select the item of interest in any of the following ways:

- By navigating in the product tree
- By using the text search function
- By directly entering the material number
- By directly entering the material short description

You have to enter the desired quantity and delivery date. The system then ascertains the quantity of the particular material that will be available to meet the delivery date you have specified. The system checks to see how much of this material is already promised to meet the requirements already confirmed. Your display will show the ATP Available to Promise quantity for each material at the material provision date; it is shown separately for each plant that is able to supply it. The provision date takes no account of any additional delays occasioned by delivery scheduling.

You can opt to have the end of the replenishment lead time reported for any material that is unavailable in the required quantity for the required date.

The browser you use to access the Available to Promise IAC must be Java enabled and set so that Java programs can run. Netscape Navigator version 3.0 and later and Microsoft Internet Explorer version 3.0 and later are suitable.

Product selection is managed by a Java *applet*, which is a program that is loaded and executed on your PC when the relevant HTML page is accessed by your browser. The Java applet loads the product catalog from files saved in the Web server. You can identify a product in the applet by navigating the product hierarchy tree or by a text search; you can have the applet copied to the field that receives input for the R/3 availability check function. This function will normally use the material's checking group and apply the Sales department's checking rule A.

N O T E A text search in an applet allows you to search using material numbers or descriptions. The wildcard * is accepted. The search does not differentiate between upper- and lowercase characters. ▨

You can create your own product catalog by accessing the R/3 Product Catalog Maintenance screen and generating the PCATALOG report, which builds the input files for the Java applet. You have to place these files on the Web server and edit the applet parameters on the relevant HTML page, so that they correspond to your catalog files.

Changing the Layout of the SD-BF-AC Available to Promise IAC   As with every SAP program module, the SD-BF-AC Internet Application Component is built from development objects that are part of the standard R/3 system and should not be changed by the user. If you do alter a development object in any way, the object is classified as a modification. However, the IAC Java applet can be controlled through its parameters, as follows:

- ▨ Products is an essential parameter that you must specify with the filename for the product file, preceded by the absolute path from the Web server's root directory.

- ▨ Hierarchy is an essential parameter that also relates the product hierarchy text file to a Web server root.

- ▨ BgColor is an optional parameter that can control the background color of the Applet frame on the browser.

Listing 11.1 is an example of an <APPLET> tag in an HTML page.

Listing 11.1   *LST11.1.CPP*—An *<APPLET>* Tag

```
<APPLET name=catalogApplet archive="catalog.zip" codebase=/sap/its/startpages/
ckav/classes
    code=catalogApplet.class width=320 height=295 mayscript>
    <PARAM name=cabbase value="catalog.cab">
    <PARAM name=products value=/sap/its/startpages/ckav/data/materials.txt>
    <PARAM name=hierarchy value=/sap/its/startpages/ckav/data/hierarchy.txt>
    <PARAM name=bgColor value=C0C0C0>
</APPLET>
```

From Here

This chapter points to some of the standard components developed by SAP. These components enable a local or distant user to connect with an SAP R/3 system via a standard Internet browser on almost any kind of computer. You might like to move on to one of the following chapters:

- ▨ Chapter 10, "Operating WebRFC Gateway Interface," extends the discussion of preparations for extensive and wide-ranging communication through the Internet.

- ▨ Chapter 11, "Programming the Internet Transaction Server," discusses the steps that you may need to take to ensure that a suitable server is available to handle large volumes of Internet business.

■ To see how a practicing consultant interprets the role of sales and distribution in the context of an integrated SAP R/3 system, look at Chapter 12, "Interpreting SD Organizational Structures."

■ Chapter 3, "Pricing Products and Services to Improve Sales," might be worth a second look to see how the basic business of sales and distribution could perhaps benefit from improved automation.

CHAPTER 10

Operating the WebRFC Gateway Interface

In this chapter

Making Use of Remote Computers

This chapter is about ideas and technology built into the WebRFC Gateway Interface. You will appreciate how to administer WebRFC and how to develop and customize it to suit your particular requirements. SAP Web Reporting is an important application of RFC technology. It's discussed in this chapter, along with Workflow Status and Time Reporting, as examples of developed RFC applications that can be used in many companies.

The SAP WebRFC Gateway Interface is designed to link applications by dynamic Internet programming over the World Wide Web and across intranets between business partners.

The WebRFC Gateway Interface uses the RFC Remote Function Call technology to provide the software that enables Web users to get immediate access to information in the R/3 system via the Internet or their local intranet. If you have the necessary authorization and can prove your identity, you can sign on to R/3 through your Web browser. You can then execute reports and manipulate the output in your browser.

As a developer, you will also benefit by having a method for writing HTML-based Web applications that interact with the users in a style with which they are probably familiar.

Accessing Data from the Web

Data in your R/3 implementation can be accessed by addressing its storage location through the mechanism of the Uniform Resource Locator (URL) . When you click an URL in a Web page, it will change color and your system will attempt to get hold of the HTML page to which it refers. If this page is already in your computer's cache, your display will show it. If not, your browser will try to locate via a connection to some other kind of computer. This other computer could be a network server or the PC of another network user.

A successful connection depends on there being a communication link between your browser and the page you are looking for. This link will include an HTTP server that is able to operate with the Hypertext Transfer Protocol, so it can receive and send communications through the Web; the standard system URLs address these communications to their intended receivers.

The HTTP server has to be asked for an HTML page that is associated with an URL. If it can find such a page, you can see it in your browser. One page can be linked to another so that an entire document can be accessed by this method. However, the HTTP server will respond only to documents written in HTML. If you want to get information from a database over the Web, you have to call on some mechanism that will locate this information and arrange it in the form of an HTML document that is acceptable to your browser.

N O T E The MIME (Multiple Internet Mail Extension) standard allows audio, graphics, and video files to be inserted in standard HTML documents so that you view or listen to them at your browser if it contains the necessary software and your terminal has the multimedia hardware configured. ▪

The Common Gateway Interface (CGI) is a currently available standard that specifies how an HTTP server can interact with a series of instructions that you have assembled in order to find the information you need. These instructions are usually called *CGI scripts* because their job is to tell the HTTP server what to do. The CGI scripts are also referred to as *server-side gateway programs*. They generate HTML pages at runtime in response to user input. They place the information they have retrieved from a database or other data source in these pages.

The CGI is therefore a standard specification that controls how a client system working on behalf of a user shall pass on a request to a gateway program. The interface also controls how the response to the client system request shall be formatted when it is passed back for the attention of the user who made the request.

Now because all communication between clients and servers is based on URLs, the CGI must also specify how each URL shall be loaded with the parameters that define what information is needed. When the gateway has successfully passed on the parameters packed into the URLs, the data source can find the necessary information and send it back to the gateway. This stream of information can be as HTML pages or any kind of image, sound, or video that can be coded as binary data and viewed or listened to in a modern Web browser.

To allow the browser to react appropriately to the stream of binary data from the gateway, the interface program will normally send a format identification string that is taken from the MIME set of identification strings.

Accessing R/3 from the Web

A programmer could write a program to access R/3 using the standards specified as the CGI. However, each transaction type would have to have a specific CGI script and it would be a great deal of work to keep them up-to-date. The SAP WebRFC Gateway Interface has been developed to perform the CGI functions by using the RFC's technology. The WebRFC Gateway Interface allows Web activities to be written as ABAP/4 function modules rather than as CGI scripts.

The SAP Internet Transaction Server (ITS) is the link that connects R/3 and HTTP servers. This performs the duties of a generic CGI program for the WebRFC. In particular, the ITS accepts HTML documents from your browser that contain your requests and commands to a distant R/3 implementation or other source of information. The ITS has instructions that enable it to issue appropriate commands to the R/3 system or other resource. When the ITS gets a reply from the distant system, it converts the information into a form that can be handled by your browser.

See Chapter 11, "Programming the Internet Transaction Server," for more information.

Understanding the Architecture of the WebRFC Gateway Interface

The way a WebRFC application is arranged as a suite of function modules is what distinguishes that application. The modules all have a common interface that can be used to call them from the Web and that they will use when they reply to the Web. This chapter discusses function modules that are programmed in ABAP/4 and therefore are compatible and integrated with SAP R/3 implementations. However, other systems that have adopted the same interface standard can be accessed the same way.

The URL is the focus of Web communications. The URL is a string of printable characters that can be packed with information. Parts of this string identify an HTTP server that will be able to interpret another part of the URL as the intended recipient's identity. Thus, an URL functions as a name and address label for the destination of the communication. Another part can be interpreted as the sender's name and address. Yet other parts contain additional information elements that are often referred to as the *parameters*.

If the destination of a communication from the Web is an SAP function module, one of these parameters will obviously have to include this module's name. When the communication reaches its destination, this function module will be invoked to perform some task for the sender. It will evaluate the rest of the parameters, locate and retrieve any information needed, and return the results.

The results can be presented as an HTML page ready for a standard browser. If the reply needs a business graphic or is in the form of an office document, the results can be streamed back to the originator in the form of binary data.

Building a Caller Module

Using the module WWW_MODEL_MODULE as a template and building a caller module is the most convenient way of setting up your system so that you can call an existing SAP R/3 WebRFC function module over a network communication channel. This should set up the call to the SAP Internet Transaction Server by first calling the WWW_DISPATCH_REQUEST special function module to specify some global variables. This has to occur because the WebRFC function modules cannot be called directly from outside if you are using the CHANGING parameters to allow for output of unpredictable dimensions.

It is typical to arrange for one function module to act as the entry point and then allow other functions to be called by URL links offered in HTML pages (generated as needed). If necessary, these links can point to other destinations in the Web by using the URL parameter technology again. Here is an example of using an URL to call a function module that must obtain the specification of a report and then compile the data:

```
/scripts/wgate.dll?~service=XGWFC&_FUNCTION=WWW_GET_REPORT&_REPORT=BTDOK
```

If you do not know the exact values for the parameters, you can leave them to be supplied by the sending user when requested to do so by an exchange of HTML messages.

Defining the Interface Parameters

Web-callable function modules have to be called by a series of characters that can be interpreted by the standardized interface. This means that your calls have to be strict in terms of their content, their syntax, their capitalization, and their punctuation. Each parameter takes the form of an internal table, which can include parameters that are themselves tables, and so on.

Understanding *QUERY_STRING* QUERY_STRING is a table that contains all the parameters from an URL that are to be passed to the function module from the Web.

Understanding *HTML*   HTML is a table that contains an HTML page that is generated by the called function module and is being returned to the Web browser.

Understanding *MIME*   MIME is a table that contains binary data, such as an image or sound segment that has been located by the called function module and is being returned to the Web browser.

> **N O T E**   A Web-callable function can return either HTML data or MIME data, but not both at the same time. ▨

Using the *CONTENT_TYPE* Parameter   CONTENT_TYPE is a parameter that can be used to tell the Web browser that what follows is HTML data. It also defines the data's format. It is therefore an alternative to signaling the type of content via a MIME or HTML parameter in the URL.

The value of CONTENT_TYPE must be the same as one of the file types your browser can recognize. Some illustrations follow:

- ▨ If the function is returning an HTML table, CONTENT_TYPE must contain the value text/html.
- ▨ If the function is returning a MIME table, CONTENT_TYPE must contain a value, such as image/gif or application/postscript, that has been taken from the list of MIME types recognized by your browser.
- ▨ If CONTENT_TYPE contains the value application/winword, your Web browser will call Microsoft for Windows in order to display the data.

Understanding the *CONTENT_LENGTH* Parameter   CONTENT_LENGTH must be set for binary data and will specify the length of the data being returned as an HTML or MIME table.

Understanding the *RETURN_CODE* Parameter   The value of RETURN_CODE determines how the communication shall be terminated. You could break the RFC connection to your R/3 system and end the session with the ITS. The following options are available:

- ▨ 0   Default, close the RFC connection after this call.
- ▨ 1   Keep the RFC connection open after this call.
- ▨ 2   Close the RFC connection and terminate this ITS session.

Performing Login Procedures

Your standard login to the R/3 system using the SAPGUI will normally demand that you enter your username and password. You might also have to signify other information, such as the language you want to work in. The system will consult the user authorizations to find out what you are allowed to do.

In the same way, if you try to access your R/3 system from a Web browser by clicking an URL that references a WebRFC application, you will have to identify yourself before the entry function module will respond. Your Web browser will be sent a login page, generated in HTML, that contains forms for you to submit your identification information.

Part

III

Ch

10

It is possible to have some of this login information already set up in the URL you use to call the WebRFC.

Understanding Login Parameters

Table 10.1 illustrates the login parameters.

Table 10.1 WebRFC Login Parameters

URL Parameter	Example	Description
~service	XGWFC	ITS service name
~client	000	Client identification
~login	WEBLOGIN	SAP username
~password	********	SAP user password
~language	E	Language is English

The ~service parameter is mandatory because its value identifies the SAP ITS file that contains the information needed to gain access to the R/3 system you are calling.

The example of a service given in Table 10.1 is the service file XGWFC. This is a standard service file that gives Web users access to SAP WebRFC applications. You could specify this service directly in an URL, such as the following:

```
/scripts/wgate.dll?~service=XGWFC&_FUNCTION=WWW_GET_TREE_LIST
```

The function module WWW_GET_TREE_LIST will connect you to the standard SAP Reporting Browser. However, this URL does not include your client, username, password, or language. The system presents you with a suitable form so that you can enter these details at your browser and thus complete the login requirements. If the URL had already specified some other parameters—your login language, for example—then there would be one less item for you to enter. Your login information is held in the ITS until you finish your terminal session.

You could have all the login parameters specified in the URL if you are operating in an environment where your login password is protected in some other way, so that you would be connected to the R/3 without further login information requests. If you need to connect to more than one R/3 system, you would need a separate version of your service file for each.

Authorizing Access to Data and Reports

Standard SAP R/3 login procedure is designed for situations where each employee in your company, and everyone on your intranet, has a separate R/3 user account and an individual password and authorization profile. However, if you expect to allow large numbers of customers to access your R/3 system for just a few transactions each, it is better to establish a single account that is given a user account name and password in the calling URL. There need be no login procedure in these circumstances. You would obviously have to be careful about controlling what each customer would be allowed to access. You could perhaps allow each customer to view, but not change, his or her own account. You would not want them to be able to inspect the accounts of all other customers.

The WebRFC application has to manage a basic customized login procedure:

- Generate an HTML page in which a customer can enter an ID and password.
- Wait for the customer to enter these values in the Web page.
- Check in the function module that this user is recognized as a genuine customer and has the authorization needed to access the information being sought.

As an alternative to customized login, you could arrange anonymous login. That is achieved by offering any customer that has reached your company's home page the choice of an URL that will carry out a particular function, such as compiling a report. The URL will have been primed with a user ID and password that are designated simply for the purpose of allowing large numbers of customers limited access to a specific WebRFC module. It is prudent to set up these ID and password arrangements so that viewers are able to gain access only to those reports they really need.

Part
III

Ch
10

Using the SAP Web Reporting Application

The SAP Web Reporting application uses the WebRFC technology to allow authorized users to access the information in an R/3 system via a remote function call to the system from their Web browsers. This is the standard technique of having URLs visible in Web pages, where they can be selected if the user wants to access the resource they point to. The SAP Web Reporting application provides the following basic services in support of the URLs:

- Allows reports to be initiated dynamically by the user and therefore compiled using the most up-to-date information available.
- Displays in the user's browser a list that has been generated beforehand when the user selects its title from a report tree.
- Allows the user to scan and select from report trees available in the SAP Reporting Browser.

Many SAP reports can be retrieved over the Web without any modification. However, reports that call other transactions or reports that perform uploads or downloads are not yet available over the Web. Some reports at the SAPGUI can be filtered interactively by using the drill-down function, where you can indicate with your cursor a data element about which you would like more detailed information. The system immediately provides this further detail. However, the current release of R/3 does not include a drill-down interactive reporting facility for use over the Web.

If you are able to create a new report, perhaps by editing an existing report structure, then you can set up URL links to other Web pages or back to the same or another R/3 system or application. Your users can thus enjoy as much reporting flexibility as you have chosen to allow them.

Understanding the SAP Web Reporting Environment

The SAP ITS manages the connections between the HTTP servers that manage your Web browser pages and one or more R/3 systems with which their readers may want to communicate. When one of your customers selects an URL in a Web page that you have prepared, the browser will interpret this as a request.

If the browser can find the location indicated by the URL (on the local hard disk, for example), it will do so and then display the result to your customer. For instance, your customer may have previously downloaded your latest product list and want to consult it again.

If your customer's browser cannot find the target, the request is forwarded to the ITS. It communicates with an R/3 system by initiating a Remote Function Call (RFC). With luck, a dispatcher program will be waiting in R/3 for such RFC requests and will demand the resources to execute them when they arrive.

Forming Requests for the ITS

There are various ways you or your customers can make a Web browser send a valid request for a reporting activity to the ITS for transmission to the appropriate application server. The neatest way is for you to have written a Web page that includes explanatory text (perhaps graphics, animation, and sound), which helps your customer make an appropriate choice between a few URLs that you have set up in the page. You have to place the text or label for the URL and you have to set up the information (that is usually hidden from the browser user) that determines what happens when the URL is clicked.

If you write a Web page and place within it a suitable URL, you can enable your user to execute a specific report, retrieve a pre-generated list, or access the SAP Reporting Browser. Which of these possibilities is activated depends on the parameters hidden in the URL. Your particular browser may refer to the "target" of the URL.

If you want your Web page to link your user to an R/3 system, you must specify one of the following function module calls as a parameter in the URL:

- WWW_GET_REPORT
- WWW_GET_SELSCREEN
- WWW_GET_TREE_LIST
- WWW_GET_TREE_NODE
- WWW_GET_NODE_LIST

The activities initiated by these SAP function module calls are discussed in the following sections. Their functions are available as components of the SAP Reporting Browser.

Executing WWW_GET_REPORT   If you call this function module from your Web browser, it gets and executes a report immediately and then displays the results in your browser. Which report? There are two choices. The URL could already contain a parameter that determines which report will be generated and displayed. Alternatively, you could be shown a selection screen of the possibilities from which you could choose your requirement.

Here is an example of an URL using this function to generate the report titled BTDOK2:

`/scripts/wgate.dll?~service=XGWFC&_FUNCTION=WWW_GET_REPORT&_REPORT=BTDOK2`

This example specifies the standard service XGWFC and instructs the function module WWW_GET_REPORT to get and execute the report BTDOK2.

N O T E The parameter/value pairs are separated by the ampersand character (&). If you have to transmit further criteria, pack them into the URL as additional parameters and separate each by the character &.

Never use single or double quotation marks within an URL string. If parameter values contain spaces, such as the name of a product, replace each space with a + sign.

If parameter values contain an &, replace the symbol with a % character and its ASCII equivalent 26 (hexadecimal)—%26. ▥

Executing WWW_GET_SELSCREEN As its name suggests, this function module can be used with reports that already have a selection screen. The function module generates the selection screen for the report that has been specified in the URL. What finally appears in your customer's browser will depend on their choices as indicated in the selection screen.

Executing WWW_GET_TREE_LIST This function module links to the standard SAP Reporting Browser, which contains all available SAP report trees. The SAP Reporting Browser can only be used to view reports and report trees that have been explicitly designated for viewing by Web users. Like all browsers, the Reporting Browser will expect to find reports in HTML format.

If you call the standard function module WWW_GET_TREE_LIST, you will be offered a hierarchical structure of report trees. Each branch of the tree leads to an executable report or a list that has been generated beforehand. However, there is no default report tree, so users have to establish their own report trees or accept report structures already available in their network.

Executing WWW_GET_TREE_NODE This function module links to a particular node in a report tree and displays the contents, which may be a further tree structure or a list of available reporting items.

Executing WWW_GET_NODE_LIST Suppose you require a list that has been previously generated; this function module will retrieve it if you supply the correct parameters.

Executing Reports Without a Selection Screen If you are setting up a link to a report that does not need a selection screen to control the output, you would call the standard function module WWW_GET_REPORT with a suitable parameter joined by the & symbol.

No selection screen would appear. Each page's layout would be in accord with a standard SAP HTML template specifically designed for the purpose. You could modify this template or create one in its place customized to your own design.

Executing Reports with a Selection Screen You have two options if the report you are looking for does have a selection screen as part of its specification:

▓ Preempt the choices that a user might make by sending the necessary information in the URL. That way the selection screen need not be displayed and processed.

▓ Set up the URL with a call to the standard function module. This generates a selection screen, if the report needs one, before it executes the report.

If you are not sure whether the report will have a selection screen, it is safer to call WWW_GET_SELSCREEN, which will simply produce the report if no selection screen is necessary. WWW_GET_REPORT will adopt the default values if, in fact, a selection screen should have been generated.

On the other hand, if you are sure about the necessary parameters, you can pack them into the URL and the receiver will get faster service. This is because there will be no need to display and process a selection screen dialog.

Using the Report Parameter Syntax in URLs

The WWW_GET_REPORT function module needs the necessary parameters in the URL to use the prescribed report parameter syntax. The format separates parameter name and value pairs with the & symbol:

```
<parameter name>=<parameter value>&<parameter name>=
↪<parameter value>&<parameter name>=<parameter value>
```

Specifying Report Variants in URLs

Your report requesters may tend to specify the same set of options each time. What you could do is build a report variant that specifies all or most of these favorite choices as parameters passed through the URL. You could preselect values for report variants, select-options, report parameters, check boxes, and radio buttons.

If you have established one or more report variants that are used to generate different outputs, you can signify which variant you require by including the following parameter in the URL that appears on the Web page:

```
_VARIANT=<variant name>
```

If the report you are calling would use a selection screen to determine the select-options, you can pack the necessary values in the URL. Any of the principal data types can be passed, namely, C, D, F, I, P, and T.

Passing Data Types in URLs

You can pass any of the principal data types when specifying values for report select-options in an URL. Normally, you have to specify low and high values to define a range. Depending on the data type required, the correct syntax for select-options is as follows:

- Data type C (Character) (text)

  `SELC_<name>-LOW=<value> and SELC_<name>-HIGH=<value>`

- Data type D (Date)

  `SELD_<name>-LOW=<value> and SELD_<name>-HIGH=<value>`

- Data type F (Floating Point)

  `SELF_<name>-LOW=<value> and SELF_<name>-HIGH=<value>`

- Data type I (Integer)

  `SELI_<name>-LOW=<value> and SELI_<name>-HIGH=<value>`

- Data type P (Packed Number)

  `SELP_<name>-LOW=<value> and SELP_<name>-HIGH=<value>`

- Data type T (Time)

  `SELT_<name>-LOW=<value> and SELT_<name>-HIGH=<value>`

If you specify just the lower limit of a range of any data type, the result will be a list corresponding to this value.

Preselecting Check Boxes

You may have some reports in which the user can select any number of check boxes to get additional information. You may find that most users choose the same check boxes. You could improve the speed of the service by preselecting these favorite check boxes in the URL and doing without a selection screen.

The URL syntax for check boxes is as follows:

`CBOC_<name>=<value>`

The only permissible values for check boxes are X or ' '. The data type is C.

Preselecting Radio Buttons

A report could offer a selection screen with a set of radio buttons from which the user can select only one. If most of your users select the same radio button, you could anticipate this by packing this choice into the URL and thus leaving out the selection screen.

The URL syntax for radio buttons is as follows:

`RADC_<radio button group>=<radio button name>`

The values are names of radio buttons and the data type is C. SAP R/3 release 3.0 uses a technical name for the radio button group. You can find this group name by looking in the standard selection screen page generated by WWW_GET_SELSCREEN.

Interacting with SAP Web Reporting

You can start executing an SAP report or make a call to a function module from a Web page if the URL you select has been packed with the necessary parameters. Interactive reporting is not possible in this type of situation. However, you can carry out interactive reporting if the SAP system sends to your Web page a list of URLs for you to choose from. This is how interactive SAP Web reporting is achieved.

There are two possibilities:

- A report that has been sent to your browser contains one or more lines that have been constructed, so that part of the line can be highlighted in your browser. You can then click this part of the line and the system will respond by sending you a particular part of the report.

- A list can be sent to your browser. That list would include URLs that execute calls to SAP R/3 function modules that have been previously set up to carry out a particular reporting task that many users are likely to require.

The reason these two possibilities have to exist is found in the way Web browsers work. If you are working at a SAPGUI, you will be able to make use of the drill-down function. With it you can find the information when you require it because the R/3 system has been primed to stack up certain information. Have you called your R/3 system over the Web? As soon as the first request has been dispatched to your browser, the R/3 system will assume that the transaction is completed and the stacked information will be set aside.

How these two reporting arrangements are initiated forms the subject of the next two sections.

Linking URLs to SAP Web Lists

When you are designing a report that is to be used by applying the method of linking URLs to SAP Web lists, you have to use the SAP Web function module WWW_SET_URL, as follows:

1. Generate the list line with the WRITE statement.
2. Call WWW_SET_URL directly after the WRITE statement.
3. Specify the offset of the desired link in the import parameter OFFSET.
4. Specify the length of the desired link in the import parameter LENGTH.
5. Specify the URL you want to link to as a literal or as a variable in the import parameter FUNC.

The effect is to pass an empty internal table with the structure W3QUERY to the tables parameter QUERY_STRING.

Your report will execute as normal if your user is working at a SAPGUI, but if this report is called from a Web browser, each of the list lines that you have designated with the WWW_SET_URL function will show up with the URL part as a link that can be clicked.

Linking R/3 Function Calls to SAP Web Lists

If you need to have SAP function modules perform specific tasks according to the choices made by a user at a Web browser, you can arrange for the system to automatically generate the necessary URLs.

Use the function module WWW_SET_URL in your report to implement the call to a SAP function module in the line of a Web list:

1. Fill an empty internal table with the parameters you want to pass to the function module. The table should have structure W3QUERY because it has two fields, NAME and VALUE, which correspond to the convention for URL parameters.

2. Create a list line with the WRITE statement.

3. Call WWW_SET_URL directly after the WRITE statement.

4. Specify the offset of the desired link in the import parameter OFFSET.

5. Specify the length of the desired link in the import parameter LENGTH.

6. Specify the function module you want to call in the URL as a literal or as a variable in the import parameter FUNC. This function module must have the standard WebRFC Gateway Interface.

7. Pass the internal table with the parameters to the tables parameter QUERY_STRING.

You can specify a different function module with different parameters for each URL you write.

Working with the Reporting Browser

A *report tree* is a hierarchical structure that displays the titles of SAP reports, user-defined reports, or pregenerated lists. You can always call for a specific report by checking the URL that points to it, and you may be invited to refine your requirements by completing a selection screen. However, if you enable authorization for Web users to access a specific set of report trees, they can repeatedly select branches of these trees until they arrive at the report or list they are looking for. They can then view the information in their browsers and print it if necessary.

There are some limitations to Web reporting that prohibit browser access to some of the reports that would normally be available at a SAPGUI from standard SAP report trees. You should be very selective regarding what your customers are allowed to view, so the SAP report trees are all disabled for Web reporting when your system is installed. What you have to do is explicitly identify who is allowed to see what over the Web.

The easiest method is for you to generate your own report trees that contain only those reports and lists that you want your customers to view over the Internet/your intranet.

Utilizing Standard Web Reporting Templates

As you would expect, SAP has provided some master templates that will probably cover most of your requirements. Each template is associated with a particular Web Reporting function module. Within the template are placeholders that are replaced by the actual data when the function module operates. The following Web Reporting templates are standard:

- WEBREPORTING_TREELIST provides a list of all report trees by calling WWW_GET_TREE_LIST.
- WEBREPORTING_TREENODE accesses a specific node of a report tree by calling WWW_GET_TREE_NODE.
- WEBREPORTING_SELSCREEN generates a specific report selection screen by calling WWW_GET_SELSCREEN.
- WEBREPORTING_REPORT accesses a specific report output or pregenerated list after offering the user a selection screen by calling WWW_GET_SELSCREEN.
- WWW_GET_REPORT accesses a specific report.
- WWW_GET_NODE_LIST displays a list of a specific reporting tree's nodes.

The standard templates are written in HTML, and you can modify copies to create your own templates. The standard templates may be updated by SAP at any time, so you will have to accept the updates or control which version of the standard template you are using by renaming the copy you use as a basis for your own version.

Understanding Placeholder Rules

Any placeholder in a Web Reporting template can be omitted if you do not know its function. Each placeholder must be replaced with HTML data that corresponds to the rules for that function module.

Calling WEBREPORTING_TREELIST   This standard template displays a list of report trees and is offered with three placeholders:

- `!title!` is a placeholder for an HTML document. It must be placed between `<title>` `</title>` tags on one line.
- `<!heading!>` is a placeholder for a page title. It can be placed with other tags on one line.
- `<!treelist!>` is a placeholder for a list of URLs that point to reporting trees. It must appear on a separate line.

Calling WEBREPORTING_TREENODE   This standard template displays a report tree's node and is offered with placeholders:

- `!title!` is a placeholder for an HTML document. It must be placed between `<title>` `</title>` tags on one line.
- `<!treename!>` is a placeholder for the name of a report tree to which the node belongs. It can be placed with other tags on one line.
- `<!treelisturl!>` is a placeholder for an URL to the list of all report trees. It must occur as part of an `<A HREF=…>` tag.

■ `<!treelistname!>` is a placeholder that is to be replaced by a translated string, such as `'List of all report trees'`. It can be placed with other tags on one line.

■ `<!nodedata!>` is a placeholder that can contain information about the reporting tree node, such as a list of URLs that can be accessed. It must appear on a separate line.

Calling WEBREPORTING_SELSCREEN   This standard template displays a report selection screen. It is offered with placeholders:

■ `!title!` is a placeholder for an HTML document. It must be placed between `<title>` `</title>` tags on one line.

■ `<!heading!>` is a placeholder for a page title. It can be placed with other tags on one line.

■ `<!reportname!>` is a placeholder for the name of the report to which the selection screen belongs. It can be placed with other tags on one line.

■ `!action!` is a placeholder for an URL that calls WWW_GET_REPORT. It must occur as part of a `<form action=…>` tag.

■ `<!selection_screen!>` is a placeholder for the content of a report selection screen. It must appear on a separate line.

■ `!reset!` is a placeholder for a Reset button's translated text. It must occur as part of an `<input type=reset …>` tag.

■ `!submit!` is a placeholder for a Submit button's translated text. It must occur as part of an `<input type=submit …>` tag.

Calling WEBREPORTING_REPORT   This standard template displays a report output. It is offered with placeholders:

■ `!title!` is a placeholder for an HTML document. It must be placed between `<title>` `</title>` tags on one line.

■ `<!listname!>` is a placeholder for the name of a report or a list. It can be placed with other tags on one line.

■ `<!listbody!>` is a placeholder for the output of a report or a list. It must appear on a separate line.

Customizing Web Reporting Templates

If you modify any of the standard templates for Web reporting, you may have to specify the modified templates in the URLs. Two parameters are provided for this purpose: `_TEMPLATE` and `_TEMPLATE_SET`.

Using the _TEMPLATE Parameter   Suppose you modified a standard Web Reporting template such as WEBREPORTING_SELSCREEN and renamed it as MODTEMP. You can specify it in an URL via the `_TEMPLATE` parameter, as follows:

```
/scripts/wgate.dll?~service=XGWFC&_FUNCTION=WWW_GET_SELSCREEN&
➥_REPORT=BTDOK1&_TEMPLATE=MODTEMP
```

In this example, the Web browser calls the function module WWW_GET_SELSCREEN to execute the report program BTDOK1 and display the output according to the modified template MODTEMP.

However, if your Web user wants to call another report, the function module will revert to standard SAP report format, as in the standard Web Reporting template. The solution is to build a set of templates, all of which have been customized to your specific requirements. They could be copied from the four standard templates.

Using the _TEMPLATE_SET Parameter If you need to use customized templates, the WEBREPORTING prefix will have to be replaced by a prefix of your choosing, so that the modified templates will always be referenced if the Web user calls for subsequent reports. If SAP subsequently updates the standard reporting templates, your renamed set will not be affected.

For example, if you had copied the four standard Web Reporting templates and prefixed them with MYCOPY, you could access any of them by referring to the _TEMPLATE_SET parameter:

```
/scripts/wgate.dll?~service=XGWFC&_FUNCTION=WWW
➥GET_TREE_LIST&_TEMPLATE_SET=MYCOPY
```

In this example, a browser user calls the function module WWW_GET_TREE_LIST by clicking this URL. The processing is carried out by the customized version of the standard SAP Reporting Browser via the template set MYCOPY. Further function module calls would use the same template set.

Understanding the Workflow Status WebRFC Application

The WebRFC application-specific technology is a method of setting up the SAP WebRFC Gateway Interface to allow Web users direct access to a particular set of R/3 business functions. Two such applications have been developed and are available as the following modules:

- Workflow Status Reports in the Internet (BC-BEW-WFM)
- Time Statements in the Internet (PA-TIM-EVA)

This section discusses the WFM application module.

Using the BC-BEW-WFM Status Reports Application

The WFM module's purpose is to allow employees to execute certain parts of a workflow reporting system by remote function calls over the Internet. In particular, employees can use the Internet to access their parent company R/3 system in order to carry out the following tasks:

- Display completed work items
- Display work items that are linked to a particular object
- Display work items that are linked to a particular purchase requisition, which will be defined as the object type BUS2009

If an employee has access to the Internet through a browser, interchanges with the parent R/3 system can be used to control the standard functions of SAP business workflow within the limits imposed by that employee's authorization profile.

This application is for employees who are distant from the parent system. However, there are distinct advantages for local employees to use their familiar browser to access what may be very limited functionality from their parent R/3. If they are already using their browser for business, they can address R/3's workflow reporting system without leaving their browser.

Using the Standard Internet Workflow Reports

The WFM module's standard version provides a useful range of functions that you may use as models from which to develop your own variants. The following sections discuss some examples.

Calling for Completed Work Items   If you are working with a complex workflow, you may well need to know how the various tasks are proceeding. For example, you may want to inspect the status of all dialog work items and workflow items that satisfy a set of criteria.

The Completed Work Items report is comprised of a display of the current agent and the process time of all work items that meet the criteria. You are allowed to refine the set of items displayed by entering any or all of the following selection parameters:

- Date   Defined as the period within which the work items completed processing.
- Agent   Defined as the current agent of the work items.
- Task   Defined as a single-step task that is represented by the work items.

You may omit the selection parameters if you are prepared to receive a report of all work items.

Selecting Work Items by Purchase Requisition   This report displays workflows and single-step work items if they are related to a particular item of a purchase requisition that you specify when you call for the report. The following information items are reported:

- Type
- Status
- Start date
- Work item text

You have to establish the purchase requisition number and the item number (selection parameters) to specify this report.

Workflow items are not reported individually because the workflow is treated as a coherent item; it is reported as a unit. However, you can double-click a work item text that represents a workflow and be branched to the step log, where you can inspect the status of the individual components.

Setting Up the BC-BEW-WFM Application

You will be sending service messages over the Internet. Therefore, the following system settings must be established specifically for the BC-BEW-WFM Status Reports module:

- Authorizations/Security—Controlled by reference to an authorization group to which each type of Internet report is assigned. This authorization has to be in the employee's authorization profile.

- Standard Settings and Default Values—To display completed work items or work items related to a purchase requisition.

- Modification Options—Used when you have added variants of your own to the standard reports provided.

Understanding the Time Statements WebRFC Application

Many people talk about it, some achieve it, some like it, and some hate it. There are several names for it:

- Home working
- Telecommuting
- Flexible work location
- Virtual office working
- Networking

None of these names covers all the aspects of the type of activity associated with the telephone, either as a voice channel or as a multimedia channel—one of these media is likely to be a computer. The telephone link may be replaced by another channel, but the point of this preamble is to recognize that there is a way of doing work that does not entail regularly attending a place of work, that does not demand working during set hours of the day, and that need not be confined to interactions with a single company or a single language community.

As a shorthand for this flexible working, let us simply refer to the Internet as a good example of how people can communicate and do business. They may operate an intranet where you need a membership to sign on; they may be potential customers who are seeking a goods or services supplier.

Of course, they may all be employees of a single parent company. If you are the manager, you will want to know who is working on what and when they can be contacted. You need to know the status of each of their work items.

The SAP R/3 PA-TIM-EVA Time Statements application is a software module designed to facilitate flexible yet effective staff time management, wherever and whenever they work.

There is an essential requirement—they must clock in and clock out at the PA-Personnel Administration's TM-Time Management module. If this requirement is met, employees can check how many hours they have worked in the current or previous payment period. As you would expect, a valid R/3 ID and password are required.

If you were such an employee, you could use the Internet to make sure that you met minimum working-time requirements and that you did not exceed the maximum. You could probably estimate your earnings from the hours you had worked.

As an employer, you would perhaps find that your work force found the Time Statements useful and a small compensation for having to always clock in and clock out.

The PA-TIM-EVA Time Statements application depends on standard settings and default values. For example, there must be a 0105 Communications infotype established for each individual in the Personnel Administration System. This provides a unique personnel number that is associated with any Time Statement records.

You can specify that some of the fields be included or excluded, and you can determine the appearance of the reports from this scenario by requiring certain background or text colors and by having your company logo included in the Internet display.

Part
III

Ch
10

From Here

This chapter is about some the ways in which SAP R/3 can provide services across the Internet or through your company intranet via the Remote Function Call mechanism, which sets in motion a piece of software held on a distant computer.

You might like to move on to one of the following:

- Chapter 11, "Programming the Internet Transaction Server"
- Chapter 12, "Interpreting SD Organizational Structures"

Programming the Internet Transaction Server

Using Your Browser to Access R/3

This chapter is about how the ITS is controlled. For most purposes, you will be able to use a standard function or template and make, at most, only minor editorial adjustments. However, the HTML-Business language is only slightly different from standard HTML, and you may be very familiar with this format. This chapter will perhaps invite you to develop your browser HTML skills to include HTML-Business.

The Internet Transaction Server (ITS) is an interface between the Internet and your SAP R/3 system. The role of this interface is to translate between the communication protocols of an Internet HTTP server and the SAP R/3 system. It may also be necessary to adjust the format of data passing between them.

The ITS also manages the tasks of establishing connections and allocating systems resources. When an Internet HTTP server is triggered by a request from a user, the server gets in touch with the R/3 system; in particular it connects with its DIAG interface. The ITS talks to the DIAG as if it were a normal SAPGUI. When the R/3 has completed the processing needed to respond to the user's request, the DIAG transmits the reply to the ITS, where it is converted to an HTML document. Once in this format, the reply to the user request can be handled by an HTTP server that will eventually route it to the Web browser, where the user can view it.

N O T E As in all Internet communications, an HTML document can be addressed to a specific person through the person's Internet address rather than to a specific terminal device. The user who made the request to the R/3 system can see the reply at a different terminal if need be.

The ITS will have to make a translation in the reverse direction if the user has logged on to a Web browser. The request for a service will be transmitted in HTML document form and then have to be converted to the equivalent of R/3 screen data, so that it is indistinguishable from information input through an SAPGUI.

R/3 transactions are the elements that take part in the SAP standard business processes, which are conducted by the ABAP/4 programming language functions. However, standard ABAP/4 functions have to be adjusted to comply with various special requirements necessary where the Internet is used as part of a communication linkage. For example, the design of screens that will be viewed through a Web browser has to be in accord with the international standards that are recognized by the popular browsers. In addition, SAP has standardized the conduct of Internet business processing by maintaining strict control through the use of Business Application Interfaces (BAPI). A BAPI's essential characteristic is that processing takes place only through precisely defined methods and works exclusively with strictly formed business objects. The role of a business object is to ensure that every field of data is able to be correctly and unambiguously interpreted by every integrated application and across all worldwide client/server systems that comply with this standard.

A BAPI is available from SAP for just about every common type of business transaction.

Using the ITS Programming Guide

Although the process of setting up an ITS is complex and has to be tailored to your particular requirements, the SAP ITS Programming Guide is available to prompt you and check the correctness of your specifications. Of course, you will want to be familiar with R/3 screen technology, HTML standards, and Web concepts before you set out on this task. The sections that follow show you what sort of work is entailed in preparing your company to do profitable business on the Internet.

Using the ITS in the Parallel Debugging Mode

The ITS Debugger is an operating mode of the ITS. It allows the ITS to connect a standard SAPGUI in parallel during communication with a Web transaction. The transaction is visible in both the Web browser and the SAPGUI at the same time. You can then call upon the R/3 Debugger in the SAPGUI to conduct error analysis while a Web transaction is running.

> **N O T E** The parallel debugging facility will be disabled once your ITS has completed its development and is released in its operational version. ▦

You can set up Web transactions for SAP Internet Application Components by using SAP dialog programming tools. There are two main differences between SAP R/3 transaction screens for a normal dialog and one intended for use over the Internet:

- The screens of Web transactions must have special ITS control fields.
- Special dialog control rules must be observed when programming IACs.

Each IAC screen has to be associated with an HTML template so that the information in the IAC fields is converted to a format that allows HTML to display the contents in the same way as an SAPGUI. The template also controls how any data entered by the user at a Web browser is transferred to corresponding IAC fields.

If you are running the ITS in the debugging mode, you will be able to discern any errors or discrepancies between the R/3 transaction and the user interactions taking place at the Web browser. The tools already available in your R/3 system can be used to troubleshoot problems in the SAP Internet Application Components.

The ITS in the debugging mode displays the status of a transaction simultaneously in the SAPGUI and in the Web browser. You can therefore make a direct check of the correspondence of the two screens. If the SAPGUI transaction screen contains the required information, there is probably an error in the HTML template. If the SAPGUI transaction screen contains the wrong information, there is probably an error in the SAP transaction.

The SAPGUI will accept input at any moment, and the ITS mimics each action as it sends the appropriate message to the application server. Thus, you can inspect an IAC transaction by logging on to the ITS using an SAPGUI the same way you would access an application server. If you use the Web browser to change any aspect of an SAP transaction, the ITS will immediately respond to your changes through the SAPGUI.

Part

III

Ch

11

It is impossible to synchronize the transaction status as shown on the Web server when a transaction is updated from the SAPGUI. What you can do is enter /H in the SAPGUI command line. Next time an action is executed in the Web browser, the ITS will process the transaction and display the results in the SAPGUI, together with any debugging messages.

Operating the ITS in the Debugging Mode

First you must call the Windows NT Registry Editor regedt32, for which you must be authorized to the administrator level. Then set the following key in the Windows NT Registry to 1:

`HKEY_LOCAL_MACHINE\Software\SAP\ITS\Agate\AdminEnabled`

Restart the ITS Mapping Manager by the following command sequence:

`Settings   Control Panel   Services`

On the SAPGUI system, call the ITS service that you want to analyze in a Web browser. Open the SAP Logon window and log on to the ITS using the same procedure you use for an application server.

Your logon should include the following information:

- A brief description
- The name of the application server
- The number of the system (the default is `sapdp00`); if you want to use a different number, assign it to the Windows NT Registry entry.

  `HKEY_LOCAL_MACHINE\Software\SAP\ITS\Agate\SAPguiDebuggerPort`

When you start an action in the Web browser, the transaction screen will appear. You can then start the ABAP/4 Debugger by entering /H in the SAPGUI command line. The ITS will now be in the debugging mode, which will cause the ABAP/4 Debugger to appear in the SAPGUI as soon as an action is executed in the Web browser. A message stating that a debugging is operating appears in the browser window.

If you want to discontinue the ITS Debugger, you should deactivate the ABAP/4 Debugger in the SAPGUI. The SAPGUI window will not close until the ITS service in the Web browser has been exited.

Defining the HTML-Business Language for the ITS

HTML-Business expressions are sequences of printable characters in HTML pages. These sequences are recognized by the `SAPJulep.dll` interpreter when an HTML page is called up in a Web browser. Data from an R/3 screen can be integrated dynamically into HTML pages, which become HTML-Business pages. Any authoring tool for Web pages can be used to create the HTML pages, provided you enclose the R/3 name of each field between the `<server>` and `</server>` tags.

The Internet Transaction Server is provided with an interpreter interface that can be set to apply any scripting interpreter, including SAPJulep.dll.

N O T E   HTML does not support embedded tags, so you cannot place an HTML-Business expression within a pair of HTML tags. For these situations, an alternative JavaScript marker is available to signify HTML-Business expressions. The back tick (`` ` ``) is used to open and close an HTML-Business expression in place of the <server> and </server> tags. ▪

In most other respects, the conventions of HTML, JavaScript, and the C language are applicable to HTML-Business. An HTML comment starts with <!-- and ends with -->. You can use these tags to comment on HTML-Business expressions, and you can embed comments on parts of the expression within the text of the HTML-Business expression. Statements may be linked using a semicolon or at least a single-character HTML code.

Using Variable Substitutions

HTML-Business has to place values from R/3 screens in corresponding places in a Web page. It does this by matching identifiers that correspond between R/3 and the HTML page shown on the Web browser.

HTML-Business identifiers follow the programming conventions of many modern languages. They start with a letter (a–z, A–Z), an underscore (_), or a tilde (~). The identifier can be of any length and can include the digits 0–9 and hyphens (-). Other characters may be included if they are enclosed in single quotation marks.

One of the aspects of using a general communication channel like the Internet is that any word may appear in a message. You have to be careful that your system does not respond to a command word when it is not intended. In particular, SAP keywords may not be used as HTML-Business identifiers because the system may not be able to discern their significance from the context in which they are used.

For example, to include the contents of the field VBCOM-KUNDE on the R/3 screen in an HTML page, enclose it in back ticks:

```
Customer number: <server> vbcom-kunde</server>
<p> Customer number: `vbcom-kunde`   </p>
```

Specifying the Attributes of an HTML-Business Identifier

A business identifier that is recognized in the context of an HTML page has to have been previously defined in the R/3 system that is processing the page. If you want a particular business identifier to be recognized and to elicit a specific reaction, you have to provide R/3 with a table of values. Table 11.1 illustrates the kind of format standard for these tables.

Table 11.1   Matching Variables by Substitution

Nonterminal	Derivation
field	{ ^ } identifier [[expression]] [. attribute]
attribute	dim ¦ maxSize ¦ visSize ¦ disabled ¦ label

The following are possible identifier attributes:

- `dim`   The number of values for a field (stands for dimension).
- `maxSize`   Maximum permitted number of characters in the field.
- `visSize`   Maximum number of characters displayed by the field in the screen.
- `disabled`   Is the screen field ready for input? This attribute is not yet supported. In future releases of the ITS it will be possible to use it to determine whether a field is ready for input.
- `label`   Text describing the input field of the same name.

Using Identifiers as Indirection Pointers

The caret character (^) preceding an identifier signifies an indirection pointer that can retrieve the identifier's value. For example, if the variable `Field_Name` has the value `vbcom-kunde`, you can write the following HTML statement and cause the value of field VBCOM-KUNDE to be sent to the browser:

```
<p> The value of the field 'Field_Name` is '^Field_Name` </p>
```

The browser will display the label's text, followed by the actual name of the field and its value.

Working with Identifier Attributes

You can find the maximum input length and the field's maximum visible length by using the attributes `maxSize` and `visSize`. The following paragraph of code shows the type of programming language that has been developed to work with SAP variables in the HTML environment:

```
<p>Please enter your customer number
<input type =text name = "vbcom-kunde"
size = 'vbcom-kunde.visSize'
maxSize='vbcom-kunde.maxSize'>
</p>
```

Using the Identifier *label* Attribute

If an input field on the screen has a description with the same field name, it is possible to access this description using the `label` attribute. For example, you could use the logon language to associate a label text in the correct language:

```
<p> 'vbcom-kunde.label': <input type=text name="vbcom-kunde">
</p>
```

This technique can be used to call up resource files for purposes other than language resolution.

Using the *dim* Attribute

dim indicates how many values are associated with a field. You might like to interpret this as the dimensions of an array or as a multi-value field. The dimensions are used when step loops are used to progress through all the values. For example, a field may have 15 rows. This field's dim will be 15. A field that is not defined will return a dim value of 0. You can signify the value of any particular row in a multidimensional field by entering the row number in square brackets ([ ]).

Interpreting Expressions in HTML-Business

Expressions are interpreted in HTML-Business according to the standard programming language syntax:

- **Terminals** in bold.
- [Optional derivations in square brackets].
- {Zero or more repetitions of this expression in curly brackets}.
- alternative | alternative | alternative | options separated by the vertical bar.
- Parentheses () can be used to ensure that a logical combination is unique.

Table 11.2 sets out the HTML language in the strict grammatical format used to define logical languages.

Table 11.2   HTML-Business Grammar

Nonterminal	Derivation
expression	simpleexpr[compop simpleexpr]
simpleexpr	term { addopr simpleexpr}
term	factor { mulopr factor}
factor	(! ¦ ++ ¦ --) factor (expression) ¦ function call ¦ ➥assignment ¦ lvalue [++ ¦ --] ¦ constant
function call	internalfn (argument {, argument}) ¦ ➥externalfn (expression {, expression})
internalfn	**write** ¦ **writeEnc** ¦ **wgateURL** ¦ **archiveURL** ¦ **imageURL** ¦ **assert**
mulopr	* / % &&
addopr	+—& ¦¦
compop	== ¦ != ¦ > ¦ < ¦ >= ¦ <=

Bracketing with parentheses is supported if the evaluation sequence of the operators has to be broken. Operators with identical weighting are grouped and are evaluated from left to right.

The following permitted operators are listed in decreasing weighting:

Operator	Semantics
!	Not
++	Increment
--	Decrement
=	Assignment
*	Multiplication
/	Division
%	Modulus
&&	Logical and
+	Addition
-	Subtraction
&	Concatenation
¦¦	Logical or
==	Equal to
!=	Not equal to
>	Greater than
<	Less than
>=	Greater than or equal to
<=	Less than or equal to

Here are examples of correct expressions:

```
vbcom-kunde
nCustomers % 10
!fExists
a > b*2+1
name != "Walt"&" "&"Whitman"
(x-y) * (a+b) & " US$"
cond1 && (cond2 ¦¦ cond3) && cond4
```

Recognizing Reserved Key Words

HTML-Business uses the following tokens as reserved key words:

archiveURL	assert	by	declare
define	else	elseif	elsif
end	for	from	if
imageURL	in	include	repeat
times	to	wgateURL	with
write	writeEnc		

These key words cannot be used as identifiers unless they are enclosed in simple ticks (').

Using HTML-Business Standard Functions

The following functions are available as part of HTML-Business:

- write
- writeEnc
- wgateURL
- archiveURL
- imageURL
- assert

These standard functions are described in the next sections.

Introducing the *write()* Function

The write() function allows you to place expressions as output in an HTML page. Individual arguments are included to form the expression terms in the HTML page.

The format is as follows:

```
<p>    write ( expression {, expression} ) </p>
```

Introducing the *writeEnc()* Function

The writeEnc() function is used like write(). However, the output included in the page is URL coded. All non-alphanumeric characters are converted into the relevant hexadecimal coding. This enables you to set up an URL that contains fields that include special characters or blanks.

The format is as follows:

```
<p>    writeEnc ( expression {, expression} ) </p>
```

If you attempt to specify a field name composed of two words, the HTML server will attempt to process the two words as separate entities unless the writeEnc() function is deployed.

Introducing the *wgateURL()* Function

The purpose of the wgateURL() function is to send parameters to the ITS server software. It allows templates to be easily portable between servers.

The format is as follows:

```
<p>    wgateURL ( identifier = expression {, identifier = expression} )
</p>
```

In addition to including system information such as the field ~State, the function codes all parameters in accordance with URL requirements.

Introducing the *archiveURL()* Function

The purpose of the archiveURL() function is to access the iXOS archive system.

The format is as follows:

```
<p>    archiveURL ( command, archiveID=expression, docID=expression) </p>
```

The individual parameters for this function are taken from the product description of the appropriate Archive-Web-DLL driver file, which has to be present on the Web server. The URL used by archiveURL() has to be taken from the SAP HTML-Business global service description.

Introducing the *imageURL()* Function

The purpose of the imageURL() function is to access images according to their language and the theme of their contents, if these images have been stored directly in the HTTP server's file system.

The system will generate an URL by responding to your specifications. Those specifications should be in accord with the following basic directory structure:

```
<imageURL>/<type>/<language>/<theme>/<name>
```

> **N O T E** During Customizing, undefined or empty value placeholders are removed from the directory structure that is used to search for images. ▓

The ~imageURL dimension is defined in global.srvc.

The image type (~type) could be one of your company screen backgrounds named compbg1 and the language English so that the following call to your Internet Transaction Server might be made with the resulting substitutions:

```
<img src="`imageURL(~type="backgrounds", ~name="compbg1.gif")`">
<img src="/sap/its/graphics/backgrounds/E/ compbg1.gif">
```

The dimensions ~language and ~theme will be taken from the service description file unless you overwrite them by making explicit entries when you call the imageURL() function. No theme is specified in the example.

Introducing the *assert()* Function

The purpose of the `assert()` function is to copy error messages from the R/3 system to Web pages.

If an error is detected in the R/3 system when a user submits an entry for checking, the cursor position, or *focus*, on the screen is queried to determine which field caused the error. The error message then appears in the system field ~MessageLine.

When an HTML page is being assembled, the system reports any `assert()` statement that includes a field in which the cursor has been placed because an error was detected. The way this error message appears in HTML can be specified by the system field ErrorMarker in the global service description `global.srvc`.

Understanding Conditional Substitutions

The HTML-Business page is a template and therefore is not generated in a fully dynamic form at runtime. In particular, the current status of the application will not be determined. HTML-Business has an `if` statement for this purpose and can perform a conditional substitution to generate a different HTML page according to the current application status. The following format is adopted:

```
if ( expression ) htmlbusiness
➡{ [elsif ¦ elseif] ( expression ) htmlbusiness }
[else htmlbusiness ] end
```

Nesting

Nesting of any kind is permitted, and therefore HTML-Business statements can contain conditional or repeated statements. The key words `elsif` and `elseif` are equivalent. The expression will be evaluated to zero as FALSE or not equal to zero as TRUE.

Developing Repeated Substitutions

Where the R/3 system screen is built using step loops, HTML pages can be developed through the following HTML-Business types of `repeat` statement:

```
loop    repeat expression times htmlbusiness end
➡¦repeat with register in field htmlbusiness end
➡¦repeat with register from expression to expression
➡ [by expression] htmlbusiness end ¦for
➡ ( expression ; expression ; expression ) htmlbusiness end
```

This definition's components are described in the sections that follow.

Part
III

Ch
11

Specifying the *repeat* Expression A familiar programming format is used to specify loops:

```
loop    repeat expression times htmlbusiness end
loop
        repeat
                4 * z
        times
                <td>
end
```

Specifying the *repeat with register in...* Expression This function is used when an HTML-Business command is to be applied to each of an entire array of values as they are placed in a register in succession. The following format is applied:

```
loop
    repeat with
        register
    in
        field
htmlbusiness
end
```

Specifying the *repeat with register from...* Expression This expression allows you to develop HTML outputs that are selective when extracting information from arrays in R/3. The following format is applied:

```
loop
    repeat with
        register
        from
            expression
        to
            expression
                [by expression]
htmlbusiness
end
```

Iteration is only permitted over a single column of a step loop. If several columns are to be addressed in parallel, the individual field values should be pointed to by using an index, as in the variant illustrated as follows:

```
<table>
   'repeat with index from 1 to xlist-posnr.dim'
          <tr> <td> 'xlist-posnr[i]'   </td>
          <td> 'xlist-matnr[i]'   </td>
          <td> 'xlist-arktx[i]'   </td>
          <td> 'xlist-kwmeng[i]'  </td> </tr>
   'end'
</table>
```

You can specify that an increment is not equal to 1 via output to a table in the reverse sequence where the increment, for example, is –1.

```
<table>
  'repeat with index from xlist-posnr.dim to 1 by "-1" '
        <tr> <td> 'xlist-posnr[i]'  </td>
        <td> 'xlist-matnr[i]'  </td>
        <td> 'xlist-arktx[i]'  </td>
        <td> 'xlist-kwmeng[i]' </td> </tr>
  'end'
</table>
```

Specifying the *for()...loop* Expression   Again, the familiar programming format is applied as follows:

```
loop    for ( expression ; expression ; expression )
htmlbusiness
end
```

N O T E   You cannot list several expressions separated by commas because such a list could be interpreted as a simple set of values rather than a definition of a multidimensional nested loop structure. ▪

Summarizing HTML-Business Grammar and Syntax

Table 11.3 specifies the grammar and syntax available with HTML-Business expressions.

Table 11.3   HTML-Business Grammar and Syntax

Nonterminal	Derivation
htmlbusiness	([html ¦ script[;]] htmlbusiness)¦ **eof**
html	**bytestream**
script	(declaration ¦ expression ¦ conditional ¦loop)
declaration	**declare** externalfn { , externalfn } **in** module
externalfn	identifier
module	constant
function	funcname (argument {, argument})
argument	[identifier =] expression
expression	simpleexpr [compop simpleexpr]
simpleexpr	term { addopr simpleexpr}
term	factor { mulopr factor}

continues

Table 11.3   Continued

Nonterminal	Derivation
factor	(! ¦ ++ ¦ --) factor(expression) ¦ function call ¦ assignment ¦ lvalue [++ ¦ --] ¦ constant
function call	internalfn (argument {, argument}) ¦ externalfn (expression {, expression})
internalfn	**write** ¦ **writeEnc** ¦ **wgateURL** ¦ **archiveURL** ¦ **imageURL** ¦ **assert**
mulopr	*** / % &&**
addopr	**+ - & ¦¦**
compop	**==** ¦ **!=** ¦ **>** ¦ **<** ¦ **>=** ¦ **<=**
lvalue	field ¦ register
field	{ ^ } identifier [**[** expression **]**] [. attribute]
attribute	**label** ¦ **visSize** ¦ **maxSize** ¦ **dim** ¦ **disabled**
assignment	lvalue = expression
conditional	**if** (expression) htmlbusiness {(**elsif** ¦ **elseif**) (expression) htmlbusiness } [**else** htmlbusiness] **end**
loop	**repeat** expression **times** htmlbusiness **end** ¦**repeat with** register **in** field htmlbusiness **end** ¦**repeat with** register **from** expression **to** expression **by** expression htmlbusiness end ¦ **for** (expression ; expression ; expression) htmlbusiness **end**
register	identifier
identifier	{ ~ ¦ _ ¦ - } char { char ¦ **digit** ¦ _ ¦ ~ ¦ - } ¦ **"bytestream"**
constant	**digit** {**digit**} ¦ **"bytestream"** #identifier
char	**a..z** ¦ **A..Z**

Utilizing ITS National Language Support Facilities

National Language Support is comprised of the ability to handle several character sets or code pages at three distinct interfaces:

■ The interface between the ITS and the HTTP server, such as an Internet Information Server or Netscape Enterprise Server

■ The interface between the ITS and the file system where the ITS templates and service descriptions are held

■ The interface between the ITS and the R/3 application server where the DIAG-protocol is appropriate

N O T E   The ITS supports the Unicode character set (ISO 10646) as used by the Windows NT 4.0 operating system. It does not accept multibyte character sets (MBCS), although the Web server and the R/3 application server can operate with these characters if configured to do so. ■

You must maintain the configuration parameters if you need the ITS to recognize several code pages in one installation. Global parameters that control the access to ITS internal configuration files, such as the `global.srvc` file, are stored in the Windows NT Registry as Registry keys. Service-specific parameters are stored in the service description files, such as `global.srvc` and the associated service files. It is prudent to maintain the `global.srvc` file and thus change the attributes of all services, because each service file inherits the attributes of the `global.srvc` file.

Modifying the ITS Default Configuration

The standard ITS configuration will run in a one-code page, single-byte environment that needs no changes for most installations in the Western part of the world. If your R/3 system uses a multibyte character set (MBCS), or if you want to use an MBCS to offer an online catalog with Japanese help texts made from your templates, you will probably need to develop a modified set of configuration parameters.

Developing a Custom ITS Code Page Configuration

The following parameters in the Windows NT server registry can be altered:

■ `CodePageGlobal` has default value 0 and is a Win32 code page used to load the `global.srvc` file.

■ `CodePageSystem` has default value 0 and is a Win32 code page used to load the system templates.

■ `CodePageService` has default value 0 and is a Win32 code page used to load all other `.srvc` files.

■ `CodePageHttp` has default value 0 and is a Win32 code page used to load the `http.header` file.

Part

III

Ch

11

If any code page is not specified in the Registry, the default is `CodePageGlobal`. The value `0` specifies the system's default ANSI code page. These entries will not normally need to be altered unless, for example, you want to transmit HTML system messages in Japanese using the ShiftJIS character set, which you would implement by specifying `CodePageSystem=932`.

Windows Code Pages and SAP Code Pages

The Internet Transaction Server is a Windows NT 4.0 system and requires Windows NT code pages. However, an R/3 system to which the ITS may be connected will be running on any available R/3 platform. It will have code pages to provide the local national language support.

A routine has to be provided to explicitly associate Windows NT code page numbers with SAP code page numbers. These assignments are stored in the file `cp2sap.def`. This reference file contains the common Windows NT code page numbers and their equivalent SAP code page numbers. Should you need to support languages other than those specified in `cp2sap.def`, you will have to enter the corresponding SAP code pages used for the languages in your R/3 configuration.

Providing Language Independence

The Internet Transaction Server can work with any of three ways of generating language-independent HTML templates:

- Language resolution via the R/3 system
- Language resolution via language-dependent HTML templates
- Language resolution via language resource files

These technologies are discussed in the sections that follow.

Managing Language Resolution in the R/3 System

When you log on to the R/3 system, language-dependent texts appear on the screens. You can have these texts evaluated in an HTML template and therefore passed on to a user's browser. The `.label` attribute is used as shown in the following example:

```
<table>
  <tr> <th> 'text-posnr.label'  </th>
       <th> 'text-matnr.label'  </th>
       <th> 'text-arktx.label'  </th>
       <th> 'text-kwmeng.label' </th> </tr>
  'repeat with index from 1 to xlist-posnr.dim'
       <tr> <td> 'xlist-posnr[i]'  </td>
       <td> 'xlist-matnr[i]'  </td>
       <td> 'xlist-arktx[i]'  </td>
       <td> 'xlist-kwmeng[i]' </td> </tr>
  'end'
</table>
```

This variant works well if the details in any of the supported languages can be suitably placed in the screen; otherwise, one of the additional methods should be used.

Language Resolution via Language-Dependent HTML Templates   An individual set of HTML templates is written for each language supported. Your logon language determines which set is used. You can also define variant pages for the same transaction screen so that the appearance will depend on the HTML variant you specify when you define the service. The disadvantage is that any changes you make to the screen will have to be replicated for all the variant HTML pages.

Language Resolution via Language Resource Files   You may be content to have the same HTML templates used for all supported languages. In that circumstance you can employ language resource files, one for each language. They are files stored with the HTML templates.

From Here

This chapter was about how the Internet Transaction Server can be set up to moderate business data processing as it passes between an R/3 application and a network of users served by the Internet (or by the World Wide Web and therefore likely to be using any of several different Web browsers).

You might like to move on next to Chapter 12, "Interpreting SD Organizational Structures."

On the other hand, you might like to look again at some of the ways of developing sales activities touched on in the following chapters:

- Chapter 3, "Pricing Products and Services to Improve Sales"
- Chapter 6, "Trading Worldwide"
- Chapter 8, "Using Modern Sales Systems"

CHAPTER 12

Interpreting SD Organizational Structures

A Consultant's Perspective on Sales and Distribution

In this chapter

Sales Areas

The exact structure of your enterprise—the Sales and Distribution departments in particular—will have been represented in your implementation at the stage of customizing for Sales and Distribution. However, there are some structures that work better than others. You may have the opportunity to influence how they are established and used.

Sales orders are processed through sales areas, which are composed of sales organization, distribution channel, and division. Customers are set up by sales areas, and sales-relevant data can be varied by sales area on the customer master, as well as by sales organization and distribution channel. The sales area also controls the link between SD and several of the other modules, like MM and FI.

Try to keep the sales areas to a minimum; remember that the end users will have to enter the sales area before starting the SD process. Reporting needs are not a valid reason for using multiple sales areas; there are many fields on the customer and material masters that can be used for this purpose.

Shipping Points

Deliveries are processed through shipping points. Shipping points are linked to plants; a plant can have several shipping points, and a shipping point can be linked to more than one plant—although the plants should be physically located in the same area.

Master Data

The most important master data in SD are the customer master, product master, customer-material master, and condition records (pricing, output, and so on). If you create master data in more than one sales area, you can map it at distribution channel and division level. If you use mapping, it will reduce the amount of data you need to set up. However, if you do not need to vary the master data per sales area, why are you using multiple sales areas?

Sales Orders

SAP comes with a variety of standard sales documents, which may well fit your business requirements. If they do not, copy the one that is closest to your requirements—do not amend the standard documents. Again, keep it simple. Try to keep the number of document types in use to a minimum. End users have to enter the sales document type when they begin processing. The purpose of the sales document type should be clear to them, and it should be easy for them to decide in what circumstances to use the sales document types.

SAP sales order processing comes with a cornucopia of features, some of which are mentioned in more detail later in this chapter. A word of caution: Just because a feature exists does not mean you have to use it. It is unforgivable to complicate a business procedure just because it's fun to set it up in SAP. Always remember that some poor end user will have to use the system after the consultants and management have finished with it.

Most of the decisions about the steps in order processing are made at sales order entry. If master data is set up correctly, an end user will only have to enter the sales order type, sales area, customer, material, date, and quantity required. All subsequent processing can take place automatically, with only exceptions interrupting the flow—for example, the stock on the computer not matching the stock in the warehouse.

Pricing

The comprehensive pricing function is the jewel in the crown of SD. As you may have gathered from Chapter 3, "Pricing Products and Services to Improve Sales," you can arrange for just about every customer to enjoy an individual pricing policy. However, pricing is also the area in which some consultants get a little carried away. It is a wonderful concept, but it extracts a penalty in terms of system performance. As always, keep it simple and enjoy the ride.

Availability Checking

When all the promised orders have had the goods set aside, and when all the incoming replenishments have been unloaded, what you have left in your warehouse is ATP (Available to Promise). It can get more complicated. You need to know what will be available to promise at the time the order you are considering is scheduled for picking, throughout the time between now and your planning horizon date.

The major problems are when the basis on which the commitment in the sales order changes; for example, when the availability check in the sales order confirms a schedule line against a shipping notification from the vendor. The *shipping notification* is a document linked to a purchase order; it is supposed to be created when the goods are shipped from the vendor and the date slips. If this happens, the sales order should be rescheduled to reflect the new commitment date. Mass rescheduling of sales orders eats your resources and is not an option for most businesses.

The problem is essentially one of procurement. The problem should not exist if the date is entered in the purchase order or production order and the procurement lead times are reasonably accurate. This is not always the case. If accurate procurement times are not always available, minimize the amount of rescheduling. Consider restricting rescheduling to critical products on sales orders due for delivery within a restricted period and only reschedule for delays within a critical window.

Shipping

In SAP, the delivery document created is the first step in the delivery process; this is a concept I found very difficult to deal with when I began using SAP—you print the document as the last

Part III
Ch 12

step. It is the basis for all shipping. SAP shipping has greatly improved in recent releases and is well integrated with WM and MM. Another SAP feature is that the goods issue and the invoice create are separate functions, and consequently, the financial updates are separate events.

Shipping should occur seamlessly—all relevant decisions have been made in the sales order, and sales orders lacking critical shipping information should be blocked for delivery. Chapter 7, "Managing the SD Communications," discusses the processing of incomplete sales documents lists.

Billing

This is the last step in the SD process. It is where SD updates FI and, if appropriate, COPA. The invoice documents sales area is linked to only one company code, and the values are posted to this company's chart of accounts. The SD invoice is a separate document to the FI invoice. In practice, they are usually created at the same time, but they can be created separately if it's required. An invoice can be re-priced or the price can be copied from the price calculated at order entry. Taxes, of course, should be re-priced at invoice time.

When you enter an order, the shipping decisions are usually taken by reference to previous arrangements or by directly specifying the details. At the order entry time, the various accounts to which the transaction must be posted are suggested as defaults; they have to be confirmed before posting. The usual practice is for the order to be attributed to a specific sales area, which will have been defined in certain terms.

Obviously, the Financial Accounting and Controlling departments will have agreed to the details of the posting and authorized certain codes to initiate them. In practice, the billing document should require little manual intervention once set up.

Credit Management

Although it is a financial area, credit management is usually configured by an SD consultant. This area requires close cooperation between Sales, Distribution, and Finance. Don't let the credit management people go mad. This is an excellent tool for managing and minimizing your credit exposure. Clumsily implemented, however, it can cause chaos in the warehouse. Most problems can be avoided by thinking ahead and achieving a balance between reducing the credit exposure and delivering goods to the customer. As before, keep it simple.

Integration

This is a critical part of the implementation process and should be considered from the very start of the process. This may seem obvious, but many projects set up an integration management team without considering what the team should do. Integration team members must be part of every process team. They should always have a "helicopter" view of the project and help teams become aware of integration issues within SAP. The glass walls that exist between departments must be removed when implementing SAP. If possible, build cross-departmental teams. At the very least, hold cross-functional workshops. A design phase cannot be considered complete until it has been integration tested. A company implementing SAP should ensure that its staff are closely involved in the design phase. Do not rely only on consultants; make sure the consultants train your staff as they work on the project. You may even consider formalizing this process by setting targets.

From Here

SAP is a wonderful, functionally rich product that is being enhanced with every release. As an SAP consultant, it is great fun to work on and is the best business software on the market today!

CHAPTER 13

Glossary of SD Terms and Concepts

ABAP/4—Advanced Business Application Programming/4 is a fourth-generation language in which SAP R/3 application software is written. It has been developed by SAP.

ABAP/4 Native SQL—A method for accessing a specific database by using its proprietary commands to implement the Structured Query Language.

ABAP/4 Open SQL—A portable method for accessing all supported databases by the Structured Query Language commands.

ABAP/4 Query—User tool for generating special report programs without requiring any knowledge of ABAP/4.

ABAP/4 Repository—Store for all objects managed by the ABAP/4 Development Workbench.

ABAP/4 Repository Information System—Navigation aid for the ABAP/4 Repository.

ABAP/4 Workbench—Development environment that contains all the necessary tools for creating and maintaining business applications within the R/3 system.

ABC Analysis—Analysis of, for example, materials, may be conducted according to several criteria, (importance or consumption value, for instance):

- Important part or a material with high consumption value
- Less important part or material with medium consumption value
- Relatively unimportant part or material with low consumption value

Account Assignment—Specification of accounts open for posting during a business transaction.

Account Assignment Element—Work breakdown structure element to which actual or commitment postings can be made.

Active SAP R/3 Repository—The directory currently in operational use that contains descriptions of all of an enterprise's application data and their relationships, including how they are used in programs and screen forms. During ABAP/4 program development, a separate development repository directory is maintained for versions of the program components undergoing development or modification.

Activity (Controlling)—Internal or external; physical measure of the activity output of a cost center according to activity type.

Activity (Project System)—An instruction to perform a task within a network in a set period of time. Work, general costs, or external processing can be associated with it.

Activity Input—Transaction to plan the secondary cost quantities on a receiver cost center that uses activity from a sender cost center.

Activity Logs—Records of all activities in the SAP R/3 system for each transaction and for each user.

Activity Type—Classification of an activity and the data structure. The following are examples:

- Number of units produced
- Hours
- Machine times
- Production times

Actual Costs—All the costs accruing to an object in a period.

ALE (Application Link Enabling)—SAP method for using documents to carry messages that control distributed applications while maintaining integration and consistency of business data and processes across many systems.

Allocation Group—Defines which orders within one controlling area are to be settled together, as follows:

- By settlement timing—monthly, weekly, and so on
- By order types—repair, capital spending, and so on
- By settlement receivers—cost center, GL account

Allocation Receiver—Object to which the costs of a cost center or order are allocated.

APC Acquisition or Production Costs—Value of an asset that is used in some types of depreciation calculation.

API (Application Programming Interface)—Interface to support communication between applications of different systems.

ASCII—American Standard Code for Information Interchange, which associates each readable character or command to an input or output device with a specific pattern of binary numbers.

Assembly Order—Request to assemble premanufactured parts and assemblies to create finished products according to an existing sales order.

Asset Class—A grouping of fixed assets that is depreciated in a specified manner.

Asset Under Construction—An asset that is still being produced when the balance sheet is prepared.

Asynchronous Database Updating—A method of updating a database separately from the management of the transaction's dialog section.

Availability Check—Stock or inventory check that is automatically carried out after every goods movement. This check should prevent the book or available inventory balance of the physical inventory from becoming negative.

Background Process—Non-interactive execution of programs, sometimes using prepared file data to replicate the user dialog so as to utilize the same standard functions.

Part
III

Ch
13

Backward Scheduling—Scheduling a network where the latest start and finish dates for the activities are calculated backward from the basic finish date.

Batch (Lot)—A subset of the total quantity of a material held in inventory. This subset is managed separately from other subsets of the same material. A batch of material may have to be identified by its date and place of origin. Delivery lots and lots comprised of particular quality grades can be differentiated.

Bill-To Party—Person or company that receives the invoice for a delivery or service. The bill-to party receives the bill but is not necessarily the payer who settles the bill.

Billing Document—Generic term for invoices, credit memos, debit memos, and cancellation documents. A billing document is comprised of a header of data that applies to the whole document plus any number of items.

Billing Element—A data object to which you can post invoices and revenues in a work breakdown structure.

Bill of Material (BoM)—A complete, formally structured list of all the subassemblies, parts, and materials that go into an assembly or product. It includes a description, quantity, and unit of measure for each of the constituent parts.

Block—A mechanism that enables credit controlling personnel to stop a customer from taking part in any transaction.

Budget—Prescribed and binding approved version of the cost plan for a project or other task over a given period.

Business Area—A legally independent organizational unit within a client, for which internal reporting balance sheets can be created. The boundaries of a business area are normally determined on the basis of the sales organization, the division responsible, or the delivering plant.

Business Segment—Intersection of criteria defined in a particular controlling area to suit the relevant operating concern. The following are examples:

- Country, U.S.
- Industry, farming
- Product range, animal feeds
- Customer group, wholesale

Business Segment Criterion—Either chosen from SAP proposal list or existing tables, or created manually. Comprised of a field name and a field value.

Business Segment Value Field—Holds a number, a code, or a string.

Business Transaction—A recorded data processing step representing a movement of value in a business system, such as cost planning, invoice posting, and movement of goods.

Calculated Costs—An order's progress toward completion represented in value terms. There are two methods for determining the calculated costs: calculation on a revenue base and calculation using quantity produced as a base. There are two corresponding methods for calculating the (interim) profit realization if planned revenue is more than planned costs regarding an order.

Calculated Revenue—The revenue that corresponds to the actual costs incurred for an order, determined from results analysis as:

> actual costs × planned revenue / planned costs

Capacity (Cost Accounting)—Output of a cost center and activity that is technically possible during a specific period. Differentiated by category and arranged hierarchically.

Capacity (Production Planning)—Capability of a work center to perform a specific task. Capacities are differentiated according to capacity category. Arranged hierarchically under a work center.

Capacity Planning—Includes the following:

- Long-term Rough-Cut Capacity Planning (RCCP)
- Medium-term planning
- Short-term detailed planning (CRP)

Capital Investment Measure—A project or order that is too large or contains too much internal activity to be posted to fixed assets as direct capitalization. A capital investment measure's master record stores both the actual cost data and the planned values.

Capitalized Costs—Difference between the actual costs and the calculated costs of an order, calculated by results analysis. With deficit orders, this figure is reduced to allow for the loss realized.

Capitalized Profit—Calculated in results analysis by subtracting the capitalized costs from the value of the inventory from which revenue can be generated.

Cardinality—The number of lines in a dependent table to which the table under consideration, in principle, can or must relate. A line in a table may be related to another dependent line in a cardinality of one-to-one correspondence. The relationship may be one-to-many if there can be several dependent lines for any referenced line.

CCMS—Computing Center Management System, which is an SAP product designed to provide efficient management of an R/3 system and any associated systems.

Characteristic—A property of an object, such as length, colors or weight, used to describe and distinguish the object. Characteristics are also used to differentiate data objects in a database.

CIM—Computer Integrated Manufacturing, which is the concept of controlling a manufacturing plant by a linked network of computers that is elaborated as an SAP product of the same name.

Classification—When an object is assigned to a class, values for the object are assigned to characteristics belonging to the class.

Client—The highest level in SAP R/3. Within the R/3 system, "client" refers to the highest level in the organizational hierarchy. Each master record in the SAP R/3 database is associated with only one client, so that the data is not corrupted. The data of one client may not be accessed by another client. A client may represent a group of related companies. There are often a training client and a testing client, in addition to the client code that represents your group or corporate identity and under which the SAP system runs normal business. Some data is managed at the client level because everyone in the corporate group of companies will want to refer to exactly the same information and be certain that it is up-to-date. Vendor addresses are an example of data managed at the client level.

Client Caches—Work areas set up in the database application servers for data frequently accessed by the client's applications.

Collective Invoice—A billing document for several deliveries to one customer; initiated by the vendor at the end of a billing period.

Company Code—A unit within a client that maintains accounting balances independently and creates the legally required balance sheet and the profit and loss statement.

Compiler—A tool that translates source code statements written in a general programming language into statements written in a machine-oriented programming language.

Condition—A data element, term, or rule that defines price, taxes, and output according to criteria determined by the user.

Condition Record—A data record that stores a condition and perhaps refers to condition supplements. Condition records can include the following:

- Prices
- Discounts and surcharges
- Taxes
- Output

Contingency Order—A results analysis object on which the costs of complaints are collected. Reserves are created by results analysis for the expected cost of complaints; they are drawn from as costs are incurred.

Control Indicator—Determines, in cost accounting, which application components is active, how certain data is stored, and what types of validation are to take place.

Control Key—Determines how an activity or activity element is to be processed in such operations as orders, costings, and capacity planning.

Controlling Area—Area within an organization that shares a cost accounting configuration—normally the same as company code. For cross-company cost accounting, one controlling area may be assigned to multiple (more than one) company codes of one organization.

Controlling Area Currency—Default currency in cost accounting objects, cost centers, orders, and so on.

Consignment Stock—A particular inventory made available by the vendor and stored on the purchaser's premises; remains the vendor's property until withdrawn from stores for use or transferred to the purchaser's own valuated stock.

Contact Person—A person at the customer location who deals with the vendor's Sales or Marketing department.

Contract—A long-term agreement with a vendor that is fulfilled by individual release orders; initiated according to the customer's requirements.

Conversion—Translation from one data format to another, from decimal to binary code, for example.

Cost—The expenditure involved in buying or manufacturing a product.

Cost Center—Place in which costs are incurred. A unit within a company distinguished by area of responsibility, location, or accounting method.

Cost Component—A group of cost origins.

Cost Component Layout (Product Cost Accounting and Cost Center Accounting)— A technical term. Controls how results of a product cost estimate are saved. Assigns cost elements to cost components and determines the following:

- How the costs for raw materials, finished, and semi-finished products are rolled up in a multilevel assembly structure
- What portion of the costs is treated as fixed costs
- Which costs are treated as the cost of goods manufactured
- Which are sales and administration costs
- Which is the cost of goods sold

Cost Element—Mandatory criterion for classifying costs arising in a company code and the name of the balance sheet account to which these costs are assigned. Examples follow:

- Direct cost elements for goods and services procured externally. Direct cost elements are maintained in the general ledger master records.
- Indirect (internal activity) cost elements. Indirect cost elements have no counterpart in the financial accounts and are maintained exclusively in Cost Accounting.

Cost Element Group—A technical term for a conjunction of cost elements used to select records and to define lines and columns in reports. They can be used for planning purposes.

Cost Element Planning—Planning primary and secondary costs on a cost center, order, or project.

Cost Element Type—Classification of cost elements by uses or origin—material cost element; for example, settlement cost elements for orders, cost elements for internal cost allocations.

Cost Object—An account assignment term for individual cost objects to which actual data (costs, budgets, and sales revenues for instance) can be assigned. It can consist of individual products, such as product groups, or local situations based on classification criteria, such as shop floor areas.

Cost Object Hierarchy—Structure of cost objects as nodes to which actual data can be assigned.

Cost Origin—Logical category to which costs may be assigned. Activity types and cost elements are cost origins.

Cost Planning—Planning the costs to be incurred during a transaction.

Cost Planning Type—A technical term that indicates the purpose of a cost planning method. Examples follow:

- Rough planning: estimating costs to be incurred for an order or for an element in a work breakdown structure
- Cost element planning
- Unit costing

Cost-of-Sales Accounting—Form of results analysis. Sales deductions and unit costs are assigned to the sales transaction.

Costing—Calculating total production costs of individual product units (which may be a piece, a batch, a lot, or an order, for example). Costing may also take place on the provision of services.

Costing Type—Technical term used to control unit costing and product costing. The costing type determines the following:

- For which reference object a costing may be used
- Which costing object will be updated
- How the key of the costing file is made up
- Which costing application can use this costing type

Costing Variant—Technical term for determining criteria for a cost estimate. Comprised of mainly the following:

- Costing type
- Valuation variant
- Organizational level
- Quantity structure determination, which includes the date control parameter

Costing Version—Technical term for determining the quantity structure when cost estimates are created. There can be more than one product cost estimate for a material when production alternatives exit. Cost estimates with different production alternatives are given different version numbers.

CPI-C—Common Programming Interface-Communications. A set of standardized definitions for communications between programs.

Credit Memo Request—Reference document for creating a credit memo. If a customer applies for a credit memo, the Sales department initiates a credit memo request, which is blocked until it has been checked. The credit memo block is removed if the request is approved.

Customer Billing Document—Statement of payment due as a result of the business transaction referred to in the document.

Customer Credit Group—A group of customers defined by industry sector, by country, or by any characteristic useful to credit management. Credit representatives can generate reports for statistical analysis and retrieve information, such as credit holds, for processing customer credit groups.

Customer Delivery—A collection of sales products that are delivered together.

Customer Group—A set of customers nominated or specified in any way for the purpose of statistical reporting or other management tasks.

Customer Hierarchy—A method of representing complex customer structures, such as a buying group. Pricing and other information that is valid for all members of a customer hierarchy can be stored in the master record.

Customer Inquiry—Request from a customer to a sales organization for a price and availability check of the in-hand inventory.

Customer Quotation—An offer submitted by a sales organization to a customer for the delivery of goods or the provision of services according to fixed terms.

Customer-Material Information Record—A collection of information and references to be used in specifying material for a particular customer.

Customizing—A procedure and an SAP tool, provided as part of the SAP R/3 system, composed of two components: implementation guides and customizing menus and their associated functions. It does not change the program coding. This tool supports all the activities necessary for the following:

■ Initial configuration of the SAP system before going into production

■ Adjustment of the system during production

■ Implementation of additional SAP applications

Data Element of a Field—A description of the contents of a record or field in terms of their business significance.

Database Interface—A work area to receive data from ABAP/4 Data Dictionary tables and from which any data that is changed may be passed to the database.

Date of Next Credit Review—The date can be entered manually and be used to trigger an automatic credit review, which issues a warning or a block if anyone attempts to process a sales order after that date.

Part

III

Ch

13

DBMS—Database Management System, which is a software system used to set up and maintain a database. It includes SQL facilities.

DDL—Data Definition Language, which is used to define database objects under the DBMS.

Debit Memo Request—A document created either because of a discrepancy in the price or quantity or as a result of a customer complaint. The debit memo request has to be approved before a debit memo can be created.

Decentralized Shipping—Round-the-clock shipment processing that is independent of the host computer. The following functions can be included:

- Copying data from the central Sales and Distribution System
- Shipping processing in the decentralized Shipping system
- Confirmation of goods issued on the goods issue date to the central Sales and Distribution System

Delivering Plant—Storage plant from which a customer's goods are to be delivered.

Delivery—A sales and distribution document for processing a delivery of goods that stores information needed for the following tasks:

- Planning material requirements
- Picking
- Creating shipping documents
- Creating shipping units
- Transportation
- Billing

Delivery Due List—A work list that serves as the basis for creating deliveries. The delivery due list comprises all sales orders and scheduling agreements that are due for delivery within a specified period.

Delivery Scheduling—The result of determining all dates relevant for shipping of the goods referred to in a goods issue note. The system determines when the delivery plant must start picking and packing activities to ensure meeting the requested loading date.

Delta Management—System of transferring only data that has changed when using Remote Function Call (RFC).

Dialog Module—A group of dialog steps in a program.

Direct Cost—Costs that are directly and fully identifiable with a reference object according to the costs-by-cause principle.

Distribution Channel—An organizational unit that determines how a product reaches the customer. A distribution channel indicates how a company generates business and which organizations are involved in distribution activities.

Distribution (Controlling)—A business transaction used to allocate primary costs. The original cost element is retained on the receiver cost center. Information on the sender and the receiver is documented in the cost accounting document.

Distribution Key—Contains rules on how the costs are to be distributed. It is used for the following:

- Planning to spread costs over the planning period
- Assessment
- Distribution of direct costs in order to divide the costs of a sender cost center among the receivers

Division—An organizational unit that has been set up to supervise distribution and monitor the profitability of a particular product. Customer-specific arrangements such as partial deliveries, prices, or terms of payment can be defined for each division.

DLL—Dynamic Link Library, which is integral to the functioning of the windows architecture at runtime.

DMS—Document Management System, which is a specialized set of functions provided in R/3 for controlling documents of all kinds and recording any changes made to them.

Document—A printable record of a business transaction in sales and distribution processing. There are three kinds of printed documents in SD:

- Sales documents
- Shipping documents
- Billing documents

Document Date—Date on which the sales document becomes valid for SD processing. The document date is different for each document in a sales sequence. In the quotation, the document date is the date from which the quotation is valid. In the order, it is the date from which the agreement becomes binding. For example, the order creation date can differ from the date on which the agreement stipulated in the order becomes binding. In such a case, the agreement date is taken as the document date.

Document Flow—A stored representation of the sequence of documents necessary for one particular business transaction. For example, a particular document flow could be defined as a quotation, a sales order, a delivery, and an invoice.

Domain—A description of the technical attributes of a table field, such as the type, format, length, and value range. Several fields with the same technical attributes can refer to the same domain.

Dynamic Credit Limit Check with Credit Horizon—The credit exposure of a customer is split into a static part and a dynamic part. The static part is composed of open items, open billing, and delivery values. The dynamic part is the open order value, which includes all orders that are not yet delivered or are partially delivered. The value is calculated on the shipping

Part
III
Ch
13

date and stored in an information structure using a time period that you specify (days, weeks, or months). When you define a credit check, you can specify a particular horizon date by nominating a number of these time periods. When evaluating credit, the system has to ignore all open orders that are due for delivery after the horizon date. The sum of the static and dynamic parts of the credit check may not exceed the credit limit you have set for the credit horizon time period.

Dynpro—A dynamic program that controls the screen and its associated validation and processing logic to control exactly one dialog step.

EBCDIC—Extended Binary-Coded Decimal Interchange Code, which is an extension of the ASCII system; defines a binary pattern for each data object or command that may need to be sent from one system to another.

EDI—Electronic Data Interchange is a standardized scheme for exchanging business data between different systems via defined business documents, such as invoices and orders.

Enqueue Service—An SAP R/3 system mechanism for the management of locks on business objects throughout client/server environments.

Entity—An entity is the smallest possible collection of data that makes sense from a business point of view and is represented in the SAP R/3 system.

Entity Relationship Model—Entities may be linked by logical relationships that have business significance. Entities and their interrelations can be used to build static models of the enterprise, which in turn are portrayed in the respective computer application with its tables.

Environment Analyzer—A Help program that generates a list of the development objects that belong together and the boundaries between development classes.

EPC—Event-driven Process Chain. A process chain describes the chronological and logical relationship of functions of the R/3 system and business system statuses; those systems initialize the functions or are generated as a result of function execution.

Equivalence Number—A specification of how any given value is to be distributed to the different receiving objects.

Event (Reference Model)—A status that has business relevance. It can trigger an SAP system function, or it can be the result of such a function.

Event (Workflow Management)—A collection of object attributes that describes the change in the state of an object.

External Activities—Non-stock components or activities in a production order that are produced or performed outside the company.

External Credit Data—Credit data about a customer from external sources, such as the Dun & Bradstreet data, which is standard for SAP R/3. You refer to the D & B credit information number (DUNs number) that identifies the customer and append the D & B indicator and rating. You can also enter the date on which you last acquired this data.

Float—Period of time that allows you to start a network or activity at a later date without incurring a delay in scheduling.

Follow-Up Costs—Incurred after the actual manufacturing process has been completed (costs of rework and warranties, for example).

Forecasting—A forecast is an estimate of future values based on historical data. An SD forecast is carried out using a statistic model that you can select, or you can allow the system to select automatically after conducting a "best fit" analysis.

Foreign Key—A foreign key defines a relationship between two tables by assigning fields of one table (the foreign key table) to the primary key fields of another table (the check table).

Forward Scheduling—A means of scheduling a network, starting from the basic start date and adding durations to determine the earliest start and finish dates for successive activities.

Free Float—Time that an activity can be shifted into the future without affecting the earliest start date of the following activity or the end date of the project. Must not be less than zero or greater than the total float.

Function Module—A program module that has a clearly defined interface and can be used in several programs. The function module library manages all function modules and provides search facilities in the development environment.

Function-Oriented Cost Accounting—Assigning costs to a business function for the purpose of analysis.

General Costs Activity—General costs incurred during the lifetime of a project are planned via this type of activity in a network. Examples of such planned costs are insurance, travel, consulting fees, and royalties.

Goods Issue—The decrease of warehouse inventory resulting from a withdrawal of material or a delivery to a customer.

Goods Issue Document—A statement that verifies goods movement and contains information for follow-up tasks. A corresponding material document is initiated for the subsequent outflow of material with the goods issue document in the delivery. The material document contains one or more items and can be printed as a goods issue slip for the actual physical movement of goods.

GUI—Graphical User Interface. The SAPGUI is designed to give the user an ergonomic and attractive means of controlling and using business software.

Hypertext—Online documentation that is set up like a network, with active references pointing to additional text and graphics.

IDoc—Intermediate document. The SAP R/3 system EDI interface and the ALE program link enabling both to use standardized intermediate documents to communicate.

IMG—Implementation Guide is a component of the SAP R/3 system that provides detailed steps for configuring and setting the applications.

Imputed Costs—Value changes that do not represent operational expenditure or correspond to expenditures in either content or timing. Examples include depreciation and interest.

Incompletion Log—A list that indicates what information is missing in a sales document. You can set up conditions to specify the information that has to be included in a document.

Indirect Costs—Costs for which one single receiving object cannot be directly and fully identified according to the cost-by-cause principle. The following are examples:

- Indirect expenses, such as building insurance
- Indirect labor cost, such as supervisor wages
- Indirect materials cost, such as coolant cleaning materials

Initial Cost Split—Cost component split for raw materials procurement, showing such details as the following:

- Purchase price
- Freight charges
- Insurance contributions
- Administration costs

Inquiry—A request from a customer to a sales organization for a price and on-hand availability.

Inventory from Which Revenue Can Be Generated—The revenue expected in view of the costs that have already been incurred can be divided into capitalized costs and capitalized profits. It is calculated as Calculated Revenue minus Actual Revenue. Results analysis calculates the inventory for profit orders.

Invoice—Sales and distribution document used to charge a customer for a delivery of goods or for services rendered.

Invoice Date—Date on which a delivery is due for settlement. Invoices are processed periodically in some firms. All deliveries that are due at the same time can be combined and settled in a collective invoice. As soon as the next billing date determined by the calendar is reached, the orders and deliveries are included in the billing due list and can be billed.

Invoice List—Method of billing by combining all billing documents for a specific period for a particular payer. Additional discounts, such as factoring discounts, can be granted on the basis of the total value of an invoice list. The list may include individual and collective documents.

Invoice Split—Creation of several billing documents from one reference document, such as an order or delivery. The split may be on the basis of materials, for example.

Item—Element of a document that carries information on the goods to be delivered or the services to be rendered.

Item Category—An indicator that defines the characteristics of a document item. The following item categories are predefined:

- Items kept in inventory
- Value items
- Text items

The item category controls the following tasks:

- Pricing
- Billing
- Delivery processing
- Stock posting
- Transfer of requirements

Job Order Cost Accounting—Instrument for the detailed planning and controlling of costs. Serves for the following:

- Collecting
- Analyzing
- Allocating the costs incurred for the internal production of non-capitalized goods

Joint Products—Made in the same manufacturing process.

Kerberos—A technique for checking user authorizations across open distributed systems.

Library Network—Generic network structure that can be used by many projects. Used in project system for repetitive processes or for process planning.

Line Item—Display of posting according to activity and document number.

Loading Date—Date by which goods must be ready to be loaded and the vehicles required to transport them must be available.

Loading Group—A key that identifies the equipment needed to load the goods. For example, "crane or fork lift truck" could be defined as a loading group.

Loading Point—Place within a shipping point where goods are loaded.

Logical Database—A set of predefined paths for accessing the tables in a specific database system. Once they're defined and coded, they can be used by any report program.

Logical System—A system on which applications integrated on a common data basis run. In SAP terms, this is a client in a database.

Loop—Circular path through activities and their relationships.

Lot-Size Variance—Variances between the fixed planned costs and the fixed allocated actual costs that occur because part of the total cost for an order (or a cost object) does not change with output quantity changes. Setup costs that do not change no matter how often the operation is carried out are an example.

LU6.2—IBM networking protocol used by the SAP R/3 system to communicate with mainframe computers.

LUW—Logical Unit of Work is an elementary processing step that is part of an SAP transaction. A LUW is either executed entirely or not at all. In particular, database access is always accomplished by separate LUWs, each of which is terminated when the database is updated or when the COMMIT WORK command is entered.

Make-to-Order Production—Type of production where a product is normally made only once, although it or a similar product may be made again in the future. The costs of goods manufactured by this type of production are collected on a sales order item or an internal order and settled to profitability analysis.

MAPI—Messaging Application Programming Interface, which is part of the WOSA, Microsoft Windows Open Service Architecture.

Master Data—Data relating to individual objects; remains unchanged for a long time.

Matchcode—An index key code attached to the original data that can be used to perform quick interactive searches for this data.

Material Requirements Planning—Generic term for activities involved in creating a production schedule or procurement plan for the materials in a plant, company, or company group.

Material—Product, substance, or commodity that is bought or sold on a commercial basis or is used, consumed, or created in production. A material master record can also represent a service.

Material Availability Date—The date on which a material has to be available. On the material availability date, the vendor has to start the activities relevant for delivery, such as picking and packing the goods. The material availability date should allow time for the goods to be completely prepared by the loading date.

Material Determination—The process of conducting an automatic search for a material master record during the creation of SD documents; you use a key instead of the actual material number. The key can be a customer-specific material number or the EAN number of the material.

Material Exclusion—A restriction that automatically prevents the sale of specific materials to a particular customer.

Material Listing—A restriction that controls the sale of specific materials to a customer. Customers can only buy materials included in the material listing assigned to them. The system does not allow you to enter in a sales document for particular customer materials that are not included in the material listing.

Material Requirements Planning (MRP)—A set of techniques that uses BoM, inventory data, and the master production schedule to calculate requirements for materials.

Material Substitution—Automatic replacement by another material for technical reasons or during a sales promotion.

Material Type—An indicator that divides materials into groups (such as raw materials, semi-finished materials, operating supplies, services) and also determines the user screen sequence, the numbering in the material master records, the type of inventory management, and the account determination.

Maximum Document Value—A specific value that the sales order or delivery may not exceed. The value is defined in the credit check and is stored in the currency of the credit control area. Checking is initiated by a risk category, which is defined specifically for new customers if a credit limit has not yet been specified.

Maximum Number of Dunning Levels Allowed—The customer's dunning level may not exceed this specified maximum.

Measuring Point—Physical or logical place at which a status is described. Examples include the following:

- Temperature inside a reactor
- Speed of revolution of a wind wheel

Menu Painter—An SAP R/3 system tool for developing standardized menus, function keys, and pushbuttons in accord with the SAP Style Guide.

Metadata—Information about data structures used in a program. Examples of metadata are table and field definitions, domains, and descriptions of relationships between tables.

Milestone—An operation or task that also confirms the completion of processing previous tasks. When you confirm a milestone, the system backflushes its component operations to confirm their completion.

Mode—A user-interface window in which an activity can be conducted in parallel with other open modes.

Modified Standard Cost Estimate—A costing type; uses the quantity structure that has changed during the planning period to calculate the cost of goods manufactured for a product.

Moving Average Price—Value of the material divided by the quantity in stock. Changes automatically after each goods movement or invoice entry.

Network—In SAP R/3, activity-on-node structure containing instructions on how to carry out activities in a specific way, in a specific order, and in a specific time period. Made from activities and relationships.

Network Type—Distinguishes networks by their usage. The network type controls the following:

- Costing variants for plan, target, and actual costs
- Order type

- Number ranges
- Open items
- Status profile
- Authorizations

Object Currency—The currency of the controlling area is the default currency of a cost accounting object, such as cost center, order, and so on.

Object Dependency—Product variants may entail certain combinations of parts and exclude other combinations. If the customer chooses one variant, certain options may not be available for technical or commercial reasons. These reciprocal relationships are represented in the system by object dependency. A special editor is provided in the classification system to maintain the object dependency for characteristics and the characteristic values. You can also store object dependency in a BoM. The system uses this information during BoM explosion. Object dependency controls whether all possible components are taken into account in materials planning.

Object Master Data—Information stored in order to produce variants for a standard product. BoMs list of the parts needed and routings store instructions for combining the individual parts.

Object Master Data and Object Dependency—Master records for the manufacture of products with many variants. Information on the objects involved and their relationships is stored as object master data and object dependency.

Object Overview—Customized list of data and line display layout: routings, inspection plans, maintenance tasks, and networks, for example.

ODBC—Open Data Base Connectivity, which is a Microsoft standard based on SQL Access Group definitions for table-oriented data access.

Oldest Open Item—The oldest open item may not be more than a specified number of days overdue.

OLE—Object Linking and Embedding, which is a Microsoft technology to enable the connection and incorporation of objects across many programs or files.

One-Time Customer—Term for a collective customer master record used to process transactions involving any customer that is not a regular customer. The customer data must be entered manually if a transaction is entered for a one-time customer.

Open Item—Contractual or scheduled commitment that is not yet reflected in Financial Accounting, but will lead to actual expenditures in the future. Open item management provides for early recording and analyzing for cost and financial effects.

Operating Concern—An organizational unit to which one or more controlling areas and company codes can be assigned. Certain criteria and value fields are valid for a specific operating concern. The criteria define business segments, and the value fields are then updated for these objects.

Operating Level—The planned or actual performance of a cost center for a period: output quantity, production time, and machine hours, for example.

Operating Rate—Ratio of actual and planned operating level. Measures the effective utilization of a cost center or activity.

Operating Resources—Personnel and material necessary to carry out a project. Can be used once or many times. Defined in value or quantity units. Planned for a period or a point in time. Includes, for example, materials, machines, labor, tools, jigs, fixtures, external services, and work centers.

Operational Area—A technical term used to signify a logical subdivision of a company for accounting or operational reasons and therefore indicated in the EDM-Enterprise Data Model. An operational area is an organizational unit within logistics that subdivides a maintenance site plant according to the responsibility for maintenance.

Operations Layout—List, sorted by operations, of costing results from product costing and final costing.

Order—Instrument for planning and controlling costs. It describes the work to be done in a company in terms of which task is to be carried out and when, what is needed to carry out this task, and how the costs are to be settled.

Order Category—The SAP application to which the order belongs—SD, for example.

Order Combination—A combination of complete sales orders, of individual order items from different sales orders, or of partial deliveries of individual order items in a delivery. Order combination in a delivery is only possible when you authorize it for the customer in the customer master record or when you manually authorize it for individual sales orders in the sales order document header.

Order Group—Technical term for grouping orders into hierarchies. Used to create reports on several orders, to combine orders, and to create order hierarchy.

Order Hierarchy—Group of orders for processing at the same time, as in order planning and order reporting.

Order Phase—System control instrument for the order master data. Prohibits operations on orders depending on the phase or stage: opened, released, completed, or closed.

Order/Project Results Analysis—Periodic valuation of long-term orders and projects. The O/P results analysis evaluates the ratio between costs and a measure of an order's progress toward completion, such as revenue or the quantity produced. The results analysis data include the following:

- Cost of sales
- Capitalized costs or work in progress
- Capitalized profits
- Reserves for unrealized costs

- Reserves for the cost of complaints and commissions
- Reserves for imminent loss

Order Settlement—Complete or partial crediting of an order. The costs that have accrued to an order are debited to one or more receivers belonging to Financial or Cost Accounting.

Order Status—Instrument that controls whether an order may be planned or posted to. Reflects the operational progress and the order phase. Determines the following:

- Whether planning documents are created during cost element planning
- The transactions allowed at the moment (phase), such as planning, posting actual costs, and so on
- When an order may be flagged for deletion

Order Summarization—Allows you to summarize data by putting orders into hierarchies. Also allows you to analyze the order costs at a higher level.

Order Type—Differentiates orders according to their purpose—repair, maintenance, marketing, and capital expenditure, for example.

Outline Agreement—Generic term for contracts and scheduling agreements. The outline agreement is a long-term agreement with the vendor involving delivery of products or rendering of services according to specified requirements. These requirements are valid for a limited period of time, a defined total purchase quantity, or a specified total purchase value. A further transaction determines when deliveries and services take place.

Output—Information sent to the customer by various media such as mail, EDI, or fax. Examples of output include the following:

- Printed quotation or order confirmations
- Order confirmations sent by EDI
- Shipping notifications sent by fax

Overall Network—Network resulting from the relationships between all the existing networks.

Overdue Open Items—The relationship between the total value of open items that are more than a specified time overdue and the customer balance may not exceed a nominated percentage.

Overhead—Total cost of indirect expenses, indirect labor, and indirect materials (indirect costs). Allocated to cost objects by means of overhead rates.

Overhead Cost Management—The entirety of cost accounting activities for planning and controlling the indirect costs, as follows:

- Responsibility-oriented overhead cost management by cost centers
- Decision-oriented overhead cost management by action-oriented objects, which are orders and projects

Overhead Costing—Most common method in product cost accounting. The method is as follows:

- Assign the direct costs to the cost object.
- Apply the indirect (overhead) costs to the cost object in proportion to the direct costs, expressed as a percentage rate.

Overhead Group—Key that groups materials to which the same overheads are applied.

PA Settlement Structure—To settle costs incurred on a sender to various business segments depending on the cost element. The profitability analysis settlement structure is a combination of assignments of cost element groups to profitability segments.

Partial Delivery—A quantity of goods received that is smaller than the quantity ordered after making allowance for the underdelivery tolerance.

Partial Payment—Payment that only partially settles the invoice amount outstanding.

Partial Quantity—Quantity of a product that deviates from the standard packaging quantity. In the warehouse management system, bin quantities containing less than the standard pallet load defined in the material master are regarded as partial pallet quantities.

Partner—An individual inside or outside your own organization who is of commercial interest and who can be contacted in the course of a business transaction. A partner can be a person or a legal entity.

Payer—Person or company that settles the bill for a delivery of goods or for services rendered. The payer is not necessarily the bill-to party.

Period Accounting—One basis for profitability analysis. Costs are identified in the period in which they occur, irrespective of the period in which the corresponding revenue occurs.

Pick/Pack Time—Time needed to assign goods to a delivery and to pick and pack them. The pick/pack time depends on the loading point, the route, and the weight group of the sales order.

Picking—The process of issuing and grouping certain products from the warehouse on the basis of goods requirements from the Sales or Production department. Picking can take place using transfer orders or picking lists. The procedure distinguishes between picking from fixed storage bins and random picking.

Plan Version—Control parameters for comparative analyses in planning in Cost Accounting. The plan version determines whether:

- Planning changes are documented
- A beginning balance is to be generated
- The planning data of another version can be copied or referenced

Planned Activity—The planned cost center activity required to meet the demand, measured in the corresponding physical or technical units.

Part

III

Ch

13

Planned Delivery Time—Number of days required to procure the material via external procurement.

Planning—Assigning estimates of the costs of all activities that will be required to carry out the business of an organizational unit over the planning period.

Planning Document—Line item for documenting planning changes.

Planning Element—Work breakdown structure (WBS) element on which cost planning can be carried out.

Plant—The plant is the main organizational entity for production planning and control. MRP and inventory maintenance are often conducted at the plant level.

Pooled Table—A database table that is used to store control data, such as program parameters or temporary data. Several pooled tables can be combined to form a table pool, which corresponds to a physical table on the database.

Price Group—Grouping of customers for pricing purposes.

Price Difference Account—To record price differences for materials managed under standard prices, or differences between purchase order and billing prices.

Price Variance—Occurs if planned costs are evaluated in one way and the actual costs in another. The planned standard rates for activities might change in the meantime, for example. Can also be the result of exchange rate fluctuations.

Pricing Element—A factor that contributes to pricing. Any or all of the following can be identified as pricing elements:

- Price
- Discount
- Surcharge
- Freight
- Tax

Pricing Procedure—Definition of the conditions permitted for a particular document and the sequence in which the system takes these conditions into account during pricing.

Pricing Scale—Scale within a condition record where prices, discounts, or surcharges are defined for different customer order quantities or values.

Pricing Type—Controls whether prices are copied from a reference document to a new document or whether they are recalculated in the new document.

Primary Cost Planning—By values and as quantities.

Primary Costs—Incurred due to the consumption of goods and services that are supplied to the company from outside. Costs for input factors and resources procured externally. These are examples:

- Bought-in parts
- Raw materials
- Supplies
- Services

Process Manufacturing—A production type; continuous manufacturing process from raw materials to finished product.

Product Costing—Tool for planning costs and setting prices. It calculates the cost of goods manufactured and the cost of goods sold for each product unit using the data in the PP-Production Planning module. Product costing based on bills of material and routings is used for the following:

- Calculating production costs of an assembly with alternatives
- Showing the costs of semifinished products
- Detailed estimate of the cost components down to their lowest production level

Product Proposal—Product groupings, combinations, and quantities frequently ordered. You can save time by referring to and copying from product proposals. You can also define a product proposal for a particular customer. The system automatically enters the customer-specific product proposal when you create an order for this particular customer.

Production Costs, Total—The costs of finished products bought for resale, or the costs of goods manufactured plus sales overhead, special direct costs of sales, and administration overhead.

Production Cycle—A manufacturing process in which the output of the final manufacturing level (or part of it) becomes input for lower manufacturing levels of the same process (recycle).

Production Order—For the Production department to produce a material. It contains operations, material components, production resources and tools, and costing data.

Production Resources and Tools (PRT)—A specification of the objects needed for carrying out operations at work centers. They are assigned to activities for whose execution they are necessary.

PRT include the following:

- Job instructions
- Tools
- Test equipment
- Numerically controlled programs
- Drawings
- Machinery and fixtures

PRT are stored in master records, as follows:

- Material master
- Equipment master
- Document master

Profit Center—Area of responsibility for which an independent operating profit is calculated; responsible for its own profitability. Separate divisional result is calculated.

Profit Order—Order whose planned revenue is greater than the planned costs. Results analysis uses the profit percentage rate of a profit order to calculate the inventory from which revenue can be generated and to calculate the cost of sales.

Profit Percentage Rate—Planned revenue divided by planned costs of an order.

Profitability Analysis—In SAP R/3, by cost-of-sales approach or period accounting.

Project Definition—Framework laid down for all the objects created within a project. The data, such as dates and organizational data, are binding for the entire project.

Project Management—An organizational structure created just for the life of the project, to be responsible for planning, controlling, and monitoring the project.

Project Structure—All significant relationships between the elements in a project.

Project Type—Capital spending or customer project, for example.

Q-API—Queue Application Program Interface, which supports asynchronous communication between applications of different systems by using managed queues or waiting lines.

Quantity Structure—The quantity-related basis for calculating costs. The bill of material, the routing form, the quantity structure for product costing, and the preliminary costing of a production order.

Quantity Variance—Difference between the target costs and the actual costs, which results from the difference between the planned and actual quantities of goods or activity used. The following are examples:

- More raw materials from stock for a production order
- Fewer activities from a cost center than were planned for

Rate of Capacity Utilization—Ratio of output to capacity. Fixed costs can be divided into used capacity costs and idle time costs.

Realized Loss—Usage of reserves for imminent loss by results analysis. Loss can be realized when actual costs are incurred and when revenue is received. Results analysis realizes loss as the difference either between the actual costs and the calculated revenue, or between the calculated costs and the actual revenue:

- Actual costs minus calculated revenue
- Calculated costs minus actual revenue

Rebate—Price discount that a vendor pays to a customer after the sale. The amount of the rebate usually depends on the total invoiced sales that the customer achieves within a specified time period.

Rebate Agreement—Agreement between a vendor and a customer regarding the granting of rebates. A rebate agreement contains relevant information such as the rebate basis, rebate amount, rebate recipient, and validity period.

Reference Date—Using the reference dates and the offsets, the start and finish dates of the sub-operation or the production resource/tool usage are determined. A time within an activity—the start date, for example. You can enter time intervals for reference dates.

Reference Document—Document from which data is copied into another document.

Relationship (Project System)—Link between start and finish points of two activities in a network or library network. In SAP R/3, the relationship types are the following:

- SS   start-start
- FF   finish-finish
- SF   start-finish
- FS   finish-start

Repetitive Manufacturing—A production type. Many similar products are manufactured together or one after another. In SAP R/3, bills of materials and routings are created for each product.

Reserves for Costs of Complaints and Sales Deductions—Inventory cannot be created for certain costs—costs arising under warranties or because of sales deductions, for example. Results analysis creates reserves equal to the planned costs for such costs. These reserves are then used when (and if) actual costs are incurred.

Reserves for Imminent Loss—Results analysis creates reserves equal to the planned loss. These reserves are reduced as (and if) this loss is realized.

Reserves for Unrealized Costs—Calculated in results analysis by subtracting the actual costs from the cost of sales.

Resource-Usage Variance—Occurs if the used resource is different from the planned one—for example, if the actual raw material used is different from the planned raw material.

Results Analysis—Periodic valuation of long-term orders. Results analysis compares the calculated costs and the actual cost of an order as it progresses toward completion. It calculates either inventory (if actual costs are greater than calculated costs) or reserves (if actual costs are less than calculated costs).

The data calculated during results analysis is stored in the following forms:

- Cost of sales
- Capitalized costs

- Capitalized profit
- Reserves for unrealized costs
- Reserves for costs of complaints and commissions
- Reserves for imminent loss

Results Analysis Account—General ledger account that records the figures calculated during results analysis.

Results Analysis Data—The data includes the following:

- Work in progress and capitalized costs
- Reserves
- Cost of sales

Results Analysis Key—The results analysis key controls valuation of the relationship between costs and the computational base, such as revenue or produced quantity, as an order progresses toward completion. The results analysis key determines at least the following characteristics:

- Whether revenue-based, quantity-based, or manual
- Whether to use planned or actual results
- How profits are to be realized
- Whether to split inventory, reserves, and cost of sales

Results Analysis Version—Describes the business purpose for which results analysis was carried out. It determines the following, for example:

- Whether in accordance with German and American law
- Whether for financial accounting purposes
- Whether for profitability analysis
- To which results analysis accounts to post the results
- How the life cycle of an object is to be broken down into open and closed periods

Returnable Packaging—Packaging material or transportation device used to store or transport goods. The returnable packaging is delivered to the customer along with the goods and has to be returned to the vendor afterwards or incur a charge.

Returns—Return of goods by a customer. Returns are planned by means of a returns order. A receipt of returns records the arrival of goods, which are then posted to inventory.

Revenue—The operational output from an activity, valued at the market price in the corresponding currency for the normal sales quantity unit. The revenue from a single unit multiplied by the number of units sold equals the sales revenue.

Revenue Account Determination—Notifies the revenue accounts to which prices, discounts, and surcharges are to be posted. The system uses predefined conditions to determine the appropriate accounts.

RFC—Remote Function Call, which is a protocol, written in ABAP/4, for accessing function modules in other computers. RFC-SDK is a kit for integrating PC applications so that they can access SAP R/3 functions.

Risk Category—Enables the credit manager to classify customers according to commercial risk. The risk category helps determine, along with the document type, which kind of credit check the system automatically carries out. For example, you may decide to carry out stringent checks at order receipt for high risk customers, but waive a credit check for customers with an acceptable payment history.

RPC—Remote Procedure Call, a protocol for accessing procedures residing in other computers from C programming environments. Corresponds to RFC.

Sales Activity—A data record that contains information on interactions with customers, including sales calls, telephone calls, conferences, or presentations.

Sales and Distribution Document—A document that represents a business transaction in the SD module. SD documents include the following:

- Sales documents
- Shipping documents
- Billing documents

Sales and Operations Planning (SOP)—The creation and maintenance of a meaningful sales plan and a corresponding operations plan that includes a forecast of future customer demand.

Sales Area—An organizational unit that is responsible for three facets:

- Sales-related aspect (sales organization)
- Customer-related aspect (distribution channel)
- Product-related aspect (division)

Sales Document—A document that represents a business transaction in the Sales department. Sales documents include the following:

- Inquiry
- Quotation
- Sales order
- Outline agreement such as contracts and scheduling agreements
- Returns, credit, and debit requests

Sales Document Type—Indicators that control processing of various SD documents by allowing the system to process different kinds of business transactions, such as standard orders and credit memo requests, in different ways.

Sales Order—Contractual arrangement between a sales organization and a sold-to party concerning goods to be delivered or services to be rendered and an SAP document that contains information about prices, quantities, and dates.

Sales Organization—The division or other organizational unit responsible for negotiating sales and for distributing products and services. Sales organizations may be assigned to subdivisions of the market by geographical or industrial criteria. Each sales transaction is carried out by one sales organization.

Sales Plan—A sales plan is the overall level of sales, usually stated as the monthly rate of sales per product groups or product family. The plan is expressed in units identical to the operations plan for planning purposes and represents a commitment by the Sales and Marketing management to take all reasonable steps necessary to achieve actual customer orders that add up to the sales forecast.

Sales Unit—Unit of measure in which a product is sold. If several alternative sales units of measure have been defined for one product, conversion factors are applied by the system to convert them to the base unit of measurement.

Schedule Line—A subdivision, according to date and quantity, of an item in a sales document. If the total quantity of an item can only be delivered in partial deliveries, the system creates schedule lines corresponding to each partial delivery and determines the appropriate quantities and delivery dates for each schedule line.

Scheduling—The calculation of the start and end dates of orders and of operations within an order. Network scheduling determines earliest and latest start dates for activities and calculates the required capacity, as well as floats.

Scheduling Agreement—A type of outline agreement. The scheduling agreement is a long-term agreement with a vendor or customer that defines the creation and continuous updating of schedules. Schedules specify timing of partial deliveries for each item in schedule lines.

Screen Painter—An ABAP/4 Development Workbench tool that can be used to create, modify, display, and delete dynpros.

Secondary Cost Element—Cost centers require services from other cost centers to produce activity of their own. These are secondary costs. Planned assessment is used to plan the secondary cost quantities. Activity input is used to plan the secondary cost values.

Settlement Parameters—Control data required for order settlement. That data includes the following:

- Allocation group
- Settlement cost element
- Settlement receiver

Settlement Rule—The settlement rule consists of the sender and the settlement distribution rule, which includes the settlement receiving accounts, the distribution factor, the settlement type, and the validity period.

Ship-To Party—Person or company that receives goods. The ship-to party is not necessarily the sold-to party, the bill-to party, or the payer.

Shipping Conditions—A statement of the general strategy for shipping goods to a customer. If one of the shipping conditions states that goods must arrive at the customer location as soon as possible, the system will automatically suggest the shipping point and route that will deliver the goods the fastest.

Shipping Document—A document that defines a shipping transaction. SD shipping documents include the following:

- Delivery
- Material document containing goods issue information
- Grouped deliveries

Shipping Material—Material used for packing and transporting products. Shipping material includes crates, pallets, or containers. A shipping unit master record normally specifies a shipping material.

Shipping Point—Location that carries out shipping activities, such as a mail department or rail depot. Each delivery is processed by one shipping point.

Shipping Type—An indicator that shows which means and mode of transport are used to carry out a shipment of goods.

Shipping Unit—Combination of products packed together in a shipping material at a particular time. Shipping units may contain delivery items or items that are themselves shipping units.

Simultaneous Costing Process—Displays the actual costs incurred to date for such things as an order. The process describes all costings of an order in the SAP system, including order settlement. These costings come in the form of preliminary costings and actual costings. The values can then be analyzed in final analysis.

Sold-to Party—Person or company that places an order for goods or services. The sold-to party can also perform the functions of the payer, bill-to party, or ship-to party.

Spooling—Buffered relaying of information to output media, across multiple computers if necessary.

SQL—Structured Query Language, defined by ANSI (American National Standards Institute) as a fourth-generation language for defining and manipulating data.

Standard Cost Estimate—Calculates the standard price for semi-finished and finished products. Relevant to the valuation of materials with standard price control. Usually created once for all products at the beginning of the fiscal year or a new season. The most important type of costing in product costing. The basis for profit planning or variance-oriented product cost controlling.

Standard Hierarchy—Tree structure for classifying all data objects of one type. For example, the cost centers belonging to a company from a cost accounting point of view are represented by a standard hierarchy copied from the R/3 reference model and customized.

Standard Price—Constant price with which a material is evaluated, without taking into account goods movements and invoices. It is used for semi-finished and finished products, where they are part of product costing.

Static Credit Limit Check—The customer's credit exposure may not exceed the established credit limit. The credit exposure is the total combined value of the following:

- Open sales documents
- Open delivery documents
- Open billing documents
- Open items in Accounts Receivable

The open order value is the value of the order items that have not yet been delivered. The open delivery value is the value of the delivery items that have not yet been invoiced. The open invoice value is the value of the billing document items that have not yet been forwarded to Accounting. The open items represent documents that have been forwarded to Accounting but are not yet settled by the customer.

Status—Order items with the item category TAK are made to order and have an object status that passes through the following phases:

- 1 Released—The system sets this status automatically when the item is created. It indicates that production can be initiated.
- 2 Revenue Posted—The system sets this status automatically, as soon as revenue for an item is posted for the first time.
- 3 Fully Invoiced—This status must be set manually, as soon as all revenues have been posted for the item.
- 4 Completed—This status must be set manually when the procedure is completed.

No more revenues can be posted after the 3 Fully Invoiced status has been set. No further costs can be posted if the 4 Completed status is set.

Stock—A materials management term for part of a company's current assets, also known as *inventory*. It refers to the quantities of raw materials, operating supplies, semi-finished products, finished products, and goods on hand in the company's stores or warehouse facilities.

Stock Transfer—The removal of materials from storage at one location and their transfer to and placement into storage at another. Stock transfers can occur either within a single plant or between two different plants. The removal of inventory from storage at the first location and its placement into storage at the other can be posted in the system in either one or two steps.

Style Guide—A collection of the SAP design standards for uniform design and consistent operation routines for SAP applications.

Sub-Item—An item in a sales document that refers to a higher level item. Services and rebates in kind can be entered as sub-items belonging to main items.

Summarization Object—An object containing data calculated during order summarization, project summarization, or the summarization of a cost object hierarchy. A summarization object can, for example, contain the costs incurred for all the orders of a specific order type and a specific responsible cost center.

Surcharge—Supplement, usually as a percentage, used to apply overhead in absorption costing.

Target Costs—Calculated using the planned costs, along with the following:

- The planned activities divided by the actual activities (for cost centers)
- The planned quantities divided by the actual quantities of goods manufactured (for orders)

Target Document—A document to which the data from a reference document is copied.

Task List Type—Distinguishes task lists according to their functionality. In production planning task lists, for example, a distinction is drawn between routings and reference operation sets.

Tax Category—A code that identifies the condition that the system is to use to determine country-specific taxes automatically during pricing.

Tax Classification—Specification of the method for calculating the customer's tax liability based on the tax structure in his or her country.

TCP/IP—Transmission Control Protocol/Internet Protocol, the standard network protocol for open systems.

Text—A system function that provides a note pad, where you can store any related text about the current customer. The system indicates in the Credit Management status screen whether there is any text already available about this customer.

Text Type— A classification for various texts that users can define in master records or in documents. Text types include the following:

- Sales texts
- Shipping texts
- Internal notes

Third-Party Business Transaction—Commerce in which goods or services are delivered directly from the vendor to the customer.

Time Interval—Period of time between at least two activities linked in a relationship. The relationship type determines how start and finish times are used in the calculation.

Total Float—Time that an activity can be shifted out into the future—starting from its earliest dates—without affecting the latest dates of its successors or the latest finish date of the network.

Part
III

Ch
13

Transaction—The series of related work steps required to perform a specific task on a business data processing system. One or more screens may be required. It represents a self-contained unit from the point of view of the user. In terms of dialog programming, it is a complex object that consists of a module pool, screens, and so on, and is called with a transaction code.

Transaction Currency—Currency in which the actual business transaction was carried out.

Transportation Lead Time—The time needed to organize the transportation of goods. For example, the interval between the booking of the freight space (transportation scheduling date) and the loading of the goods onto the means of transport (loading date) is called transportation lead time. The transportation lead time may be dependent on the route.

Transportation Planning Date—The date when the organization of goods transport must begin. The transportation planning date must be selected early enough so that the means of transport is available on the loading date.

Transportation Scheduling—Determination of all dates relevant for transportation; based on the delivery date. The system determines when transport activities must start to ensure meeting the requested delivery date.

Transportation Zone—The zone in which the ship-to party is located. Zones are used by the system as a factor for determining the route. Transportation zones could be defined according to postal code or zip code areas, or according to the territory conveniently covered by the means of transport.

Unit Costing—Method of costing where bills of material and routings are not used. Used to determine planned costs for assemblies or to support detailed planning of cost accounting objects, such as cost centers or orders.

Unit of Measure—A standard measurement recognized by the SAP R/3 system. The following are examples of units of measure:

- Base unit of measure
- Unit of entry
- Unit of issue
- Order unit
- Sales unit
- Weight group

Grouping is used in delivery processing. It refers to the weight of a convenient quantity of a material. The weight group is one of the factors the system uses to determine the route. It is also used in delivery scheduling to determine the pick/pack time.

Usage Variance—Difference between planned and actual costs caused by higher usage of material, time, and so on.

User-Defined Field Types—A classification code used to interpret the meaning of a user-defined field. For example, a user may designate a specific field as one of the following types:

- General field of 20 characters to be used for codes or text
- Quantity fields with a unit
- Value fields with a unit
- Date fields
- Check boxes

User-Defined Fields—Entry fields that can be freely defined for an activity or a work breakdown structure element (Project System) or an operation (Production Planning).

User Exit—An interface provided by an SAP R/3 application that allows the user company to insert into a standard R/3 component a call to an additional ABAP/4 program. That program will be integrated with the rest of the application.

Valuation Date—Date on which materials and internal and external activities are evaluated in a costing.

Valuation Variant—Determines how the resources used, the external activities, and the overheads are to be valued in a costing (at what prices, for example).

Variance Category—Distinguishes variances according to their causes:

- Input—Price and usage variances
- Yield—Scrap, mix variances, labor efficiency variances, schedule variances
- Allocation—Fixed cost variances, over-absorption variances, under-absorption variances

Variance Key—Technical term; it controls how variances are calculated. Assigning a variance key to an object determines, for example, whether variances are calculated for the object by period or for the life of the object, which may be a cost center, an order, or a cost object identifier.

Variance Version—Technical term that specifies the basis for the calculation of variances:

- How the target costs are calculated
- Which actual data is compared with the target costs
- Which variance categories are calculated

View—A relational method used to generate a cross-section of data stored in a database. A virtual table defined in the ABAP/4 dictionary can define a view by specifying how and what will be selected from targeted tables.

Volume Variance—Cost difference between the fixed costs estimated for the products based on standard capacity and the allocated fixed costs that are either too low or too high (due to operating either below or above capacity).

Part
III

Ch
13

WBS—See Work Breakdown Structure.

WBS Element—A concrete task or a partial task that can be divided.

Work Breakdown Structure—A model of a project. Represents, in a hierarchy, the actions and activities to be carried out on a project. Can be displayed according to phase, function, or object.

Work in Progress—Unfinished products, the costs of which are calculated by subtracting the costs of the order that have already been settled from the actual costs incurred for the order or by evaluating the yield confirmed to date.

Work Order—Generic term for the following order types:

- Production order
- Process order
- Maintenance order
- Inspection order
- Network

Work Process—An SAP R/3 system task that can be assigned independently to (for instance) a dedicated application server. Examples include dialog processing, updating a database from change documents, background processing, spooling, and lock management.

Workflow Management—Tool for automatic transaction processing used in a specific business environment.

Index

Q

ASAP WORLD CONSULTANCY
SAP specialists – author of this book – (Established 1996)

ASAP World Consultancy is a high quality international consultancy specialising in SAP and other Enterprise Applications including, Peoplesoft, Baan, Oracle Applications, J D Edwards etc., which operates worldwide from its UK Headquarters. The ASAP group comprises of a number of focused divisions and companies.

ASAP For Companies Implementing SAP

SAP Documentation Consultancy & Authorship • SAP Training • SAP Access and Security Consultancy
• SAP Recruitment - Permanent and Contract • SAP Internal & External Communications Consultancy
• SAP System Testing Consultancy & Resourcing • SAP Human Issues Consultancy • SAP Resource
Planning Consultancy • Business Process Re-engineering and Change Management Consultancy
• Hardware and Installation Consultancy • SAP Implementation Consultancy • Introductory
SAP Courses: USA, UK & Singapore & Other Countries • SAP Skills Transfer to Your Employees
• Consultancy for the procurement of SAP systems and services.

ASAP For SAP Business Partners and Other Consultancies

We can work on a subcontract basis for local SAP partners and other consultancy firms. We can also work with and alongside other consultancies. We engage in SAP market research, acquisitions and joint ventures and the development of complementary solutions.

Why Use ASAP World Consultancy?

The most important ingredient of your SAP project are the people who implement, support and operate it. We are fully committed to providing the best people and applying the best techniques and methodologies. ASAP World Consultancy has a career development strategy that enables us to;

- Recruit the best quality SAP project managers and experienced SAP consultants.
- Recruit and select for SAP training the brightest potential and the best experience
  in your industry and in the complementary technologies that are involved in your SAP realisation.
- Help you to make the best use of internal recruitment and cross-training your own staff in SAP,
  with full consideration of the economic and human issues involved.
- Transfer skills locally and internationally

We deliver people as teams or individuals, and offer highly cost effective solutions, whether your need is management consultancy, a full project management service, a particular project service, or an individual with specific skills. Having authored the world,s biggest and most recognised independent SAP book, we have a team of leading SAP communicators, and offer special capability in systems documentation services, with top quality standards of presentation and accuracy.

Are you interested in joining the ASAP Group?

Why Join the ASAP team?

We are a fast growing dynamic group of companies operating globally in an exciting new virtual environment. We have the simple aim to be the best at what we do. We therefore look to recruit the best people on either contract or permanent basis

If you are any of the following, we would like to hear from you.

1. Highly Skilled and Experienced SAP Consultant.

You will have been working with SAP systems for many years and will be a project manager or consultant of standing in the industry. If you are willing to assist in the training and development and perhaps recruitment of your team, then we will be able to offer you exceptional financial rewards and the opportunity of developing the career of your choice.

2. Skilled in Another Area and Looking to Cross Train

You may be a computer expert or a business person with expertise in a particular area, perhaps, logistics, finance, distribution or H.R. etc., and/or with a particular industry knowledge. If you are committed to working with SAP systems in the long term, we will be able to offer you SAP cross training and vital experience. You must have a proven track record in your field and must be prepared to defer financial advancement whilst training and gaining experience. If you have the commitment and the skill you will in time be able to receive from us the high financial rewards and career development choice above.

3. A Person who has worked in a functional job
for an End User Company and who has been involved in all aspects of an SAP project from initial scoping to implementation and post implementation support.

You will have an excellent understanding of the industry or business function you are in. You are likely to have a good degree, ambition, drive, flexibility and the potential to become a top SAP consultant. You will thrive on the prospect of travel and living and working in other countries, jetting off around the world at short notice and working as part of a highly motivated and productive team. You must be committed to a long term career working with SAP. We will be able to offer you an interesting and rewarding career, giving you training and experience in a number of different roles. If you can prove yourself, you can expect rapid career development, with excellent financial rewards. Your only limit is your ability and your aspirations.

How To Contact Us
ASAP World Consultancy, ASAP House, PO Box 4463,
Henley on Thames, Oxfordshire RG9 6YN, UK
Tel:+44 (0)1491 414411   Fax: +44 (0)1491 414412

ASAP - 24 Hour - Virtual Office - New York, USA
Voice Mail: (212) 253 4180 Fax: (212) 253 4180

E-Mail: info@asap-consultancy.co.uk

Web site: http://www.asap-consultancy.co.uk/index.htm

A S A P
WORLD CONSULTANCY™

ASAP Worldwide

Enterprise Applications Resourcing & Recruitment

The company established in July 1997 has ambitious plans to become the world's largest global recruitment company specialising entirely in "the placement of permanent, temporary and contract staff who will be engaged in the implementation, support, training and documentation of systems known as enterprise applications". These include: SAP, BAAN, Peoplesoft, Oracle Applications, System Software Associations, Computer Associates, JD Edwards, Markam, JBA etc.

The company benefits from:

- Detailed knowledge of the market, its requirements and dynamics.

- Use of one of the world's most advanced recruitment systems.

- Access to large databases of candidates.

- A global approach to the staffing problems of a global market.

- Unique and innovative solutions for solving the staffing problems of a high growth market.

- A commitment to offer clients and candidates a professional, efficient and high quality service that is second to none.

- A commitment to the continual development of the services that we offer.

- Reciprocal partnership arrangements with other recruitment companies worldwide.

A S A P
WORLDWIDE™

Services to companies looking for staff

Permanent, Contract & Temporary Recruitment

ASAP Worldwide has a deep understanding of the enterprise application resourcing market, its requirements and dynamics. Whether your requirement is for a single individual or a team of hundreds, we offer the best practices and standards of service you would expect from one of the world's most professional recruitment companies to solve your staffing requirements.

In such a high growth market where the right people are at a premium, it takes a very different approach to find and place candidates. We offer a unique range of services to companies of all sizes and in all sectors worldwide. We leave no stone unturned in our search for candidates and we have unique techniques for selecting the very best candidates to offer you. We offer originality and innovation that make us stand out from the crowd.

Service to people looking for work

We believe that there is far more to our work than simply trying to fill job vacancies. We believe that we are providing a service of equal value to both employers and candidates looking for work. We are genuinely interested in your personal and career development and we undertake to try our very best to find you the work that best meets your requirements. Because of the size of our network, we are able to offer a truly global service, so whatever part of the world you would like to work in, whatever the type of employer and whatever the type of work you would like, we believe that we are better placed to give you what you want.

Send us a copy of your C.V./resumé and receive a free copy of our "Career Development Programme" booklet, designed to help you advance your SAP career.

How to contact us:

ASAP Worldwide
PO Box 4463 Henley on Thames
Oxfordshire RG9 6YN UK
Tel: +44 (0)1491 414411
Fax: +44 (0)1491 414412

ASAP Worldwide - 24 Hour - Virtual Office - New York, USA
Voice Mail: (212) 253 4180 Fax: (212) 253 4180

E-Mail: enquiry@asap-consultancy.co.uk

Web site: http://www.asap-consultancy.co.uk

ASAP
WORLDWIDE™